return

SUCCESS

at Key Stage 3
Mathematics

Sheila Hunt and Philip Hooper

with Tony Buzan

Hodder & Stoughton

A ME   CLC LIBRARY BOOK   E GROUP

ISBN 0 340 72511 7

First published 1998
Impression number   10 9 8 7 6 5 4 3 2 1
Year   2001 2000 1999 1998

Designed and produced by Gecko Ltd, Bicester, Oxon
Printed in Great Britain for Hodder & Stoughton
Educational, a division of Hodder Headline Plc,
338 Euston Road, London NW1 3BH by Scotprint Ltd,
Musselburgh, Scotland.

Mind Maps: Peter Bull
Illustrations: Gill Bishop, Peter Bull, Joe Little, John Plumb
and Chris Rothero

Cover design: Amanda Hawkes
Cover illustration: Paul Bateman

Contents

Shortcuts to success

Would you like your homework to be fun and a lot easier? Would you like to be able to remember things better? Would you like to read faster and understand more? To find out how, read the next three pages and follow the suggestions throughout this book.

Your *amazing* brain

Your brain is like a super, *super*, *SUPER* computer. The world's best computers have only a few thousand chips. Your brain has brain cells – 12 *million* MILLION of them! This means you are a genius just waiting to discover yourself! All you have to do is learn how to get those brain cells working together, and you'll not only do better at school, you'll do your homework more quickly and therefore have more free time too.

Your *magnificent* 'Memory Muscle'

Your memory is like a muscle. If you don't use it, it will grow weaker and weaker, but if you do keep it exercised, it will grow stronger and stronger.

Here are four tips for improving your Memory Muscle:

1 Work for between 20 and 40 minutes at a time, and *then take a break*

The break allows your Memory Muscle to rest and lets the information sink in. This also makes your Memory Muscle stronger for your next learning session.

2 Go back over your work

If you wait for a little while after you have been learning something, and you then look back at it later, you'll catch your brain at the top of the memory wave and remember even more.

3 Make connections

Your Memory Muscle becomes stronger when it can link things together. You can use your brain's amazing power to conjure up a huge number of pictures and ideas at once to help you to remember information. Join the separate facts together in some way to make a picture, for example on a Mind Map, and they'll come back to you all together, in a flash!

4 Think BIG

Your Memory Muscle gets stronger if what it is trying to remember is special in some way, so 'think big' and make what you are learning brightly coloured, funny, peculiar, special.

Your new *magic* learning formula – The Mind Map

When people go on holidays or journeys they take maps to give them a general picture of where they are going and to help them find their way around when they get there. It is exactly the same with your memory and schoolwork. If you have a 'map' of what you have to cover, everything is easier.

The Mind Map is a very special map. It helps you to find your way around a subject easily and quickly because it mirrors the way your brain works. Use it for organising your work both at school and at home, for taking notes and planning your homework.

The Mind Maps in this book

Below you will see a Mind Map on numbers.

In the centre of this Mind Map is a picture of the number pool, which summarises the theme of the topic. Coming out from this there are two branches, each one covering an important part of the topic.

You see how easy it is! You have summarised an entire topic on just one page, and this is now firmly logged in your brain, for you to get at whenever you want! If you look at this Mind Map five times over the next five months, the information it contains will be in your brain for many, many years to come.

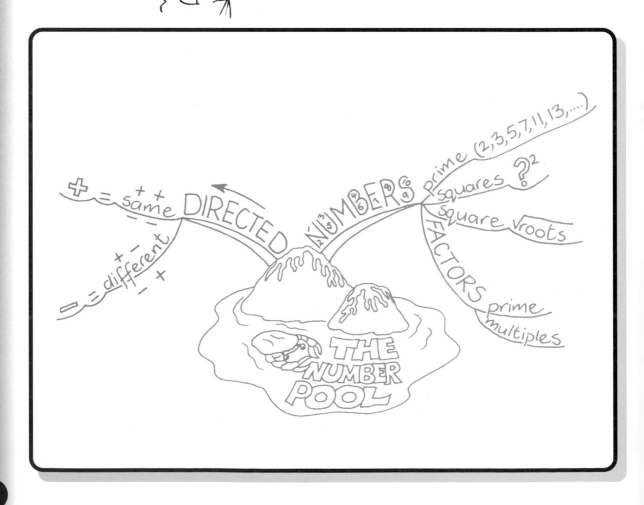

How to read a Mind Map

1. Begin in the centre, the focus of your topic.

2. The words/images attached to the centre are like chapter headings: read them next.

3. Always read out from the centre, in every direction (even on the left-hand side, where you will have to read from right to left, instead of the usual left to right).

How to draw a Mind Map

1. Start in the middle of the page with the page turned sideways. This gives your brain the maximum width for its thoughts.

2. Always start by drawing a small picture or symbol. Why? Because a picture is worth a thousand words to your brain. And try to use at least three colours, as colour helps your memory even more.

3. Write or draw your ideas on coloured branching lines connected to your central image. These key symbols and words are the headings for your topic.

4. Then add facts, further items and ideas by drawing more, smaller, branches on to the main branches, just like a tree.

5. Always print your word clearly on its line. Use only one word per line.

6. To link ideas and thoughts on different branches, use arrows, colours, underlining, and boxes.

Make life *easy* for your brain

When you start on a new book or topic there are several things you can do to help get your brain 'on line' faster:

1. **Quickly scan through the whole book or topic,** as you would do if you were in a shop deciding whether or not to buy a book or magazine. This gives your brain *control*.

2. **Think of what you already know about the subject.** You'll often find it's a lot more than you first thought. A good way of doing this is to do a quick Mind Map of *everything you know* about the subject after you have skimmed through it.

3. **Ask 'who?' 'what?' 'why?' 'where?' 'when?' and 'how?' questions about the topic.** Questions help your brain fish the knowledge out.

4. **Have another quick scan through.** Look at the diagrams, pictures and illustrations, and also at the beginnings and ends of sections – often most information is contained at the beginnings and ends.

5. **Build up a Mind Map.** This helps your brain to organise and remember information as you go.

6. **Mark up any difficult bits and move on.** Your brain *will* be able to solve the problems when you come back to them a little while later – much like saving the difficult bits of a jigsaw puzzle until last. They all fall into place in the end.

7. **Have a final scan.** Look through the book or topic quickly one more time. This will lodge it permanently in your memory banks.

And finally...

1. *Have fun while you learn* – people who enjoy what they are doing understand and remember it more.

2. *Use your teachers* as resource centres. Ask them for help with specific topics and with more general advice on how you can improve your all-round performance.

3. *Personalise your* **Success at Key Stage 3 Science** by underlining and highlighting, by adding notes and pictures. Allow your brain to have a conversation with it!

Your brain is an amazing piece of equipment. The more you understand and use it, the more it will repay you. I wish you and your brain every success.

Tony Buzan

Welcome to New-Mer-a-Sea!

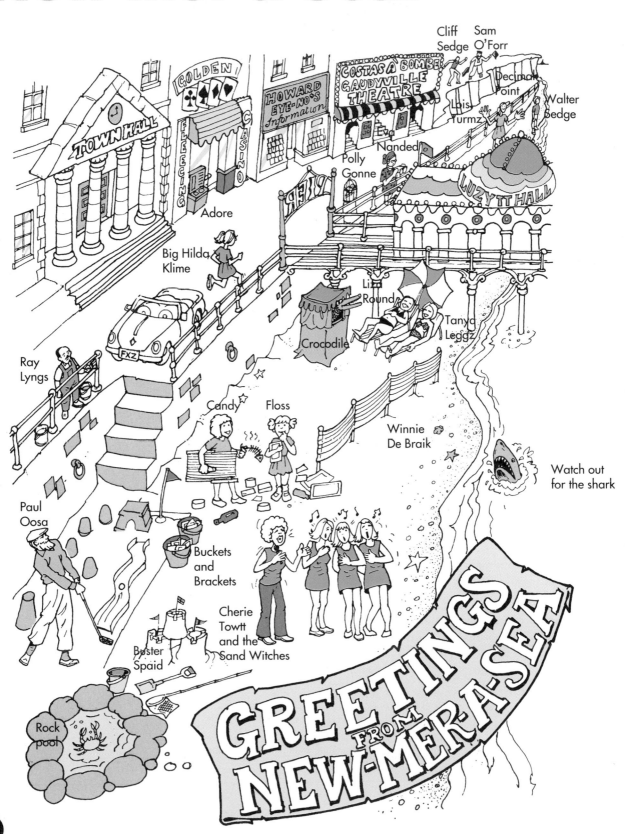

Tourist information

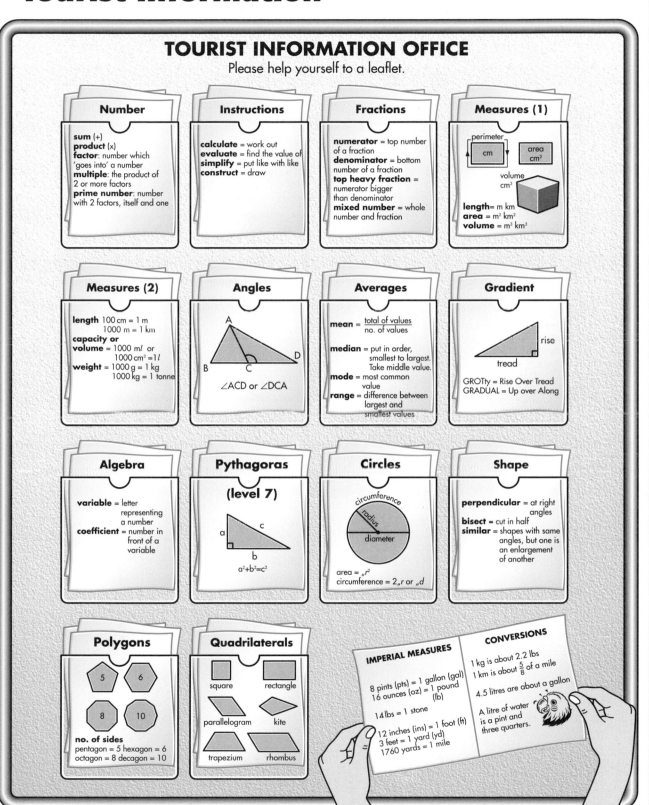

TOURIST INFORMATION OFFICE
Please help yourself to a leaflet.

Number
- **sum** (+)
- **product** (×)
- **factor**: number which 'goes into' a number
- **multiple**: the product of 2 or more factors
- **prime number**: number with 2 factors, itself and one

Instructions
- **calculate** = work out
- **evaluate** = find the value of
- **simplify** = put like with like
- **construct** = draw

Fractions
- **numerator** = top number of a fraction
- **denominator** = bottom number of a fraction
- **top heavy fraction** = numerator bigger than denominator
- **mixed number** = whole number and fraction

Measures (1)
perimeter
cm
area cm²
volume cm³
- **length** = m km
- **area** = m² km²
- **volume** = m³ km³

Measures (2)
- **length** 100 cm = 1 m
  1000 m = 1 km
- **capacity or volume** = 1000 m*l* or
  1000 cm³ = 1*l*
- **weight** = 1000 g = 1 kg
  1000 kg = 1 tonne

Angles
∠ACD or ∠DCA

Averages
- **mean** = $\frac{\text{total of values}}{\text{no. of values}}$
- **median** = put in order, smallest to largest. Take middle value.
- **mode** = most common value
- **range** = difference between largest and smallest values

Gradient
rise
tread
GROTty = Rise Over Tread
GRADUAL = Up over Along

Algebra
- **variable** = letter representing a number
- **coefficient** = number in front of a variable

Pythagoras
(level 7)
a, b, c
$a^2 + b^2 = c^2$

Circles
circumference
radius
diameter
area = πr^2
circumference = $2\pi r$ or πd

Shape
- **perpendicular** = at right angles
- **bisect** = cut in half
- **similar** = shapes with same angles, but one is an enlargement of another

Polygons
5   6
8   10
no. of sides
pentagon = 5 hexagon = 6
octagon = 8 decagon = 10

Quadrilaterals
square   rectangle
parallelogram   kite
trapezium   rhombus

IMPERIAL MEASURES
8 pints (pts) = 1 gallon (gal)
16 ounces (oz) = 1 pound (lb)
14 lbs = 1 stone
12 inches (ins) = 1 foot (ft)
3 feet = 1 yard (yd)
1760 yards = 1 mile

CONVERSIONS
1 kg is about 2.2 lbs
1 km is about $\frac{5}{8}$ of a mile
4.5 litres are about a gallon
A litre of water is a pint and three quarters.

On behalf of the council, our newly appointed tourist information officer, Howard Eye-No, is delighted to introduce you to our town's attractions. Whether you have lost your sense of direction with directed numbers, can't tell the difference between a millimetre and a millilitre, or are simply going round in circles over π, we are sure that our bang up-to-date guide book will be able to help.

Howard Eye-No gives you a guided tour

We've packed a lot into this book. In fact, we've packed all the Maths that most people meet during school years 7, 8 and 9, so we don't expect you to read it from cover to cover all in one go. Use it like you would any other guide book – to help you get to know unfamiliar surroundings. Whenever you have a new Maths topic, or you have a problem with an old one, you can turn for help to the citizens of New-Mer-a-Sea.

This book contains the material you need for Key Stage 3 SATS at Levels 4–7. However, because not all of you will study Level 7 material until years 10 and 11, you will find it clearly marked like this

when it just forms the tail-end of a topic. Otherwise, it has its own special chapter. If you are studying for Levels 4–6 you can safely leave it out – unless, of course, you fancy a lick!

If you find that you have romped through all of this and you are contemplating sitting Key Stage 3 SATS at levels 6–8, you will find a list of the level 8 attractions at the end of the book, on page 166.

Howard Eye-No has all sorts of ideas and suggestions to make your stay at New-Mer-a-Sea more memorable. The authors would like to join him in wishing you an enjoyable and unforgettable visit.

1 A toe in the water – the numbers pool

checklist

Into this chapter we have packed …

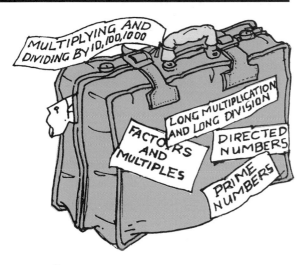

Basics

Catching crabs

Welcome to the number pool! You can find it, crammed with all sorts of numbers masquerading as sea creatures and plants, at the foot of our famous area of outstanding natural beauty known as Decimal Point.

The crabs get to grips with numbers!

By this stage, you can already read numbers such as 54, 108, 4500 etc. In the number pool you will find an assortment of crabs displaying different number values.

Multiplying by 10, 100, 1000 etc.

You probably know that $3 \times 10 = 30$, $7 \times 10 = 70$, $12 \times 10 = 120$, $35 \times 10 = 350$ etc. You don't have

to be a mathematical genius to work out that when you multiply any whole number by 10, you simply put a zero on the end of your original number. This is because multiplying by 10 moves all the digits (figures) one place to the left and the zero is written in the space at the end, to show the new positions. In the number pool, as the '× 10' wave swooshes in, all the crabs move sideways one place, and a 'zero' crab sneaks into the gap.

Of course, if you have a more powerful wave, '× 100', then the crabs are knocked two places sideways, leaving room for two 'zero' crabs.

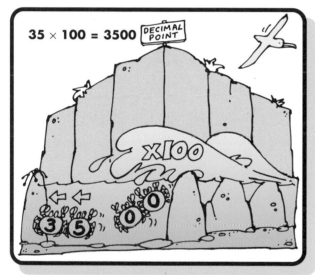

35 × 100 = 3500 DECIMAL POINT

In fact, every time the wave becomes ten times as powerful (or adds a zero to itself), you add an extra zero to the answer.

35 × 1000 = 35 000 DECIMAL POINT

Shark attack!

Everybody knows that you have to take care when there's a shark about. This sign tells you that you are in dangerous waters and that you need to watch out. Don't let the shark gobble you up!

Remember, the digits in numbers that are greater than 9999 are always grouped in threes.

One thousand, two hundred and forty-seven is written in figures as: 1247
Seventeen thousand, three hundred and eight is written in figures as: 17 308

Watch the birdie!

Have you seen those stuffed mechanical birds that speak when you pass by them? Not to be outdone, New-Mer-a-Sea has its very own stuffed parrot – a wise old bird called Polly Gonne. Her icon shows you when she is going to pass on an explanation or a helpful hint.

You will find that some books use commas instead of spaces.
Sixteen thousand and one = 16,001 = 16 001

Be careful to put in a zero where necessary.
207 = two hundred and seven
2007 = two thousand and seven

Example 1.1

$38 \times 10 = 380$ $23 \times 100 = 2300$
$174 \times 1000 = 174\,000$
and so on.

Adding a nought after your original number
when you multiply by 10, or two noughts
when you multiply by a hundred etc. is a very useful
short-cut provided that you are dealing only with a
whole number, *not one involving* **a decimal**
point. *We deal with decimals in Chapter 2.*

Exercise 1.1

Work these out without using a calculator.
1 17×10 **2** 129×10
3 60×10 **4** 100×25
5 10×310

Answers
1 170   **2** 1290   **3** 600   **4** 2500   **5** 3100

Multiplication

Multiplying by 20, 30, 40 etc.

Example 1.2

Work out 43×20

Solution

20 is 'two lots of ten', so you need to calculate
$43 \times 10 \times 2$ (or $43 \times 2 \times 10$).

$43 \times 10 = 430$ $430 \times 2 = 860$

The easiest way to multiply by numbers like 20, 30,
40, 60 etc. is to write the zero in the answer first,
so that all the crabs end up in the right column, and
then multiply by the remaining digit.

Example 1.3

Work out 73×30

Solution

Step 1:
$$
\begin{array}{r}
73 \\
\times\,30 \\
\hline
0
\end{array}
$$

Step 2: Now work out 73×3

$$
\begin{array}{r}
73 \\
\times\,30 \\
\hline
2190
\end{array}
$$

Of course, if you are multiplying by a number in the
hundreds, e.g. 200, 400, 600 etc., then you start by
putting two noughts. You put three noughts for
thousands, and so on.

Example 1.4

Work out 28×400

Solution

Step 1:
$$
\begin{array}{r}
28 \\
\times\,400 \\
\hline
00
\end{array}
$$

Step 2: Now work out 28×4

$$
\begin{array}{r}
28 \\
\times\,400 \\
\hline
11\,200
\end{array}
$$

Exercise 1.2

Work these out without using a calculator.
1 36×30 **2** 71×80 **3** 29×40
4 27×700 **5** 124×600

Answers
1 1080   **2** 5680   **3** 1160   **4** 18900
5 74400

A Quick Dip!

Whenever you see this sign, you know that Howard Eye-No is suggesting a short, quick mental exercise to keep those brain cells fit and active, and to give you practice in the sort of sums that you might meet in mental arithmetic tests in the SATS. Answer the questions as quickly as you can, without using a calculator, and do not write anything down except the answer.

1 3×8 **2** 23×10 **3** 6×8
4 What is the result of taking one away from 8000?
5 Write the number seventeen thousand and five in figures.

Answers 1 24 2 230 3 48 4 7999 5 17 005

TAKE A BREAK

Long multiplication

Phil Yerbuckitt and his mate Buster Spaid like mucking about in the rock pool to help them solve long multiplication questions.

Example 1.5

When they were given the task 23×37, they decided to split the job in two. Buster agreed to shovel up 23×7 crabs. This gave him $23 \times 7 = 161$ crabs.

It was Phil's job to collect 23×30 crabs. (Look back to page 3 if you've forgotten how to do this.) Phil collected 690 crabs. Then they felt that they had been rather hard on the crabs, so they pooled their results and threw all

$161 + 690 = 851$

crabs back into the water.

Example 1.6

Work out 68×43

Solution

You can either split up the calculation like this:

$$\begin{array}{r} 68 \\ \times 3 \\ \hline 204 \end{array} \qquad \begin{array}{r} 68 \\ \times 40 \\ \hline 2720 \end{array} \qquad \begin{array}{r} 204 \\ + 2720 \\ \hline 2924 \end{array}$$

or you can set it out like this.

$$\begin{array}{r} 68 \\ \times 43 \\ \hline 204 \\ 2720 \\ \hline 2924 \end{array}$$

Remember, it doesn't matter whether you start by multiplying the units first, followed by the tens, or vice versa, because 204 + 2720 = 2720 + 204. Don't change multipliers halfway through a line, though.

If you are likely to forget where you are up to in long multiplication, try underlining or putting a ring round the figure which you are currently using.

Example 1.7

Work out 53×68

Solution

$$\begin{array}{r} 53 \\ \times 68 \\ \hline 424 \end{array} \qquad \begin{array}{r} 53 \\ \times 68 \\ \hline 424 \\ 3180 \end{array} \qquad \begin{array}{r} 53 \\ \times 68 \\ \hline 424 \\ 3180 \\ \hline 3604 \end{array}$$

Exercise 1.3

Work these out without using a calculator.
1 54×41 **2** 137×300 **3** 61×75
4 400×34 **5** 90×500

Fill in the missing numbers.
6 $38 \times \text{❂} = 380$ **7** $100 \times \text{❂} = 1700$
8 $16 \times \text{❂} = 320$ **9** $10 \times \text{❂} = 1560$
10 $6500 = \text{❂} \times 65$

Multiplying and dividing by 10, 100, ...

The movement of the tide pulls the sea creatures with it. Just as multiplying by 10, 100 etc. moves the digits to the left and zero crabs sneak into the spaces, dividing by 10, 100 etc. moves them to the right and any zero crabs swim away.

Example 1.8

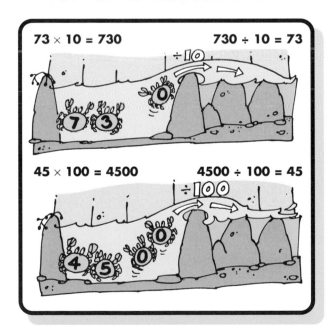

73 × 10 = 730   730 ÷ 10 = 73

45 × 100 = 4500   4500 ÷ 100 = 45

Impress your teacher!

Impress your teacher by using the word **inverse**. Using an inverse process is like running the video backwards, because it reverses everything and gets you back to where you started. Multiplication and division are inverse processes. For example, 4 × 10 = 40 and 40 ÷ 10 = 4.

Question: What is the inverse of addition?
Answer: Subtraction and addition are inverse processes (e.g. 3 + 2 = 5 and 5 − 2 = 3).

Exercise 1.4

Work these out without using a calculator.
1 4620 ÷ 10 = ☀
2 6000 ÷ 10 = ☀
3 340 ÷ ☀ = 34
4 ☀ ÷ 100 = 91
5 37 + ☀ = 96
6 96 − ☀ = 59

Remember, multiplying by 10, 100, 1000, ... by putting noughts on the end only works for whole numbers. Dividing by 10, 100, 1000, ... by crossing the last digit(s) off only works for whole numbers ending in zeros. Other numbers may involve fractions or decimals, and we shall catch them in the next chapter.

A Quick Dip!

1 430 ÷ 10   2 7 × 6
3 19 × 5 (**Hint:** Work out 20 × 5, then subtract 1 × 5.)
4 How many hundreds make two thousand?
5 How many 50p magazines could you buy for £3.50?

TAKE A BREAK

Division

Cherie Towtt is the leader of a group called the 'Sand Witches'. They like to rehearse their act by the rock pool. Sometimes they even attract an audience – well, it's a free show – and afterwards they all share in a picnic.

Short division

Example 1.9

Work out $532 \div 4$

Solution

For this sum, you would probably use this method.

$$4{\overline{\smash{\big)}\,5^13^12}}^{1\ 3\ 3}$$

This works very well when the calculations are small enough to do in your head, but when dealing with large numbers you may need to use long division. In long division you merely write down the calculations that you would otherwise make in your head.

Long division with Cherie Towtt

Cherie Towtt gets three of the Sand Witches to help her. Here they demonstrate the long division method using an easy example.

$$
\begin{array}{r}
133 \\
4{\overline{\smash{\big)}\,532}} \\
\underline{4}\!\downarrow \\
13 \\
\underline{12}\!\downarrow \\
12 \\
\underline{12} \\
0
\end{array}
$$

Share: 4 into 5 goes once and 1 left over, as **T**imes: $1 \times 4 = 4$ and **S**ubtract: $5 - 4 = 1$. In short division, you write the 1 next to the 3, in long division you **B**ring down the 3 and **S**tart all over again. **S**hare: 4 into 13 goes 3 times. **T**imes: $3 \times 4 = 12$. **S**ubtract: $13 - 12 = 1$. Bring down the 2 and **S**tart all over again. **S**hare: 4 into 12 goes 3 times. **T**imes: $3 \times 4 = 12$. **S**ubtract: $12 - 12 = 0$.

Tick each number as you bring it down, so that you can see which one to use next.
Of course, with small numbers you would probably use short division.

The last example is to show you that long division is merely short division written down in more detail.

Long division with Cherie Towtt and the Sand Witches

Cherie Towtt and the group are hoping to make the big time with their latest single, 'STSB'. The words are very easy, because they simply shout out the letters, 'S! T! S! B!' If the audience hasn't gone home by then, they shout, 'Start all over again!' and, unfortunately for those rash enough to stay, that's just what they do; they launch into 'STSB' all over again. This is how it works. Cherie Towtt gives each of her friends one task. As each one finishes her job, she passes her answer on to the next person to complete her share of the operation.

Example 1.10

Work out $975 \div 15$

Solution

Cherie Towtt shouts, 'Share!'

15 into 9 won't go, so you need to try 15 into 97. If you're not sure, write down as much of the 15-times table as you need. (You don't have to learn this. Just keep on adding 15.)

$1 \times 15 =$	15	
2	30	
3	45	
4	60	
5	75	
6	90	Nearly there!
7	105	Too big.

$$
\begin{array}{r}
65 \\
15{\overline{\smash{\big)}\,975}} \\
\underline{90}\!\downarrow \\
75 \\
\underline{75} \\
0
\end{array}
$$

'Share!' Cherie Towtt writes 6 in the answer; then the first Sand Witch shouts, 'Times!' The nearest to 97 is $6 \times 15 = 90$ so she writes that underneath ready for the next Sand Witch to shout, 'Subtract!'. The next Sand Witch shouts, 'Bring down!' and makes 75. Because they haven't finished, they shout, 'Start all over again!' and Cherie Towtt refers back to her chart to work out that $75 \div 15 = 5$. As there is no remainder, the Sand Witches don't get a look in, and the answer is 65.

Example 1.11

Work out 897 ÷ 17

Sometimes when they have finished sharing everything out fairly, they find that they have some crabs left over. They usually throw these into a pile, called **remainder** or 'rem' or 'r' for short. Sometimes they throw them at the audience instead, and then the best thing to do is to shelter around the rocks behind Decimal Point. We show you how to do that in Chapter 2 on page 34.

Solution

897 ÷ 17

It saves you work if you start by getting a rough estimate. 17 is slightly smaller than 20 and 89 is between 4 × 20 and 5 × 20, so 89 ÷ 17 is likely to be between 4 and 5. You may find it helpful to write out some of the 17-times table. You can either do this by multiplication, or by adding on 17 each time.

```
1 × 17 = 17
2        34
3        51
4        68
5        85   Don't go further than you need. You
              can add to it later if necessary.
```

```
        52    remainder 13
17 )897       Share: 89 ÷ 17 = 5 + a remainder
   85         Times: 5 × 17 = 85
   47         Subtract: 89 – 85 = 4. Bring down 7. Start all over
   34         again: 47 ÷ 17 = 2   Times: 2 × 17 = 34
   13         Subtract: 47 – 34 = 13. Bring down:
              Nothing to bring down.
              13 is the remainder.
```

When you do long division, say to yourself,

Share! **T**imes! **S**ubtract! **B**ring down! **S**tart all over again!

Our next example shows you what to do when a number 'won't go'.

Example 1.12

Work out 2475 ÷ 23

Solution

```
      107    remainder 14
23 )2475     Share: 23 into 2 won't go, but 23 into 24 goes 1.
   23        Times: 1 × 23 = 23   Take away: 24 – 23 = 1.
   175       Bring down the 7. Start all over again.
   161       Share: 23 into 17 won't go. Put a zero in the answer!
    14        It's quicker if you then skip straight to Bring down,
             followed by Start all over again! 175 ÷ 23 = 7
             rem 14. (You can write out the 23-times table if
             necessary.)
```

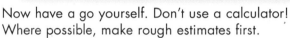

Exercise 1.5

Now have a go yourself. Don't use a calculator! Where possible, make rough estimates first.

1 436 ÷ 14   **2** 840 ÷ 24
3 561 ÷ 19   **4** 8123 ÷ 21

Answers
1 31 r 2   **2** 35   **3** 29 r 10   **4** 386 r 17

Get into the habit of making estimates, so you can see if you have made a silly mistake keying into your calculator.

TAKE A BREAK

How are you getting on?

Exercise 1.6

Do not use a calculator for this exercise.

1 Replace the stars (✲), so that the answer is always 75.

   a) 750 ÷ ✲ = 75   **b)** 70 + ✲ = 75
   c) 95 − ✲ = 75   **d)** ✲ × 25 = 75

   Now fill in the boxes with +, −, × or ÷ so that the answer is always 75.

   e) 15 ☐ 3 ☐ 30 = 75
   f) 500 ☐ 5 ☐ 25 = 75

2 Gladys Allova is buying presents to take home. She plans to buy sticks of New-Mer-a-Sea rock at 28p each. How many can she buy for £3.50? How much money will she have left?

3 Maeve Isitt is wondering whether to take the members of her youth club to stay at Ma Jinn's guest house, situated right at the edge of town, where the charge for bed and breakfast (B&B) is £16.00 per person per night.

   a) How much would it cost for seven nights' bed and breakfast for one person?

   b) How much would it cost for a group of ten to stay for seven nights bed and breakfast?

4 Millie-Anne Eyre has £850.00 to spare and has decided to splash out on a night's B&B for herself and some friends at Ma Jinn's.

   a) How many people could stay for one night? How much money would be left over?

   b) Millie-Anne Eyre wants to take six friends. How much would one night's B&B cost for the group, and how much money would Millie-Anne have left?

Answers

£850.00 − £112.00 = £738.00
b) £16.00 × 7 = £112.00 and
£2.00 left.
4 a) £850.00 ÷ 16 = 53 friends. There would be
3 a) £7 × £16.00 = £112.00 **b)** £1120.00
have 14p left.
2 350 ÷ 28 = 12 r 14. She can buy 12 sticks and
e) 15 × 3 + 30 = 75 **f)** 500 ÷ 5 − 25 = 75
c) 95 − **20** = 75 **d)** **3** × 25 = 75
1 a) 750 ÷ **10** = 75 **b)** 70 + **5** = 75

1 Write ten thousand and fifteen in figures.
2 8 × 4
3 58 + 19 (**Hint:** Try 58 + 20 − 1)
4 How many sevens make fifty-six?
5 What is the remainder when 21 is divided by 4?

Answers

1 10015 **2** 32 **3** 77 **4** 8 **5** 1

TAKE A BREAK

Negative numbers

Con Survaishun and her friends are worried about the effects of the sea on the coastline. With the help of the local council, they set up a pole in the water to monitor the tide's movements. They pick a calm day when the tide is just on the turn and mark its height on the stick with a zero. Then they keep a record of high and low water marks.

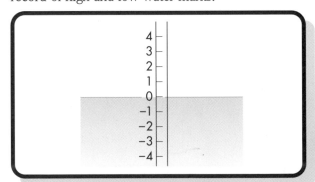

Example 1.13

a) The tide starts at level 8 on the pole. It goes down 3 levels. Where does it finish?

b) The tide starts at level 3. It rises 5 more levels. Where does it finish?

c) The tide starts at level 2. It goes down 6 levels. Where does it finish?

d) The tide starts at three levels below zero (⁻3). It rises 8 levels. Where does it finish?

e) The tide starts at ⁻2. It continues to fall another 3 levels. Where does it finish?

Solution

a) 8 – 3 = 5

b) 3 + 5 = 8

c) 2 – 6 = ⁻4 (If you found this hard, try putting your pencil or finger as a marker on the 2 and then counting down 6 places. You should finish at 4 levels below zero. This is written as ⁻4.)

d) ⁻3 + 8 = 5 (Put a marker on ⁻3 and go up 8.)

e) ⁻2 – 3 = ⁻5 (Put your finger on ⁻2 and go on down another 3 levels.)

Numbers greater than zero are positive (+) whilst those less than zero are negative (–). If you have a negative number, you must include its negative sign, e.g. a temperature of two degrees below zero is minus two (⁻2). Numbers without signs, e.g. house numbers, are assumed to be positive.

Exercise 1.7

Now try to answer these without using a calculator.

1 7 + 3   **2** 8 – 1   **3** 5 – 9

4 2 – 9   **5** ⁻4 + 4   **6** ⁻2 – 9

7 The temperature one January evening at 8 o'clock was 3° Celsius. By midnight it had fallen by another 6°. What was the temperature, in Celsius, at midnight?

Answers

5 0   **6** –11   **7** 3 – 6 = ⁻3

1 10   **2** 7   **3** ⁻4   **4** ⁻7

*Temperatures are usually measured in the **Celsius** scale (sometimes called **centigrade**). The other scale is **Fahrenheit**.*

The tide turns on directed numbers

The rock pool is full of prawns pushing the crabs around with or against the current.

Sometimes little shrimps attach themselves to the crabs, pushing or pulling them in one direction or another, turning them into directed numbers.

What happens when two signs meet?

When you are working with directed numbers, do you know what to do when you have two signs next to each other with no digit (figure) separating them? Try this exercise and see how you get on.

Exercise 1.8

Remember, numbers without a sign in front are assumed to be positive.

1 2 + ⁺5   **2** ⁻8 + ⁺6   **3** 16 + 9

4 ⁻5 + ⁻4   **5** 4 – 12   **6** ⁻5 – 3

7 5 – ⁻1   **8** ⁻10 – ⁻2

8 –8

1 7   **2** ⁻2   **3** 7   **4** ⁻9   **5** ⁻8   **6** ⁻8   **7** 6

Answers

How did you get on?

All or most of them right?

Congratulations. Many Key Stage 3 students find directed numbers a real nightmare, so you are doing well. You can skip the rest of this section, but try Exercise 1.9 on page 10, just to make sure that you haven't overlooked anything.

Any problems?

Don't worry. You're not alone. Most people find directed numbers very difficult when they first tackle them. See if the ideas in the next section help.

There's something fishy about directed numbers!

The big signs between the numbers act like big, bullying prawns, pulling or pushing the crabs according to whether they are + or −. The little signs in front of the numbers are like little shrimps pointing the crabs in a positive or negative direction. Little positive shrimps in front of numbers just muddy the waters. It's far less confusing if you let them swim away. Remember, numbers without a sign in front are positive.

$$^+5 + {}^+3 = 5 + 3 = 8$$

Negative baby shrimps are much stronger, and they always cling to their crabs.

$$^-5 + {}^+3 = {}^-5 + 3 - {}^-2$$

*Shrimps and prawns with the **same** signs always develop a **positive** relationship.*

$^+5 + {}^+3 = 8$ gives the same result as calculating $5 + 3 = 8$. (Because the little shrimps in front of each number were positive, they just swam away.)

When two creatures with negative signs meet, the nearest they can get to shaking hands to show their **positive** feelings is to lock their pincers together.

$$^+5 - {}^-3 = {}^+5 + 3 = 8 \qquad {}^-5 - {}^-3 = {}^-5 + 3 = {}^-2$$

When the sign in front of the number is negative, it clings on.

When two creatures bearing **different** signs meet, they always end up fighting. However, the result is a

foregone conclusion because the **negative** sign always wins and the positive swims away.

$$^+5 - {}^+3 = 5 - 3 = 2 \qquad {}^-5 + {}^-3 = {}^-5 - 3 = {}^-8$$

When two signs which are the **same** meet, they always develop a **positive** relationship. When two **different** signs meet, the **negative** always wins.

*When the signs are the **same**, you end up with a **plus**. (**Same** and **plus** have **four** letters.) When they're **different** you **don't**. (**Different** and **minus** have 'i' as the second letter.)*

*When you are adding or subtracting directed numbers, these rules **always** work when the signs bump into each other. However, when there are numbers in between, use the ideas demonstrated by Con Survaishun and her friends on page 8.*

$$^-5 - {}^-3 = {}^-5 + 3 = {}^-2 \qquad {}^-5 - {}^+3 = {}^-5 - 3 - {}^-8$$

Just to recap

$^+2 + {}^+3 = 2 + 3 = 5$	$^+2 + {}^-3 = 2 - 3 = {}^-1$
$^+2 - {}^-3 = 2 + 3 = 5$	$^+2 - {}^+3 = 2 - 3 = {}^-1$
$^-2 + {}^+3 = {}^-2 + 3 = 1$	$^-2 + {}^-3 = {}^-2 - 3 = {}^-5$
$^-2 - {}^-3 = {}^-2 + 3 = 1$	$^-2 - {}^+3 = {}^-2 - 3 = {}^-5$

If two signs are bumping into each other, replace them both with **one** sign.

same + plus   different − minus

Then apply the technique of Con Survaishun.

Exercise 1.9

Work these out without using a calculator.

1 $^+7 + {}^+3$	**2** $^-2 + {}^-7$	**3** $2 - {}^-3$
4 $^-20 + {}^-6$	**5** $12 - {}^-7$	

Now look back to the exercise on directed numbers on page 9 and see if you can make a better catch this time.

A Quick Dip!

1 760 ÷ 10
2 How many tens are there in 2500?
3 81 – 19 (Try 81 – 20 + 1)
4 200 ÷ 25 (Remember, 4 × 25 = 100)
5 23 × 100

2300 **5** 8 **4** 62 **3** 250 **2** 76 **1**

Answers

Types of numbers

Rod and Annette Inhand go fishing in the number pool. Because some of the fish in the pool are famous for fighting or eating each other, they have an assortment of containers in which to separate the creatures they catch. They also take hooks and nets of different sizes with them, so that they can be selective in their fishing.

Factors

Question: What do the numbers 2, 8, 18, 96 have in common?
Answer: You could have answered, 'They are all even.' Or, you may have said:
- 2 goes into them
- they are all in the 2-times table.

If one number 'goes into' another number, it is a **factor** of that number. 2 is a factor of 2, 8, 18, 96 etc. Every positive whole number except 1 itself has at least two factors.

$1 \times 5 = 5$ The factors of 5 are 1 and 5.
$1 \times 29 = 29$ The factors of 29 are 1 and 29.

Most numbers have more than two factors. The factors of 8 are 1, 2, 4 and 8, because both 1×8 and 2×4 make 8.

Numbers with **exactly 2 factors** are called **prime numbers**.

*Remember that 1 itself is **not** a prime number. Prime numbers always have exactly two factors. The number 1 is not prime because it has only one factor; i.e. $1 \times 1 = 1$.*

Multiples

Multiples are big fish which swallow up their factors.

18 is a multiple of 1, 2, 3, 6, 9 and 18.

Multiples easily get indigestion, so they swallow up only their own factors that don't leave any remainder. For instance, 6 is a multiple of 3 and 2 ($6 \div 3$ and $6 \div 2$ go exactly). 6 is not a multiple of 4 because $6 \div 4$ does not give a whole number as the answer. All numbers have the power to swallow up 1. Fish in the number pool can only swallow up other fish which are smaller or exactly the same size as they are.

Factors and multiples

Remember, 8 is the big fish that can swallow up 1, 2 and 4 – as well as another 8! These numbers all 'go into' 8, without leaving a remainder. Numbers which 'go into' or can be swallowed up by a number are called factors. Numbers which do the swallowing up are called multiples.

Example 1.14

The factors of 8 are 1, 2, 4 and 8.

8 is a multiple of 1, 2, 4 and 8.

The factors of 30 are 1, 2, 3, 5, 6, 10, 15 and 30.

30 is a multiple of 1, 2, 3, 5, 6, 10, 15 and 30.

The factors of 19 are 1 and 19.

19 is a multiple of 1 and 19.

Remember, numbers that can only swallow up 1 and themselves are called prime numbers. For example, 19 is a prime number.

Exercise 1.10

1 Write down the factors of the following numbers.
  a) 7   **b)** 24   **c)** 60   **d)** 17   **e)** 40   **f)** 1
2 Which of the numbers in question 1 are prime numbers?
3 List the numbers in question 1 which are multiples of 5.

Answers

1 a) 1, 7
b) 1, 2, 3, 4, 6, 8, 12, 24
c) 1, 2, 3, 4, 5, 6, 10, 12, 15, 20, 30, 60
d) 1, 17
e) 1, 2, 4, 5, 8, 10, 20, 40
f) 1
2 7, 17 (but **not** 1)
3 40, 60

Shortcuts to catching factors

Factor 2 The number ends in 0, 2, 4, 6, 8.
Factor 3 Add up the individual digits. If the number you get has a factor of 3, the whole number will also have a factor of 3. e.g. 258.

(2 + 5 + 8 = 15. 15 ÷ 3 = 5.

258 also divides exactly by 3. 258 ÷ 3 = 86.)

Factor 5 The number ends in 5 or 0.
Factor 6 The number is even and the Factor 3 Rule applies.
Factor 9 Use the same rule as for Factor 3, substituting 9 for 3.
(e.g. 675: 6 + 7 + 5 = 18. 9 is a factor of 18, and 675 ÷ 9 = 75.
258 gave a total of 15, which does not divide by 9. 258 ÷ 9 = 28 r 6.)
Factor 10 Probably the easiest to spot! The number always ends in 0.

There are rules which work for other numbers, but you don't need to learn them.

Exercise 1.11

Look at the following list of numbers.
2, 3, 5, 6, 9, 10
1 Which are prime numbers?
2 Which are factors of 150?

Answers

1 2, 3, 5   **2** 2, 3, 5, 6, 10

Prime factors

Now that you can recognise prime numbers, and you know what a factor is, you can put both pieces of information together to end up with **prime factors**.

Example 1.15

What are the prime factors of 20?

Solution

The factors of 20 are 1, 2, 4, 5, 10 and 20.

Of these, 2 and 5 are prime numbers, so 2 and 5 are prime factors of 20.

Expressing a number as a product of prime factors

The **product** of two numbers is the answer that you get when you multiply the two numbers together. The product of 3 and 2 is 6, because $3 \times 2 = 6$.

Example 1.16

Express 180 as a product of prime factors.

Solution

An easy way is to split 180 into two factors which will multiply together to give 180. There are various ways of doing this. Here are a couple of suggestions.

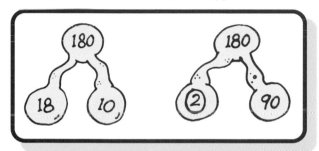

If any of the numbers which you have chosen is a prime number, ring it because it is a prime factor. Continue splitting unringed numbers into pairs until every strand ends in a ringed number.

$180 = 2 \times 2 \times 3 \times 3 \times 5$

Powers and indices

The short way of writing the answer to the last example is $180 = 2^2 \times 3^2 \times 5$. This is called using **powers** or **indices**.

A little number written at the top right-hand side of another number is called a power, or an **index number**. When you are talking about more than one of these, they are called indices.

Two to the power of four is written 2^4. It is the short way of writing $2 \times 2 \times 2 \times 2$.

In this example 4 is the index.

A number to the power of 2 is 'squared'. e.g. five squared $= 5^2 = 5 \times 5 = 25$.

A number to the power of 3 is 'cubed'. e.g. four cubed $= 4^3 = 4 \times 4 \times 4 = 64$.

When the index is bigger than 3, the number is said as '... to the power of ...'.

$2^4 = 2$ to the power of 4

$2^4 = 2 \times 2 \times 2 \times 2 = 16$. It does **not** mean $4 \times 2 = 8$.
$3^2 = 3 \times 3 = 9$. It does **not** mean $2 \times 3 = 6$.

Using a calculator to work out indices

If you need to work out a number such as 2^7, it is very time-consuming to key in ▣2▣ × ▣2▣ × ▣2▣ × ▣2▣ × ▣2▣ × ▣2▣ × ▣2▣. If it is a long calculation it is easy to make mistakes. Your calculator will probably have a button which you press between entering the number and its index. Calculators differ, however, so experiment with yours until you can find the quick way of finding the answer $2^7 = 128$.

Exercise 1.12 Powers or indices

Use a calculator to work these out.
1 2^5 **2** 3^4 **3** 5^3 **4** 7^6

Answers

Exercise 1.13

Express the following numbers as products of their prime factors.
1 108 **2** 300 **3** 175

Answers

1 $2^2 \times 3^3$ **2** $2^2 \times 3 \times 5^2$ **3** $5^2 \times 7$

Highest common factor

The **highest common factor**, or HCF, of two numbers is the biggest number which 'goes into' both numbers exactly.

Example 1.17

What is the highest common factor of 48 and 120?

Solution

Start by expressing each of the two numbers as a product of its prime factors. This is one possible route to take. There are others, but they should all lead to the same answer.

$48 = 2 \times 2 \times 2 \times 2 \times 3$ $120 = 2 \times 2 \times 2 \times 3 \times 5$

Each of these numbers has $2 \times 2 \times 2 \times 3 = 24$ in common, so 24 is the biggest fish that both 48 and 120 can swallow up.

$48 = 2 \times 24$ $120 = 5 \times 24$

Example 1.18

Find the highest common factor of 150 and 675.

Solution

$150 = 2 \times 3 \times 5 \times 5$ $675 = 3 \times 3 \times 3 \times 5 \times 5$

You can find $3 \times 5 \times 5$ in both numbers.

$3 \times 5 \times 5 = 75$,

So 75 is their highest common factor.

$150 = 2 \times 75$ $675 = 9 \times 75$

Exercise 1.14

Find the highest common factors of the following pairs of numbers.
1 72 and 160
2 45 and 80
3 60 and 360

Answers

1 $72 = 2 \times 2 \times 2 \times 3 \times 3$,
$160 = 2 \times 2 \times 2 \times 2 \times 2 \times 5$
The HCF is $2 \times 2 \times 2 = 8$
2 $45 = 3 \times 3 \times 5$, $80 = 2 \times 2 \times 2 \times 2 \times 5$
The HCF is 5.
3 $60 = 2 \times 2 \times 3 \times 5$, $360 = 2 \times 2 \times 2 \times 3 \times 3 \times 5$
The HCF is $2 \times 2 \times 3 \times 5 = 60$

TAKE A BREAK

Squares and square roots

Most calculators have a key marked x^2 for finding the square of a number.

$6 \times 6 = 6^2$ If you press 6 x^2 or 6 x^2 $=$ your calculator should display 36.

The inverse of squaring a number is to find its square root. The sign for this is $\sqrt{}$. You may also see it with an extended bar, like this $\sqrt{}$.

$6^2 = 36 \qquad \sqrt{36} = 6$

Some calculators require you to press the square root sign before you key in the number, and others work the other way round – you key in the number followed by the square root sign.

Exercise 1.15

Use a calculator to work these out.
1 14^2 **2** 25^2 **3** $\sqrt{289}$ **4** $\sqrt{3136}$

Answers
1 196 2 625 3 17 4 56

TAKE A BREAK

Common multiples

In the rock pool, 8 and 12 are swimming along, minding their own business, when along comes 48. 8 and 12 are both factors of 48 ($6 \times 8 = 48$, $4 \times 12 = 48$), so 48 gobbles them both up. 48 is a **common multiple** of 8 and 12.

There is always more than one common multiple. In this example, 24 is also a common multiple. It can

swallow up 8 ($3 \times 8 = 24$) and it can swallow up 12 ($2 \times 12 = 24$). The **lowest common multiple** or **common denominator** is the smallest number which can swallow up all the factors in the example.

Example 1.19

a) List three common multiples of 3, 4 and 6.

b) What is their lowest common multiple?

Solution

a) Fish can only swallow up other fish which are the same size or smaller than they are. The biggest number in the group is 6 and 6 can swallow up 3 but not 4. $2 \times 6 = 12$ and $3 \times 4 = 12$. 12 is therefore a common multiple and all other common multiples are in the 12-times table. You could list any of these. 12, 24, 36, ... etc.

b) The lowest common multiple of 3, 4 and 6 is 12.

Exercise 1.16

Find the lowest common multiple of each set of numbers.
1 2, 10, 15   **2** 4, 6, 8   **3** 5, 10, 25

Answers
1 30 2 24 3 50

A Quick Dip!

1 What is the square root of 81?
2 $^-9 - {}^+7$
3 $670 \div 10$
4 17×100
5 8^2

Answers
1 9 2 -16 3 67 4 1700 5 64

1

check your luggage

At the end of each chapter, we give you a chance to check up on what you have learned. Tick each item when you feel confident that you can cope with it.

HAVE YOU REMEMBERED TO PACK …

- ✓ multiplication by 10, 100, 1000, …

- ✓ long multiplication and long division

- ✓ directed numbers

- ✓ prime numbers, factors and multiples

- ✓ powers and indices

- ✓ squares and square roots?

This sign tells you that you there is more for you to get your teeth into, if you are taking SATS papers Levels 5–7 or 6–8.

Ready for more? Turn to page 131 for:
- multiplying and dividing directed numbers.

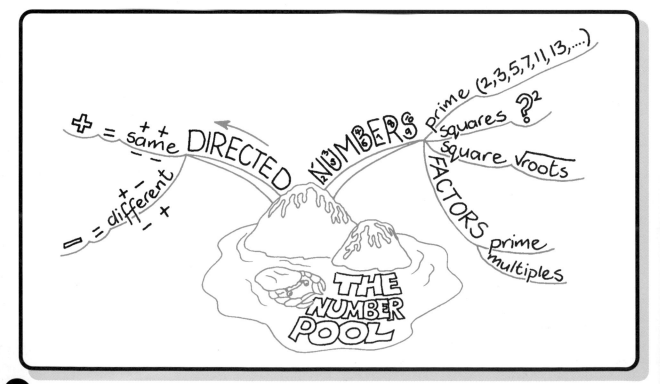

Scrambling in the rocks – fractions, decimals, percentages, ratio and proportion

2

checklist

Into this chapter we have packed ...

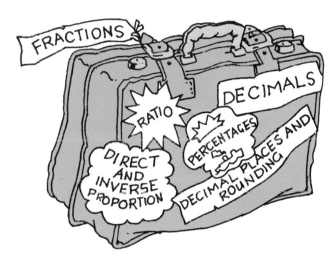

Fractions

Cherie Towtt and fractions

When Cherie Towtt is asked to divide a cake equally among four of her group, she calculates $1 \div 4 = \frac{1}{4}$.

If she has two cakes to share among three group members, she needs to work out $2 \div 3$. First of all, she cuts each cake into three pieces.

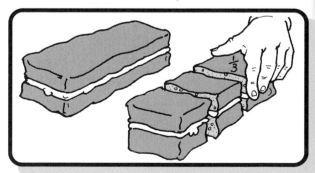

Next, she shares out one cake equally so that everybody gets $1 \div 3 = \frac{1}{3}$. Then she does the same to the other cake, so that everybody gets $\frac{1}{3}$ of that as well.

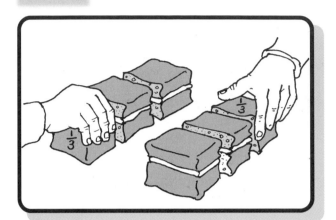

She then realises that everybody gets $\frac{1}{3} + \frac{1}{3} = \frac{2}{3}$ so you can write $2 \div 3$ as $\frac{2}{3}$.

A fraction is just another way of writing the top number divided by the bottom.

Exercise 2.1

Write the answer to each of these as a fraction.
1 $2 \div 5$ **2** $3 \div 4$ **3** $1 \div 6$ **4** $4 \div 7$

Answers

$1 \frac{2}{5}$ $2 \frac{3}{4}$ $3 \frac{1}{6}$ $4 \frac{4}{7}$

Fractions and remainders

Example 2.1

Cherie Towtt and the greediest of the Sand Witches are going to share 57 squares of chocolate equally between them. How much should each get?

Solution

Using either short or long division as in Chapter 1, would give you the answer
$57 \div 2 = 28$ remainder 1.

Dividing the remaining piece equally between them gives $1 \div 2 = \frac{1}{2}$, so $57 \div 2 = 28\frac{1}{2}$.

Similarly, $23 \div 3 = 7$ remainder 2 or $7\frac{2}{3}$.

Any number that has a remainder can be written using fractions.

Exercise 2.2

Work out the following examples, expressing any remainders as fractions.
1 $25 \div 3$ **2** $19 \div 2$ **3** $15 \div 4$ **4** $137 \div 5$

$1 8\frac{1}{3}$ $2 9\frac{1}{2}$ $3 3\frac{3}{4}$ $4 27\frac{2}{5}$

Answers

Cliff and Walter Sedge are brothers. Cliff Sedge looks down on Walter, and Walter Sedge looks up to Cliff. See what happens when they are faced with fractions.

Example 2.2

Cliff Sedge has his eye on a cake which Cherie Towtt hasn't quite finished icing. What fraction of the cake is iced?

Unfortunately for Cliff, Walter insists on having his fair share, and Cliff is forced to divide the cake down the middle.

a) How many pieces are there now?

b) How many pieces are iced and how many pieces are not iced?

c) What fraction of the cake is iced and what fraction does not have icing?

Solution

$\frac{2}{3}$ is iced.

a) 6

b) 4 iced and 2 without icing

c) $\frac{2}{3} = \frac{4}{6}$ iced and $\frac{1}{3} = \frac{2}{6}$ without icing.

Equivalent fractions

If Cliff multiplies the top digit by a number, Walter multiplies the bottom by the same number. If Walter tries to stir it by multiplying the bottom digit, Cliff, not to be outdone, multiplies the top digit by the same number.

Example 2.3

Fill in the missing numbers.

$\frac{2}{3} = \frac{4}{\text{☀}} = \frac{12}{\text{☀}} = \frac{\text{☀}}{90}$

Solution

$\frac{2}{3} = \frac{4}{6} = \frac{12}{18} = \frac{60}{90}$

These numbers are called **equivalent** fractions.

Exercise 2.3

Fill in the spaces.

1 $\frac{2}{9} = \frac{4}{\text{☀}}$ **2** $\frac{5}{8} = \frac{\text{☀}}{40}$ **3** $\frac{4}{5} = \frac{\text{☀}}{15}$ **4** $\frac{7}{18} = \frac{\text{☀}}{36}$

Answers

1 $\frac{2}{9} = \frac{4}{18}$ **2** $\frac{5}{8} = \frac{25}{40}$ **3** $\frac{4}{5} = \frac{12}{15}$ **4** $\frac{7}{18} = \frac{14}{36}$

Cancelling or reducing to lowest terms

Cliff and Walter Sedge have an enemy – Lois Turmz. Whenever she finds a fraction which they have made, she sabotages it by grabbing the common factors, i.e. the numbers which 'go into' both of them. (Look back to page 11 if you need reminding about factors.)

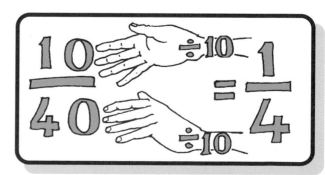

Example 2.4

Express $\frac{10}{40}$ in its lowest terms.

Solution

$\frac{10}{40}$ Both 10 and 40 have a common factor of 10. Lois Turmz grabs this from both numbers and leaves behind $\frac{1}{4}$.

$\frac{10}{40} = \frac{1}{4}$

2

Example 2.5

Reduce $\frac{125}{175}$ to its lowest terms.

Solution

Step 1:
Lois Turmz starts by taking out any common factor which she can easily spot.

5 is a factor of 125 and 175. Lois Turmz grabs that first, and leaves $\frac{25}{35}$.

$$\frac{125}{175} = \frac{25}{35}$$

Step 2:
She then sees that she can grab another factor of 5 and leave $\frac{5}{7}$.

$$\frac{125}{175} = \frac{25}{35}$$

$$= \frac{5}{7}$$

Of course, she could have grabbed 25, the HCF (highest common factor) at Step 1, and saved herself some work.

$$\frac{125}{175} = \frac{5}{7}$$

Exercise 2.4

Give these fractions in their lowest terms.

1 $\frac{15}{125}$ **2** $\frac{32}{128}$ **3** $\frac{48}{60}$ **4** $\frac{28}{120}$

Answers

1 $\frac{3}{25}$ **2** $\frac{1}{4}$ **3** $\frac{4}{5}$ **4** $\frac{7}{30}$

TAKE A BREAK

Calculators and fractions

Most calculators have at least one fraction button. Calculators differ in their procedures, however, so you need to find out how yours works.

You can often use fraction keys to give a fraction in its lowest terms.

Sometimes, however, the fraction involves more digits (figures) than the calculator can manage, so it's a good idea to be able to cancel without having to rely on it.

Example 2.6

Cliff and Walter have 28 sweets to share equally between them. How many do they each get?

Solution

An obvious solution is $28 \div 2 = 14$.
Since each would receive $\frac{1}{2}$ of the original number, you could also have worked out $\frac{1}{2} \times \frac{28}{1} = \frac{28}{2} = 14$.

When working out fractions, you can always replace 'of' with $\times$.

Example 2.7

The donkey ride along the beach extends for 150 metres. After travelling $\frac{4}{5}$ of the distance, Rhoda Weigh fell off. How far had she travelled?

Solution

$$\frac{4}{5} \text{ of } 150\,\text{m} = \frac{4}{5} \times \frac{150}{1}$$

$$= \frac{600}{5}$$

$$= \frac{120}{1}$$

$$= 120 \text{ metres}$$

Whenever you have to multiply whole numbers and fractions, as in the last example, it is easier to write the whole number in fraction form, with a denominator (bottom number) of 1. You are then more likely to multiply it correctly by the numerator (number on the top) instead of the denominator.

Lois Turmz demonstrates a quicker way!

$$\frac{4}{5} \times \frac{150}{1} = \frac{4}{1} \times \frac{150}{5} = \frac{600}{5} \qquad \text{because } 5 \times 1 = 1 \times 5$$

But $\frac{600}{5} = \frac{120}{1} = 120$

because Lois Turmz grabs a factor of 5 from top and bottom, so:

$$\frac{4}{\cancel{5}_1} \times \frac{\cancel{150}^{30}}{1} = \frac{4}{1} \times \frac{30}{1} = 120 \text{ metres}$$

Whenever you are multiplying fractions and have the same factor on the top and the bottom (i.e. the numerator and the denominator) Lois Turmz can grab it. This is often called **cancelling**.

Each time you cancel, you must have one number on the top (the numerator) which has a common factor with one number (the denominator) on the bottom.

$\frac{4}{7} \times \frac{10}{21}$ will not cancel, because there is no common factor, other than 1 itself, which is, of course, a factor in every numerator and denominator.

$$\frac{4}{7} \times \frac{10}{21} = \frac{40}{147}$$

Multiplication of fractions

As you can see, multiplication of fractions is very easy.
1 Try to cancel where possible so that the calculations are as small as possible.
2 Multiply along the line of numerators and along the denominators.
3 Always check your answer to make sure that you have given it in its lowest terms.

Work out questions 1–4 without the help of a calculator, giving your answers in their lowest terms. You will find them easier if you cancel first where possible.
Check your answers with your calculator.

1 $\frac{2}{9} \times \frac{27}{40}$ 　　　　　　2 $\frac{5}{8} \times \frac{2}{25}$

3 $\frac{6}{7} \times \frac{12}{21}$ 　　　　　　4 $\frac{7}{9} \times \frac{27}{70}$

5 Karl Aisle and Isla Wite decided to organise a day trip for themselves and six friends to the neighbouring resort of Litter-a-Sea, for which The Ricky Tea Experience, a local travel firm, was charging £12.50 per person. What was the total cost?

6 They then found that Laurie Lode, was offering the same trip on one of his vehicles, for £60.00 for a group of eight. If each person paid the same amount, what fraction of the total cost would each person pay?

7 How much would each person pay to travel with Laurie Lode?

8 Ricky Tea had a special offer – ten could travel for the price of eight. How much would each person pay now?

9 What fraction of the price would each pay?

10 Which is the greater, $\frac{1}{8}$ of £60.00 or $\frac{1}{10}$ of £100.00?

TAKE A BREAK

Mixed numbers and top-heavy fractions

Mixed numbers are just whole numbers combined with fractions.

e.g. $1\frac{3}{4}$ $10\frac{2}{5}$ $12\frac{3}{16}$

When you are working with fractions, you will sometimes find that your answer has a numerator which is bigger than the denominator.

e.g. $\frac{13}{4}$ $\frac{10}{7}$ $\frac{8}{5}$

Numbers like these are called **top-heavy fractions**. (Some books call them **improper fractions**.)

Before you can calculate with mixed numbers and fractions you need to be able to turn mixed numbers into top-heavy fractions, and top-heavy fractions into mixed numbers.

Changing mixed numbers into top-heavy fractions

Example 2.8

Change $1\frac{3}{4}$ to a top-heavy fraction.

Solution

As you have $\frac{3}{4}$ already, the fraction you need to use is quarters. $1 = 4$ quarters, or

$1 = \frac{4}{4}$, so $\frac{4}{4} + \frac{3}{4} = \frac{7}{4}$ $(1 \times 4 + 3 = 7)$

Example 2.9

Change $3\frac{2}{5}$ to a top-heavy fraction.

Solution

This time you will be using fifths. 5 fifths make a whole one, so $3 \times 5 = 15$ fifths make 3 wholes.

$\frac{15}{5} + \frac{2}{5} = \frac{17}{5}$ so $3\frac{2}{5} = \frac{17}{5}$ $(3 \times 5 + 2 = 17)$

Exercise 2.6

Change the following mixed numbers to top-heavy fractions.

1 $3\frac{4}{5}$ **2** $1\frac{3}{8}$ **3** $2\frac{5}{9}$ **4** $5\frac{3}{4}$ **5** $5\frac{2}{5}$

Answers

1 $\frac{19}{5}$ **2** $\frac{11}{8}$ **3** $\frac{23}{9}$ **4** $\frac{23}{4}$ **5** $\frac{27}{5}$

Changing top-heavy fractions to mixed numbers

Example 2.10

Change $\frac{17}{5}$ to a mixed number.

Solution

Every time you have 5 fifths, $\frac{5}{5}$, you have another whole number.

$17 \div 5 = 3$ remainder 2, or 3 whole ones and $\frac{2}{5}$ left over.

$\frac{17}{5} = 3\frac{2}{5}$

Divide the numerator by the denominator. Write any remainder as a fraction.

Exercise 2.7

Change these top-heavy fractions to mixed numbers.

1 $\frac{18}{5}$ **2** $\frac{17}{8}$ **3** $\frac{26}{3}$ **4** $\frac{19}{4}$ **5** $\frac{37}{2}$

Answers

1 $3\frac{3}{5}$ **2** $2\frac{1}{8}$ **3** $8\frac{2}{3}$ **4** $4\frac{3}{4}$ **5** $18\frac{1}{2}$

Most calculators will also do this.
For $\frac{18}{5}$ key in [1] [8] [$a^b/_c$] [5] [=] and the calculator should show $3\frac{3}{5}$.

Multiplying fractions

Example 2.11

Work out $1\frac{3}{4} \times 2\frac{4}{7}$

Solution

$1\frac{3}{4} = \frac{7}{4}$ $(1 \times 4 + 3 = 7)$

$2\frac{4}{7} = \frac{18}{7}$ $(2 \times 7 + 4 = 18)$

$\frac{^1\cancel{7}}{_2\cancel{4}} \times \frac{\cancel{18}^9}{\cancel{7}_1} = \frac{1}{2} \times \frac{9}{1} = \frac{9}{2}$

Now change your answer to a mixed number.

$\frac{9}{2} = 4\frac{1}{2}$ $(9 \div 2 = 4$ rem 1, or $4\frac{1}{2}$.)

$\frac{^1\cancel{7}}{_2\cancel{4}} \times \frac{\cancel{18}^9}{\cancel{7}_1} = \frac{1}{2} \times \frac{9}{1} = \frac{9}{2} = 4\frac{1}{2}$

Just to recap – multiplying fractions
1 Change any mixed numbers into top-heavy fractions.
2 Cancel if possible.
3 Multiply along the top and the bottom.
4 Change your answer back to a mixed number if necessary.

Exercise 2.8

Work out the following problems. Remember to give your answer as a mixed number in its lowest terms.
1 $3\frac{3}{4} \times 2\frac{4}{5}$ 2 $5\frac{1}{4} \times 2\frac{4}{7}$ 3 $2\frac{2}{3} \times 1\frac{1}{5}$ 4 $5\frac{1}{4} \times 1\frac{1}{8}$

Answers
1 $10\frac{1}{2}$ 2 $13\frac{1}{2}$ 3 $3\frac{1}{5}$ 4 $5\frac{29}{32}$

Dividing fractions

Example 2.12

Work out $10 \div 2$

Solution

For this calculation, you can either say, 'Ten divided by two' or 'How many twos make 10?' Either way, the calculation will be $10 \div 2 = 5$.

Understanding division of fractions is easier if you use the second approach.

Now try $10 \div \frac{1}{2}$

$10 \div \frac{1}{2}$ is the same as saying, 'How many halves make ten?' It is not the same as saying, 'Half of ten'. Half of ten can be written

$\frac{1}{2} \times 10$ *or* $\frac{1}{2} \times \frac{10}{1} = 5$.   *('of' = ×)*

$10 \div \frac{1}{2} = 20$ (Think of 10 cakes each cut in half. There would be 20 pieces.)

$4 : \frac{1}{3}$ (Think of 4 cakes, each cut into 3 pieces.)
$4 \div \frac{1}{3} = 12$

$5 \div \frac{1}{6}$ (How many pieces would you get if you cut 5 cakes into 6 pieces each?)
$5 \div \frac{1}{6} = 30$

Can you see the easy way to solve all of these?

$10 \div \frac{1}{2} = 10 \times 2 = 20$ $4 \div \frac{1}{3} = 4 \times 3 = 12$
$5 \div \frac{1}{6} = 5 \times 6 = 30$

Example 2.13

Work out $6 \div \frac{2}{3}$

Solution

If the question had been $6 \div \frac{1}{3}$, the answer would have been $6 \times 3 = 18$.

You need, however, groups of $\frac{2}{3}$.

$6 \div \frac{2}{3} = 6 \times 3 \div 2 = 18 \div 2 = 9$

The quick way of remembering division of fractions is 'turn the second fraction upside-down, and then multiply the two numbers together'.

$$6 \div \frac{2}{3} = \frac{6}{1} \times \frac{3}{2} = \frac{18}{2} = 9 \quad \text{or cancelling} \quad \frac{3}{1} \times \frac{3}{1} = 9$$

Example 2.14

Work out $2\frac{2}{5} \div 3\frac{1}{3}$

Solution

When you multiply fractions, you must first turn any mixed numbers into top-heavy fractions.

See if you can change $2\frac{2}{5}$ and $3\frac{1}{3}$ into top-heavy fractions before you look at the answer.

$$2\frac{2}{5} = \frac{12}{5} \qquad 3\frac{1}{3} = \frac{10}{3}$$

Now turn $\frac{10}{3}$ upside-down to become $\frac{3}{10}$ and you have $\frac{12}{5} \times \frac{3}{10}$.

Remember, to cancel you must have a common factor top and bottom. 12 and 10 have a common factor of 2, so you can make $\frac{6}{5} \times \frac{3}{5}$. Both the 6 and the 3 are in the numerator, so you can't cancel them; both the 5s are in the denominator, so you can't cancel them either.

$$\frac{6}{5} \times \frac{3}{5} = \frac{18}{25}$$

Just to recap – dividing fractions
1 Turn any mixed numbers into top-heavy fractions.
2 Turn the second fraction upside-down.

Make sure it's the second and not the first!

Note the 's' and 'd' in 'second' and 'upside-down'.

3 Treat the calculation from now on as a multiplication sum.

Exercise 2.9

1 $3\frac{3}{5} \div 2\frac{2}{5}$ **2** $4\frac{7}{12} \div 3\frac{2}{3}$

3 $8\frac{1}{3} \div 3\frac{1}{8}$ **4** $6\frac{3}{4} \div 1\frac{5}{16}$

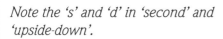

Answers

How much have you learnt so far?

Try out all your newfound skills in this exercise.

Exercise 2.10

Work out all the questions in this exercise without using a calculator. You can check them with a calculator afterwards if you wish.

1 Link up the following mixed numbers with their top-heavy fractions.

i) $5\frac{3}{5}$	**a)** $\frac{18}{5}$
ii) $2\frac{3}{4}$	**b)** $\frac{41}{4}$
iii) $3\frac{3}{5}$	**c)** $\frac{28}{5}$
iv) $7\frac{5}{8}$	**d)** $\frac{27}{8}$
v) $3\frac{3}{8}$	**e)** $\frac{11}{4}$
vi) $10\frac{1}{4}$	**f)** $\frac{61}{8}$

2 a) $10\frac{1}{2} \div 6\frac{3}{10}$ **b)** $1\frac{3}{4} \times 2\frac{3}{5}$
   c) $4\frac{5}{8} \div 1\frac{1}{2}$ **d)** $3\frac{3}{10} \times 2\frac{1}{2}$

3 Con Survaishun is doing a survey of marine life in the number pool. Of the 56 small creatures which she has caught, 24 are crabs. What fraction of the total is that?

4 a) Cherie Towtt has 24 biscuits left over from her last picnic and has decided to share them equally with Rod and Annette. What fraction of the total will each receive?
b) How many of the biscuits will Cherie keep?

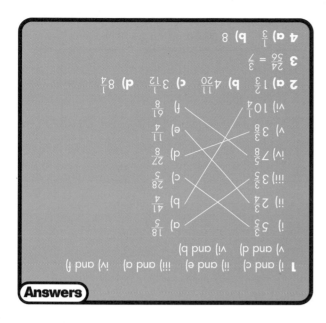

How did you get on?

All or most of them right?

Well done. You really deserve the break that's coming up.

Some right, but still some problems?

Look on the bright side! You have made a start. Take a break at this point, and then go back over the sections which caused you difficulty.

Don't even ask?

Don't worry. You are by no means the only one! Many people find fractions extremely difficult at first. Take a break at this point, and then go back slowly over the work on fractions in this chapter. Don't try to take in too much at a time.

TAKE A BREAK

Adding fractions

Example 2.15

Cherie Towtt plans to share a large cake equally among herself and four friends.

a) What fraction should each receive?

Unfortunately Big Hilda Klime has grabbed two pieces for herself, and her friend Ena Phizinuph has snatched one of the remaining pieces.

b) What fraction of the cake have they taken?

Solution

a) $1 \div 5 = \frac{1}{5}$ b) $\frac{2}{5} + \frac{1}{5} = \frac{3}{5}$

As you can see from this example, when you add fractions with the same denominator, you add the numerators, but keep the same denominator.

Do not add the denominators.

Example 2.16

Rod and Annette are sharing a pizza. Rod picks up $\frac{1}{2}$ and Annette takes $\frac{1}{4}$. What fraction of the pizza will they take between them?

Solution

$\frac{1}{2} + \frac{1}{4} = \frac{3}{4}$

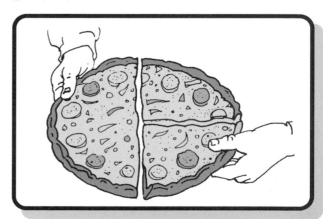

To solve the last example, you had to split up the $\frac{1}{2}$ into two quarters, i.e. $\frac{2}{4}$.

$$\frac{2}{4} + \frac{1}{4} = \frac{3}{4}$$

You can only add fractions if they have a common denominator, i.e. the same number on the bottom.

Finding a common denominator

Example 2.17

Big Hilda Klime has bought two pizzas of identical size. Her friend Ena Phizinuph has already eaten $\frac{3}{4}$ of hers, whilst Big Hilda Klime has guzzled her way through $\frac{4}{5}$ of hers.

a) Who has eaten the larger amount?

b) How much have they eaten between them?

Solution

a) It is easier to compare fractions when they have the same denominator. This is also called a common multiple, or common denominator. (Look back to page 15 if you have forgotten about lowest common multiples.) 4 and 5 'go into' 20, or are factors of 20, so, using the ideas of the Sedge brothers, change both fractions into twentieths. (Look back to page 11 for information about factors.) $\frac{3}{4} = \frac{15}{20}$ and $\frac{4}{5} = \frac{16}{20}$ so $\frac{4}{5}$ is bigger by $\frac{1}{20}$.
Big Hilda Klime has eaten more.

b) $\frac{15}{20} + \frac{16}{20} = \frac{31}{20}$

$$= 1\frac{11}{20}$$

You can always find a common denominator by multiplying the denominators of the original fractions. $4 \times 5 = 20$

Although this method will always give you a common denominator, you could end up with a number which is larger than you need, making the working out more difficult, and you would probably have more cancelling at the end.

Example 2.18

Add $\frac{2}{5} + \frac{2}{15}$

Solution

If you used the idea of multiplying the denominators, you would get $5 \times 15 = 75$.

$$\frac{2}{5} = \frac{30}{75} \text{ and } \frac{2}{15} = \frac{10}{75}$$

$$\frac{30}{75} + \frac{10}{75} = \frac{40}{75}$$

$$= \frac{8}{15}$$

Although this would be correct, you would have to use large numbers, and you could easily make mistakes. The lowest common denominator in this example is 15.

$$\frac{2}{5} = \frac{6}{15} \qquad \text{You do not need to change } \frac{2}{15}.$$

$$\frac{6}{15} + \frac{2}{15} = \frac{8}{15}$$

Example 2.19

Add $3\frac{3}{8} + 4\frac{7}{20}$

Solution

What is the lowest common denominator of 8 and 20?

A fish which is going to swallow up 8 and 20 needs to be at least as big as 20.

(Remember, no fish can swallow up a factor bigger than itself.)

20 cannot swallow up 8 without leaving a remainder, so try $2 \times 20 = 40$.

40 is the lowest common denominator.

$$\frac{3}{8} = \frac{15}{40} \text{ and } \frac{7}{20} = \frac{14}{40}$$

$$3\frac{3}{8} + 4\frac{7}{20} = 3\frac{15}{40} + 4\frac{14}{40}$$

Add the whole numbers together and the fractions together.

$$3\frac{15}{40} + 4\frac{14}{40} = 3 + 4 + \frac{15 + 14}{40}$$

$$= 7\frac{29}{40}$$

Example 2.20

Add $5\frac{5}{6} + 4\frac{7}{10}$

Solution

The lowest common denominator is 30.

$\frac{5}{6} = \frac{25}{30}$ and $\frac{7}{10} = \frac{21}{30}$

$5\frac{25}{30} + 4\frac{21}{30} = 9\frac{46}{30}$

$\frac{46}{30} = \frac{23}{15} = 1\frac{8}{15}$

Adding on the 9, gives $10\frac{8}{15}$.

Just to recap – adding fractions

1 If necessary, change the fractions so that they have a common denominator.
2 Add the whole numbers together, and the fractions together.
3 If you have a top heavy fraction, cancel, change it to a mixed number and add any whole numbers together.
4 Check again to see if it is possible to cancel.

Exercise 2.11

1 $2\frac{5}{6} + 3\frac{4}{5}$ **2** $2\frac{3}{4} + 4\frac{5}{8}$ **3** $1\frac{2}{3} + 4\frac{7}{15}$

4 $\frac{5}{8} + 4\frac{3}{16}$ **5** $9\frac{3}{10} + 1\frac{2}{5}$

Answers

1 $6\frac{19}{30}$ **2** $7\frac{3}{8}$ **3** $6\frac{2}{15}$ **4** $4\frac{13}{16}$ **5** $10\frac{7}{10}$

TAKE A BREAK

Subtracting fractions

Example 2.21

Clem Entyne and Mel Onne were sharing some fruit. They cut an apple into eight equal pieces.

a) What fraction of the whole apple is each piece?

b) Mel eats three pieces. What fraction has she eaten?

c) What fraction is left?

Solution

a) 1 whole $= \frac{8}{8}$ Each piece is $\frac{1}{8}$

b) $\frac{3}{8}$

c) $\frac{8}{8} - \frac{3}{8} = \frac{5}{8}$

As with addition, you can subtract fractions as long as they have a common denominator.

Example 2.22

Subtract $5\frac{5}{8} - 4\frac{1}{8}$

Solution

$5 - 4 = 1$ and $\frac{5}{8} - \frac{1}{8} = \frac{4}{8}$

Putting it together:

Subtracting the whole numbers and the fractions gives $1\frac{4}{8}$. Cancelling the fractions gives a final answer of $1\frac{1}{2}$.

Example 2.23

Subtract $6\frac{3}{8} - 4\frac{1}{4}$

Solution

Change $\frac{1}{4}$ into $\frac{2}{8}$ so that the two numbers have a common denominator.

$6\frac{3}{8} - 4\frac{2}{8} = 2\frac{1}{8}$

Example 2.24

Subtract $9\frac{1}{8} - 4\frac{3}{8}$

Solution

Although you have a common denominator of 8, you could run into problems if you try to calculate $\frac{1}{8} - \frac{3}{8}$.

An easy way round this is to split up $9\frac{1}{8}$ into $8 + 1 + \frac{1}{8}$. Then change the 1 into $\frac{8}{8}$, and you will have $8 + \frac{8}{8} + \frac{1}{8} = 8\frac{9}{8}$.

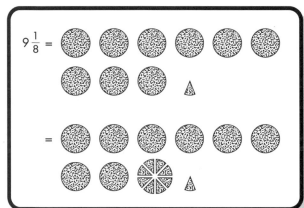

$$9\frac{1}{8} =$$

$$=$$

$8\frac{9}{8} - 4\frac{3}{8} = 4\frac{6}{8} = 4\frac{3}{4}$

Example 2.25

Subtract $8\frac{1}{2} - 1\frac{7}{10}$

Solution

The lowest common denominator is 10.

$8\frac{1}{2} = 8\frac{5}{10}$

This gives you $8\frac{5}{10} - 1\frac{7}{10}$. But $\frac{5}{10}$ is smaller than $\frac{7}{10}$.

The easiest way round this is to change one of the 8 whole numbers into $\frac{10}{10}$.

$8 = 7 + \frac{10}{10}$ so $8\frac{5}{10} = 7 + \frac{10}{10} + \frac{5}{10} = 7\frac{15}{10}$

Now it is easy to work out.

$7\frac{15}{10} - 1\frac{7}{10} = 6\frac{8}{10}$
$$= 6\frac{4}{5}$$

Example 2.26

Subtract $5\frac{1}{4} - 2\frac{3}{5}$

Solution

Find the common denominator, and change the fractions.

The common denominator is 20.

$$\frac{1}{4} = \frac{5}{20} \qquad \frac{3}{5} = \frac{12}{20}$$

$5\frac{1}{4} - 2\frac{3}{5} = 5\frac{5}{20} - 2\frac{12}{20}$

But $\frac{5}{20}$ is smaller than $\frac{12}{20}$, so change $5\frac{5}{20}$ into $4\frac{25}{20}$.

$4\frac{25}{20} - 2\frac{12}{20} = 2\frac{13}{20}$

Just to recap – subtracting fractions

1 Make sure that both fractions have a common denominator.
2 Change one of the whole numbers into a fraction if necessary so that the first fraction is larger than the second.
3 Subtract in the usual way.
4 Check the need to cancel.

Exercise 2.12

Subtract.

1 $12\frac{1}{6} - 4\frac{5}{6}$ 2 $5\frac{3}{10} - 2\frac{3}{5}$ 3 $8\frac{3}{8} - 4\frac{5}{6}$
4 $10\frac{5}{7} - 4\frac{1}{3}$ 5 $1\frac{1}{8} - \frac{3}{8}$

Answers

1 $7\frac{1}{3}$ 2 $2\frac{7}{10}$ 3 $3\frac{13}{24}$ 4 $6\frac{21}{8}$ 5 $\frac{3}{4}$

Adding and subtracting fractions – another approach

Some people learn to add or subtract mixed numbers by turning them all into top-heavy fractions first. Although this method should produce the right answer, it may involve calculating with very large numbers. It is shown here in case you come across it elsewhere.

Example 2.27

Work these out.

a) $2\frac{5}{6} + 3\frac{4}{5}$ **b)** $8\frac{3}{8} - 4\frac{5}{6}$

Solution

a) $2\frac{5}{6} + 3\frac{4}{5} = \frac{17}{6} + \frac{19}{5}$

The common denominator is 30.

$\frac{17}{6} + \frac{19}{5} = \frac{85}{30} + \frac{114}{30} = \frac{199}{30} = 6\frac{19}{30}$

b) $8\frac{3}{8} - 4\frac{5}{6} = \frac{67}{8} - \frac{29}{6}$

The common denominator is 48.

$8\frac{3}{8} - 4\frac{5}{6} = \frac{402}{48} - \frac{232}{48} = \frac{170}{48} = 3\frac{26}{48} = 3\frac{13}{24}$

Using a calculator

Most of the above calculations can be performed with the help of the fraction button. However, examiners sometimes ask you to show your working, so it can be useful to be able to work with fractions without a calculator, even if you usually use one for speed and convenience.

· ·

TAKE A BREAK

Take a break at this point, then come back prepared to tackle decimals.

· ·

On the other side of Decimal Point

In Chapter 1 you met the crabs, who get progressively 10 times bigger the further the waves push them sideways to the left from Decimal Point.

$3 \times 10 = 30$
$3 \times 10 \times 10 = 300$
$3 \times 10 \times 10 \times 10 = 3000$

and so on.

On the other side of this important landmark the crabs get progressively smaller. As you might expect, they get ten times smaller each time they are pushed one place sideways to the right, away from Decimal Point.

$3 \div 10 = 0.3$ $3 \div 100 = 0.03$ $3 \div 1000 = 0.003$
and so on.

A Quick Dip!

1 How many quarters make 6?
2 List the prime numbers between 20 and 30.
3 56×100
4 8×4
5 How many minutes are there in 1 hour 20 minutes?

Answers

1 $6 \times 4 = 24$ 2 23, 29   3 5600   4 32   5 80 minutes

Whole numbers, fractions and decimals

Sometimes Phil Yerbuckitt and Buster Spaid scoop up fraction crabs which are the same size as decimals.

$3 \div 10 = 0.3 = \frac{3}{10}$ three tenths

$3 \div 10 \div 10$ or
$3 \div 100 = 0.03 = \frac{3}{100}$ three hundredths

$3 \div 10 \div 10 \div 10$ or
$3 \div 1000 = 0.003 = \frac{3}{1000}$ three thousandths

and so on.

Example 2.28

Write these decimals as fractions. Give your answers in their lowest terms.

a) 0.7   **b)** 0.16   **c)** 0.08   **d)** 0.001

Solution

a) $7 \div 10 = 0.7$ or $\frac{7}{10}$

b) $16 \div 100 = 0.16$ or $\frac{16}{100}$

   Cancelling gives $\frac{\cancel{16}^{4}}{\cancel{100}_{25}} = \frac{4}{25}$

c) $8 \div 100 = 0.08 = \frac{\cancel{8}^{2}}{\cancel{100}_{25}} = \frac{2}{25}$

d) $1 \div 1000 = 0.001 = \frac{1}{1000}$

Turning decimals into fractions

Example 2.29

Write these decimals as fractions in their lowest terms.

a) 0.07   **b)** 0.002

Solution

a) $\frac{7}{100}$

b) $\frac{2}{1000} = \frac{1}{500}$

Be careful not to write 0.07 as $\frac{7}{10}$ or 0.001 as $\frac{1}{10}$ or $\frac{1}{100}$ The 7 is in the hundredths column and the 1 is in the thousandths column.

An easy way to turn decimals into fractions is to put a 1 on the bottom, under the decimal point (i.e. in the denominator) and a zero to represent all the other digits.

0.07 has two digits after the decimal point, or two decimal places, so the denominator is 100, and 0.001 has three decimal places, so the denominator is 1000. (Most calculators will turn fractions to decimals and some will turn decimals to fractions by the press of a button! It would be worth finding out what yours can do.)

Exercise 2.13

Write these decimals as fractions in their lowest terms, without using a calculator.

1 0.2   **2** 0.24   **3** 0.175   **4** 0. 008

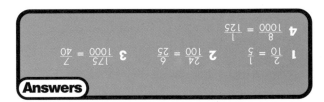

Answers

1 $\frac{2}{10} = \frac{1}{5}$ 2 $\frac{24}{100} = \frac{6}{25}$ 3 $\frac{175}{1000} = \frac{7}{40}$ 4 $\frac{8}{1000} = \frac{1}{125}$

Some common fraction and decimal equivalents

$0.5 = \frac{5}{10}$ or $\frac{1}{2}$

$0.25 = \frac{25}{100}$ or $\frac{1}{4}$

so $0.75 = \frac{75}{100}$ or $\frac{3}{4}$

$0.1 = \frac{1}{10}$

$0.2 = \frac{2}{10}$ or $\frac{1}{5}$

Decimal places

The number of decimal places is the number of digits after (i.e. to the right of) the decimal point. 3.725 has been given to three decimal places, as have 10.005 and 0.106.

Example 2.30

Write the following numbers correct to two decimal places.

a) 12.861   **b)** 3.346   **c)** 7.135

d) 12.1847   **e)** 1.297

Solution

Ray Lyngs has put up a barrier to stop people climbing down the cliffs. He is now about to paint it.

a) Underline the required number of digits, in this case there are two, which are immediately to the right of the decimal point.
12.8<u>61</u>

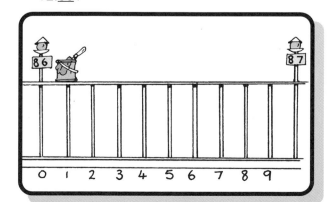

Ray Lyngs balances his paint pot on the next digit. Draw part of the barrier and label it with the number which you have underlined, and the next number. Put a ring to show where he hangs the paint pot.

Now look at the paint pot.

If it is balancing on a 5, 6, 7, 8 or 9, you are at least halfway towards the next upright.

If it is on a number that is less than 5 (i.e. 0, 1, 2, 3 or 4), you are nearer the upright from which you started.

As 1 is nearer to the 86 than it is to the 87, 12.861 = 12.86 to 2 decimal places (d.p.).

b) 3.346

Underlining the first two relevant digits, and hanging up his paint pot gives Ray Lyngs 3.3̲4̲⑥.

3.346 = 3.35 to 2 decimal places.

c) 7.135

Underlining and ringing gives 7.1̲3̲⑤.

Ring the 5.

The 5 is exactly halfway between 13 and 14.

Following the rule, 7.135 = 7.14 to 2 d.p.

d) 12.1847 = 12.1̲8̲④7 = 12.18

Ray Lyngs' paint pot is on a 4, so it is nearer *to 12.18 than 12.19. If the question had asked for three decimal places, then Ray Lyngs would have plonked his pot on 12.18̲4̲⑦ and the answer would have been 12.1847 = 12.185 to 3 d.p.*

e) 1.297

1.297 = 1.2̲9̲⑦ = 1.30 to 2 d.p.

Although 1.30 = 1.3, you must give the number of decimal places asked for in the question.

Be careful when rounding numbers such as 1.706 to 2 d.p. The answer, with a little help from Ray Lyngs, is 1.71.

2

If you have a number with fewer than three decimal places, you can check your answer by comparing it with money.

$100\,p = £1$, so every penny is one hundredth $(\frac{1}{100})$ of a pound. $0.09 = \frac{9}{100}$, and $£0.09 = 9p$ or $\frac{9}{100}$ of a pound. On the other hand, $0.9 = \frac{9}{10}$ and $£0.90 = 90p$ or $\frac{9}{10}$ of a pound.

Exercise 2.14

3.1465	4.81793	2.1478	15.9897
	6.9046	5.9999	

Write the above numbers correct to:
1 3 d.p.   **2** 2 d.p.   **3** the nearest whole number.

Answers

3 3, 5, 2, 16, 7, 6
2 3.15, 4.82, 2.15, 15.99, 6.90, 6.00
1 3.147, 4.818, 2.148, 15.990, 6.905, 6.000

Adding and subtracting decimals

If you can add and subtract money, you can add and subtract decimals.

Exercise 2.15

Try these first without using a calculator. Then check your answers with a calculator.
1 23.07 + 136.4   **2** 800.4 – 36.38
3 £14.20 – 73p   **4** 0.006 + 4.2 + 148.09

Answers

4 152.296
3 £13.47 (£14.20 – £0.73)
2 764.02
1 159.47

Multiplying and dividing decimals

Multiplying decimals by a whole number

Example 2.31

a) Enid Ashaim tried to buy tickets for herself and her five favourite nieces and nephews, at £2.40 each, for the Saturday matinee at the Gaudyville Theatre. How much would this have cost altogether?

b) Unfortunately, the theatre had sold out, so Enid generously shared the money equally among the five nieces and nephews. How much did each receive?

Solution

a) $£2.40 \times 6 = £14.40$

b) $£14.40 \div 5 = £2.88$

As you can see, multiplying or dividing decimals by a whole number is no different from multiplying and dividing tens and units, provided that you remember to put in the decimal point.

Multiplying a decimal by a decimal

Example 2.32

Multiply 0.2×0.3

Although $2 \times 3 = 6$, the answer is not 0.6.

Solution

$0.2 = \frac{2}{10}$ and $0.3 = \frac{3}{10}$

$\frac{2}{10} \times \frac{3}{10} = \frac{6}{100}$ or 0.06

$0.2 \times 0.3 = 0.06$

$$\frac{\ast}{10} \times \frac{\ast}{10} = \frac{\ast}{100}$$

tenths multiplied by
tenths = hundredths

$$\frac{\ast}{10} \times \frac{\ast}{100} = \frac{\ast}{1000}$$

tenths multiplied by
hundredths = thousandths

and so on.

*The quick way of doing this is to count the
number of digits altogether after the decimal points
in the question, and then put the same number of
digits after the decimal point in the answer.*

Esther Mait is very good at working out rough
answers. Here she helps you to put the decimal
point in the right place.

Example 2.33

Work out 4.6×3.4

Solution

Whether you use a calculator or not, you should get
the figures 1564. Esther Mait multiplies the whole
numbers and gets $4 \times 3 = 12$. The correct answer is
slightly above 12, so the answer must be 15.64 not
1564 or 1.564.

$4.6 \times 3.4 = 15.64$

Exercise 2.16

Without using a calculator, state whether each of
the following is likely or impossible. Give reasons
for your answers.
1 $3.24 \times 2.67 = 86.508$
2 $2.13 \times 2.44 = 51.9$
3 $1.3 \times 1.2 = 0.156$

Multiplying decimals without using a calculator

Example 2.34

Multiply 2.14×3.4

Solution

Start by ignoring the decimal points and treat the
calculation as an ordinary long multiplication sum.
(Look back to page 4 if you have forgotten how to do
this.)

$214 \times 34 = 7276$

In the question, there are three digits after the decimal
points, so you need three digits after the decimal point
in the answer.

$2.14 \times 3.4 = 7.276$

Check: $2 \times 3 = 6$. The answer must be slightly bigger
than 6.

Dividing a number by a decimal

Phil Yerbuckitt and Buster Spaid have six tickets
between them for the Gaudyville Theatre. Sharing
them out, they have $6 \div 2 = 3$ each.

60 tickets have been allotted to the 20 most
devoted members of Cherie Towtt's fan club. If each
fan is given the same number of tickets, how many
should each receive?

$60 \div 20 = 3$

600 tickets remain for the general public. By a
coincidence, 200 people each buy the same number
of tickets. How many do they each buy?

$600 \div 200 = 3$

Summarising these answers produces these results.

$6 \div 2 = 3 \qquad 60 \div 20 = 3 \qquad 600 \div 200 = 3$

As long as you multiply both numbers by the same
amount, the result stays the same.

2

Example 2.35

Work out $4 \div 0.5$

Solution

$0.5 = \frac{1}{2}$

Remember that this is the same as saying, 'How many halves in 4?', and not, 'What is half of 4?'

$4 \div 0.5 = 8$ This gives the same result as $40 \div 5$.

You have changed 0.5 into a whole number by multiplying by 10, so, in order not to give the correct result, you have also to multiply 4 by the same amount.

$0.5 \times 10 = 5$ $4 \times 10 = 40$ $40 \div 5 = 8$

Example 2.36

Work out $0.142 \div 0.02$

Solution

$0.02 \times 100 = 2$ $0.142 \times 100 = 14.2$

$14.2 \div 2 = 7.1$

Multiplying both numbers by the same amount won't affect the result. Multiplying only one of them will.

Example 2.37

Work these out without using a calculator. Then check your answers with a calculator.

a) $21 \div 3$ **b)** $210 \div 30$ **c)** $2.1 \div 3$

d) $2.1 \div 0.3$ **e)** $21 \div 30$

Solution

a) $21 \div 3 = 7$ b) $210 \div 30 = 7$

c) $2.1 \div 3 = 0.7$ d) $2.1 \div 0.3 = 7$

e) $21 \div 30 = 0.7$

---

*When you are dividing decimals, you must first make sure that the **divisor** (number by which you are dividing) is a whole number. You do this by multiplying the divisor by 10, 100, 1000 etc. until you have a whole number. (Look back to pages 1 and 5 if you have forgotten where the crabs go when they are affected by being multiplied or divided by a wave force of 10, 100 etc.) Then multiply your first number by the same amount.*

Exercise 2.17

Work these out without using a calculator. Then check your answers with a calculator.

1 $2.4 \div 0.4$ **2** $2.4 \div 0.04$

3 $0.24 \div 0.4$ **4** $24 \div 0.004$

Answers   1 6   2 60   3 0.6   4 6000

Multiplying and dividing by numbers less than 1

How would you work out 10×0.5?

This is the same as asking, 'What is half of 10?'

$10 \times 0.5 = 10 \times \frac{1}{2} = 5$

And can you see that $10 \div 0.5 = 20$?

This is the same as asking, 'How many halves are there in 10?'

When you multiply by a number smaller than 1, your answer will be smaller.

When you divide by a number smaller than 1, your answer will be bigger.

Remainders

Example 2.38

When Phil Yerbuckitt and Buster Spaid tried to share 27 crabs equally they found that they had one crab left over.

$27 \div 2 = 13 \text{ r } 1$

When Big Hilda Klime and Ena Phizinuph shared 27 jam tarts between them, they split the extra tart down the middle and had half each.

$27 \div 2 = 13\frac{1}{2}$

When Phyl Theeritch decided to go halves with Bjorn Loozer in a present for Vic Taurius costing £27.00, each paid £27.00 ÷ 2 = £13.50.

Writing remainders as decimals

Example 2.39

Without using a calculator, work out $74 \div 4$. Give your answer in decimal form.

Solution

$$
\begin{array}{r}
18 \quad \text{remainder 2} \\
4\overline{)74}
\end{array}
$$

If you have a remainder, write a decimal point after your original number, and add zeros.

$$
\begin{array}{r}
18.5 \\
4\overline{)7^34.^20}
\end{array}
$$

Example 2.40

Work out $175 \div 8$

Solution

Keep adding noughts after the decimal point until you have enough to finish the calculation.

$$
\begin{array}{r}
21.875 \\
8\overline{)17^15.^70^60^40}
\end{array}
$$

Recurring decimals

Example 2.41

Work these out.

a) $19 \div 3$ **b)** $81 \div 33$

Solution

a)
$$
\begin{array}{r}
6.333333... \\
3\overline{)19.^10^10^10^10^10^10...}
\end{array}
$$

b)
$$
\begin{array}{r}
2.4545454 5... \\
33\overline{)81.^{15}0^{18}0^{15}0^{18}0^{15}0^{18}0^{15}0^{18}0...}
\end{array}
$$

Even if you continued dividing for the rest of your life, you would never reach the end!

Numbers like these are called **recurring decimals** and they are usually written like this:

$6.\dot{3} \quad 2.\dot{4}\dot{5} \text{ or } 2.\overline{45}$

Turning fractions into decimals

Cherie Towtt has already shown you that any fraction is just another way of writing a **numerator** (top number) divided by a **denominator** (bottom number). This is all you need to remember to turn fractions into decimals.

Exercise 2.18

Change the following fractions into decimals. Where you have a recurring decimal, write enough digits to show the pattern.

1 $\frac{4}{5}$ **2** $\frac{7}{8}$ **3** $\frac{2}{3}$ **4** $\frac{3}{11}$ **5** $\frac{3}{1000}$

Answers

1 0.8 **2** 0.875 **3** 0.6̇ **4** 0.2̇7̇ **5** 0.003

Percentages

Most calculators will do percentages for you. Check up on yours!

Per cent means 'per hundred' or 'out of a hundred'. The sign for per cent is %. You can also write a percentage as a fraction or a decimal.

$53\% = \frac{53}{100} = 0.53$

Remember: $0.7 = \frac{7}{10} = \frac{70}{100} = 70\%$, whilst $0.07 = \frac{7}{100} = 7\%$

Exercise 2.19

Fill in the blanks. Remember to give all the fractions in their lowest terms.

Fraction	Decimal	Percentage
$\frac{9}{10}$	☀	☀
☀	0.6	☀
☀	☀	20%
☀	0.05	☀

Answers

Fraction	Decimal	Percentage
$\frac{9}{10}$	0.9	90%
$\frac{3}{5}$	0.6	60%
$\frac{1}{5}$	0.2	20%
$\frac{1}{20}$	0.05	5%

Working with percentages

There are several different ways of tackling percentage questions. Try the following exercise before you go any further, to see how you get on.

Exercise 2.20

Work out the following percentages, without using a calculator.
1 10% of 60   **2** 30% of 80   **3** 15% of 190
4 Out of an audience of 150 at the Gaudyville Theatre, 27 people demanded their money back. What percentage was that?

Answers

1 6   **2** 24   **3** 28.5   **4** 18%

How did you get on?

All or most of them right?

Congratulations. You can safely skip the next section, and move on to page 38.

All washed up?

Welcome aboard! Most people are muddled about percentages at first. Just work through the next few pages and your problems will be swept away.

What does 'per cent' really mean?

'Per cent' means per, or out of, 100. Whichever method you use, you need to know that the whole amount of something is 100%. You have probably used either fractions or decimals to solve percentage questions. We show both methods here so that you can choose the way that you have been taught, or the way that you find easier.

Fractions and percentages

Example 2.42

Find 12% of 450

Solution

$12\% = 12$ out of $100 =$ twelve hundredths $\left(\frac{12}{100}\right)$

12% of $450 = \dfrac{12}{100} \times 450 = 54$

Example 2.43

In a survey, three out of four people questioned said that New-Mer-a-Sea was a good resort for a family holiday. What percentage was that?

Solution

3 out of 4 = $\frac{3}{4}$ (Remember you can replace 'out of' by ÷ .)

Now you need to work out $\frac{3}{4}$ of 100%.

$$\frac{3}{4} \times \frac{100}{1} = 75\%$$

Fractions and percentages – the 'two ears and a bottom' way!

Some people who use the fraction method get confused as to where to put the hundred. 'Two ears and a bottom' is a quick way of checking whether you have it in the right place. The previous two examples required you to calculate:

a) 12% of 450   **b)** 3 out of 4 as a percentage.

Method

First decide whether you have an 'of' or an 'out of' calculation.

12% **of** 450 = $\frac{12}{100} \times 450$ 3 **out of** 4 = $\frac{3}{4}$

Everybody has two ears. Everybody has one bottom. You need two numbers on the top and one number on the bottom.

$\frac{12 \times 450}{100}$ You already have two numbers on the top. Write the 100 on the bottom.

$\frac{12 \times 450}{100} = 54$

$\frac{3}{4}$ You have one number on the top, so you are short of an ear! Write the 100 on the top.

$\frac{3 \times 100}{4} = 75\%$

Example 2.44

To encourage more visitors to the Gaudyville Theatre, the management reduced its prices by 16% for the Wednesday evening show. What was the reduction in price on a ticket which originally cost £3.50? (**Hint:** First change £3.50 to 350 pence.)

Solution

16% of 350p   Start by replacing 'of' and write:

16×350 You already have two numbers on the top. You need the 100 on the bottom.

$\frac{16 \times 350}{100} = 56$ The reduction was 56p.

Example 2.45

On a fishing trip, Rod and Annette caught 175 creatures altogether. Of these, 105 were crabs.

a) What percentage was that?

b) What percentage were not crabs?

Solution

a) Start by writing 105 out of 175 as $\frac{105}{175}$.

You already have one number on the bottom.

You need another 'ear' for the top.

$\frac{105 \times 100}{175} = 60$ so 60% were crabs.

b) 100 − 60 = 40 so 40% were not crabs.

2

Exercise 2.21

Work these out, using a fractional method.

1 25% of 360　**2** 12% of 150　**3** 50% of $16\frac{1}{2}$

Answers

1 90　**2** 18　**3** $8\frac{1}{4}$

Using decimals to calculate percentages

Example 2.46

Find 15% of 470

Solution

15% = 0.15　　Replace 'of' with ×.

15% of 470 = 0.15 × 470 = 70.5

Example 2.47

Out of the 20 people who went on a Ricky Tea coach trip, 13 said that they would not like to repeat the experience. What percentage was that?

Solution

Start by changing 13 out of 20 into a decimal.

13 out of 20 as a decimal = 13 ÷ 20 = 0.65.
0.65 = 65%

Example 2.48

Cherie Towtt and the Sand Witches made £650.24 from a gig. They spent 30% of it on a night out. How much was that, to the nearest penny?

Solution

30% of £650.24 = 0.3 × £650.24 = £195.072
　　　　　　　= £195.07 to the nearest penny.

Short-cut percentages

Some percentages are very easy to work out in your head.

50% = $\frac{1}{2}$　　50% of 17 = 17 ÷ 2 = 8.5 or $8\frac{1}{2}$ or £8.50 if the question refers to £17.00.

25% = $\frac{1}{4}$　　You can either divide your original amount by 4, or divide it by 2, and then by 2 again.
25% of 180 = 180 ÷ 4 = 45 or 180 ÷ 2 = 90. 90 ÷ 2 = 45.

$12\frac{1}{2}$% = $\frac{1}{2}$ of 25% or $\frac{1}{8}$ of your original amount
$12\frac{1}{2}$% of 48 = 48 ÷ 8 = 6

75% = $\frac{3}{4}$　　Find 25% and multiply your answer by 3.

10% or $\frac{1}{10}$ is very easy to find if you think back to the crabs on page 5.
　　　　　10% of 60 = 60 ÷ 10 = 6
　　　　　10% of £23.40 = 23.4 ÷ 10
　　　　　　　　　　= £2.34

15% = 10% + 5%　　Find 10%, halve it to find 5% and then add the answers together.
15% of 80 = 10% of 80 + 5% of 80.
10% of 80 = 8
5% of 80 = 8 ÷ 2 = 4
15% of 80 = 8 + 4 = 12

If you can find 10% and 5%, you can use this information to find other amounts easily.

20% = 2 × 10%　　35% = 3 × 10% + 5% etc.

$33\frac{1}{3}$% = $\frac{1}{3}$　　Divide your original amount by 3.
　　　　　$33\frac{1}{3}$% of 81 = 81 ÷ 3
　　　　　　　　　　= 27

$66\frac{2}{3}$% = $\frac{2}{3}$　　Find $\frac{1}{3}$ and then double it.
　　　　　$66\frac{2}{3}$% of 81 = 27 × 2
　　　　　　　　　　= 54

Exercise 2.22

Solve the following, using whichever method you prefer.

1 25% of £96.10
2 60% of 52
3 Esther Mait scored 28 out of 45 in a test. What percentage is that, to the nearest whole number?
4 In Millie-Anne Eyre's bundle of 12 five pound notes, three were found to be forgeries.
  a) What percentage was that?
  b) How much actual money was forged?
5 Find $66\frac{2}{3}$% of £28.14.

Answers

1 £24.03 to the nearest penny
2 31.2
3 62%
4 a) 25% b) £15.00
5 £18.76

Ratio

Winnie De Braik has taken her stressed-out family for a holiday to New-Mer-a-Sea. As it is very windy on the beach, Winnie puts up a wind-break, so that everyone can shelter behind it and enjoy a picnic with the Sand Witches when they have finished rehearsing. Winnie shares out all the food equally on individual plates, but as some members of her family are much hungrier than others, they don't always have the same number of plates each.

Example 2.49

Share 40 biscuits between two Sand Witches in the ratio 3 to 2. (This is usually written as 3 : 2.)

Solution

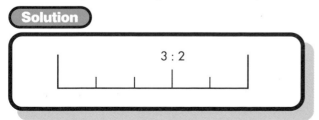

You can see that Winnie De Braik needs 5 plates.

$40 \div 5 = 8$

There will be 8 biscuits on each plate.

One Sand Witch receives $3 \times 8 = 24$, and the other $2 \times 8 = 16$.

Method for finding shares

1 Draw Winnie De Braik's wind-break and divide each section into the correct number of portions.
2 Count the number of portions altogether, then divide this into the total to find out how much is in each one.
3 Multiply each individual's share to find out how much each receives in total.

Sometimes you are given the amount after it has been shared out, and you have to work back to find the original.

Example 2.50

Rod and Annette were paid for the old drinks cans they collected from the beach at the neighbouring resort of Litter-a-Sea. As Rod collected three sacks, and Annette collected four sacks, they shared the money in the ratio 3 : 4. Rod received £6.00.

a) How much should Annette receive?

b) How much did they earn altogether?

Solution

Draw Winnie De Braik's wind-break as shown below and write Rod's portion as indicated.

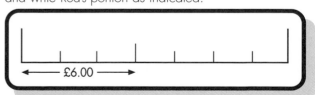

You can easily see that each section should contain $6 \div 3 = 2$.

a) Annette received $4 \times 2 = £8.00$

b) The total earned was £6.00 + £8.00 = £14.00, or £2.00 × 7 = £14.00

2

Method for finding amounts

1 Draw the wind-break and divide it into the correct number of portions.
2 Write the amount you have in the appropriate section, as shown on the diagrams.
3 Use this to work out how much is in each individual portion, and then multiply as required.

Giving ratios in their simplest form

Pause Pelling Grammar School decided to come on a day trip to New-Mer-a-Sea. Regulations state that there must be one adult for every ten pupils. In other words, the ratio of adult to pupils was 1 : 10. If 30 pupils came, the number of adults required would be three.

$$3 : 30 = 1 : 10$$

Giving ratios in their simplest form means cancelling down by taking out all the common factors. (If you need to, you can remind yourself about cancelling and factors by referring to pages 11 and 19.)

Example 2.51

Willie, Kenny and Noel Droppitt have a one-night contract to perform their juggling act at the Gaudyville Theatre. They have agreed to split the fee in the ratio of their years of experience: 10, 4 and 6 respectively.

a) If Willie received £24.50, how much did each of the others receive?

b) What was the total which they earned?

Solution

Divide through by 2, to reduce the ratios. 10 : 4 : 6 = 5 : 2 : 3 (This is not absolutely necessary, but makes the numbers more manageable.)

Draw Winnie De Braik's wind-break as usual.

Each individual portion is £24.50 ÷ 5 = £4.90

a) Kenny receives 2 × £4.90 = £9.80

   Noel receives 3 × £4.90 = £14.70

b) The total earned was £24.50 + £9.80 + £14.70
   = £49.00 (or £4.90 × 10)

Exercise 2.23

1 Maeve Isitt gave her two nieces £60.00 holiday pocket money to share in the ratio of their ages. If the girls were seven and five years old, how much should each receive?
2 Share 12 squares of chocolate between Cherie Towtt and one of her group so that Cherie Towtt receives twice as much as her friend.
3 Big Hilda Klime and Ena Phizinuph guzzled their way through a plateful of biscuits, sharing them in the ratio 5 : 3. If Ena Phizinuph wolfed six biscuits, how many did Big Hilda Klime scoff?

Answers

1 7 + 5 = 12, £60.00 ÷ 12 = £5.00
The older niece should receive 7 × £5.00 = £35.00.
The younger should receive £25.00.
2 Cherie Towtt gets 8 and her friend gets 4.
3 6 ÷ 3 = 2
Big Hilda Klime ate 5 × 2 = 10.

In the answer to question 2, if Cherie Towtt's group member gets one share, Cherie Towtt must get two shares. 12 ÷ 3 = 4, not 12 ÷ 2!

A Quick Dip!

1 Find 15% of £60.00. (Find 10%, then 5%.)
2 What is 0.25 as a fraction?
3 How many sevens make twenty-eight?
4 50% of a number is 6. What is the number?
5 Work out 64 + 19. (First try 64 + 20.)

Answers

1 £9.00 **2** $\frac{1}{4}$ **3** four
4 12 (50% = $\frac{1}{2}$. If $\frac{1}{2}$ the amount = 6, the full amount = 2 × 6 = 12.)
5 83

TAKE A BREAK

Proportion

Direct proportion

The unitary method

'The unitary method' is simply a rather grand expression which means a method of finding one, or one unit, of a quantity.

Example 2.52

It costs £7.50 to hire five sun loungers for a morning.

a) How much does it cost to hire one?

b) How much would it cost to hire eight?

Solution

Set the information out in a table.

	Sun loungers	Cost	
What does the question tell me?	5	£7.50	Divide: £7.50 ÷ 5
What do I need to find?	1		1 costs £1.50
	8		Multiply: £1.50 × 8 = £12.00

a) £7.50 ÷ 5 = £1.50

It costs £1.50 to hire one sun lounger.

b) £1.50 × 8 = £12.00

It would cost £12.00 to hire eight sun loungers.

Example 2.53

If three ice creams cost £1.35, find the cost of seven.

Solution

Start by setting the question out in a table. Leave a gap between the first and last lines.

	Ice creams	Cost	
What does the question tell me?	3	£1.35	Divide: £1.35 ÷ 3
	1		1 costs 45p
What do I need to find?	7		Multiply: 45p × 7 = £3.15

Example 2.54

Gladys Allova bought eight holiday postcards for £1.28. How many could she have bought for £2.08?

Solution

Start by listing the information in the usual way. Be sure to keep the same quantities in the same column.

Postcards	Cost in pounds
8	1.28
	2.08

Only one column will have two numbers. Link these with a '1'.

Postcards	Cost in pounds
8	1.28
	1
	2.08

The other side is the DIM side. Write DIM as shown.

		Postcards	Cost in pounds
8 ÷ 1.28 = 6.25	D	8	1.28
	I		1 (How many for £1.00?)
6.25 × 2.08 = 13	M		2.08

When you work this out on a calculator, you can simply key in 8 ÷ 1.28 × 2.08 = 13.

2

> ### Just to recap
> #### Direct proportion for the DIM!
> 1 Set out the information in a table.
> 2 Join the two amounts which are in the same column with a 1.
> 3 Write DIM vertically in the other column. Divide the number next to the D by the other number in the same row. That will give you the value for 1. Multiply by the number alongside the M to give you the final answer.

Exercise 2.24

Use the DIM method, or a method of your choice, to work these out.

1 Rhoda Weigh paid £10.50 to hire a horse for three hours. How much would it have cost her to hire it for seven hours?

2 If five sticks of rock cost 85p, how many sticks could you buy for £2.04?

3 A large bottle of washing-up liquid costs 90p for 500 ml. A giant bottle of the same brand costs £1.25 for 750 ml. Which is better value?

> The giant bottle is cheaper.
> 90 ÷ 500 = 0.18p and 125 ÷ 750 = 0.17 (2 d.p.)
> Alternatively work out the cost of 1 ml.
> money with the giant bottle.
> Giant: 750 ÷ 125 = 6 ml. You get more for your
> Large: 500 ÷ 90 = 5.6 ml, to 1 d.p.
> 3 Work out the amount you get for 1p.
> **1** £24.50   **2** 12
>
> **Answers**

Inverse or indirect proportion

Example 2.55

Laurie Lode took four hours to drive to Litter-a-Sea. He made the return journey at twice the speed. How long did he take?

Solution

If you go twice as fast, it takes you half the time. Laurie Lode took two hours.

This is very similar to a direct proportion question, except that with direct proportion, both quantities get bigger or both quantities get smaller, but with inverse proportion, one quantity gets bigger whilst the other gets smaller.

Example 2.56

It would take three workmen eight days to repair the sea defences. How long would four men take?

Solution

	Men	Time in days
What does the question tell me?	3	8
What do I need to know?		4

Try solving this the MAD way. Start by working out how long one man would take. Remember, he has to do everyone's job. Having spent 8 days on his part, he has to spend the next 8 days on the next man's section, and then the next 8 days etc.

Men	Time in days
3	8
1	3 × 8 = 24

There are 24 days' work altogether which 4 men are going to share.

4	24 ÷ 4 = 6

To summarise:

	Men	Time in days	
Multiply	3	8	3 × 8 = 24
And then	1	24	
Divide	4	24 ÷ 4 = 6	

*If you cannot do direct proportion, you are downright DIM (**D**ivide to find **1** and then **M**ultiply), but inverse proportion can drive you MAD (**M**ultiply **A**nd then **D**ivide.)*

Exercise 2.25

Work out the following. Decide whether your answer should be larger or smaller than your original amount.

1 Three of the Sand Witches took six hours to do the washing up after a picnic. How long would two of them have taken?
2 Rod and Annette paid £35.10 for three new fishing lines. How much would five cost?
3 Ricky Tea's coach took $2\frac{1}{2}$ hours to complete a trip. It made the return journey at half the speed. How long did it take?

Answers

1 9 hours   2 £58.50   3 5 hours

check your luggage

HAVE YOU REMEMBERED TO PACK ...

- fractions
- decimals
- decimal places and rounding
- percentages
- ratio
- direct and inverse proportion?

Ready for more? Turn to pages 132–3 for:
- smallest and largest values of a rounded number
- rounding to one significant figure.

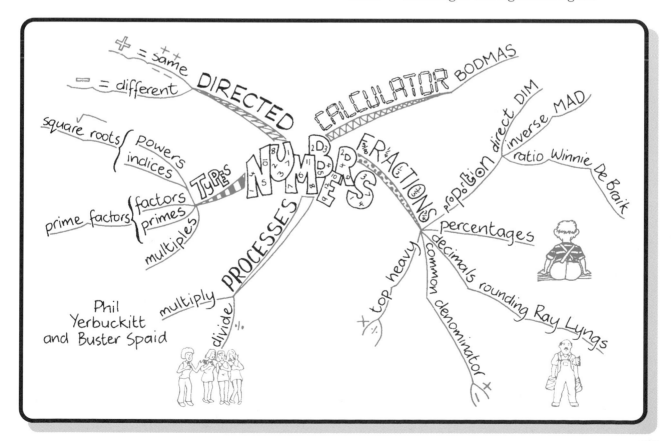

Number review

1 Multiply the following numbers by 100.
   a) 34
   b) 0.0045
   c) $\frac{1}{2}$

2 Divide the following numbers by 10.
   a) 530
   b) 67.2
   c) 3.6

3 The Great Barry O'Reefe, the famous Irish conjuror now resident in Australia, can be seen throughout the summer performing at The Gaudyville Theatre. One of his tricks involves a pack of special cards. Some of the cards look like this.

The audience shouts out numbers and The Great Barry O'Reefe makes them using two cards from his pack. He can only use any card just once in every question.
Barry O'Reefe always produces two cards. Which two cards would he have used?
   a) ☼ + ☼ = $^{+}$18
   b) ☼ − ☼ = 19
   c) ☼ + ☼ = 0

4 **a)** Seventeen of Cherie Towtt's fan club want to come to her next concert. Tickets are priced at £12.50 each. How much should the club pay?
   b) The club is allowed a 10% discount. How much is the discount?
   c) How much will the club be charged?

5 Find 1400 as a product of its prime factors.

6 What is the lowest common multiple of 12 and 30?

7 **a)** Big Hilda Klime has eaten $\frac{3}{5}$ of a pizza.
   Ena Phizinuph has eaten $\frac{1}{2}$ of the remainder. What fraction of the original pizza has Ena Phizinuph eaten?
   b) What fraction of the original pizza is left?

8 Work out 0.2 × 0.4

9 At a concert at the Gaudyville Theatre, 54 people out of an audience of 360 said that they had not enjoyed the show. What percentage was that?

10 **a)** Winnie De Braik planned to share out some chocolate drops amongst the youngest three members of her enormous family in the ratio of their ages. If the youngest three were aged two, three and seven, and she had 72 chocolate drops, how many should each receive?
   b) Unfortunately two of the older members had already grabbed them and shared them between them so that one had twice as many as the other. How many did each receive?
   c) When Rod and Annette compared how many crabs they had caught, they found that Rod had three times as many as Annette. If Rod had 24 crabs, how many had Annette caught?
   d) How many crabs had they caught altogether?

Algebra

checklist
Into this chapter we have packed ...

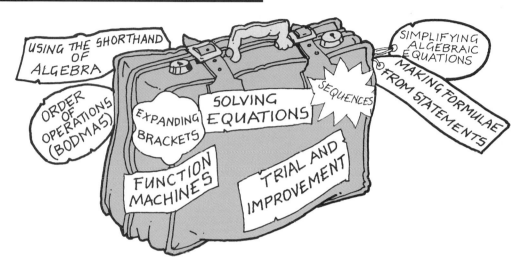

USING THE SHORTHAND OF ALGEBRA

ORDER OF OPERATIONS (BODMAS)

EXPANDING BRACKETS

SOLVING EQUATIONS

SEQUENCES

SIMPLIFYING ALGEBRAIC EQUATIONS

MAKING FORMULAE FROM STATEMENTS

FUNCTION MACHINES

TRIAL AND IMPROVEMENT

Cracking the code – the shorthand of algebra

This page from Howard Eye-No's guide book gives the shorthand that we use to write algebra.

$$ab = a \times b$$

$$\frac{a}{b} = a \div b$$

$$3a = 3 \times a$$

$$a^2 = a \times a$$

$$3a^2 = 3 \times a \times a$$

$$(3a)^2 = 3a \times 3a = 9a^2$$

Order of operations

BODMAS is renowned throughout the resort – he appears on all public walls, bus shelters, garage doors, and even on the dirt on the side of vans and lorries. It is a problem, but the council have finally found a way to deal with it. At long last they have realised that BODMAS gives an easy way of remembering the order in which to carry out mathematical tasks.

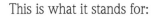

This is what it stands for:

Brackets
Of (e.g. '2 to the power **of**', or '$\frac{1}{2}$ **of** 16')
Division
Multiplication
Addition
Subtraction

Example 3.1

Evaluate $20 - (3 + 1)$

Solution

Evaluate means 'find the value of'.

Working through BODMAS from the start, carry out the operation inside the brackets first, then subtract.

Brackets: $20 - (3 + 1) = 20 - 4$
Subtract: $= 16$

Example 3.2

Evaluate $26 - 5 \times 3$

Solution

BODMAS says, 'Do the multiplication before the subtraction.'

Multiply: $26 - 5 \times 3 = 26 - 15$
Subtract: $= 11$

Example 3.3

Evaluate $(1 + 4)^2$

Solution

BODMAS says, 'Carry out the operations inside the brackets before performing any of the operations outside them.'

Brackets: $(1 + 4)^2 = (5)^2$
$= 25$

Example 3.4

Evaluate $\dfrac{60}{4 + 2}$

Solution

This is the same as $60 \div (4 + 2)$.

So $\frac{60}{4 + 2}$ could be written as $\frac{60}{(4 + 2)}$.

Brackets: $\frac{60}{(4 + 2)} = \frac{60}{6}$
Division: $= 10$

Example 3.5

Evaluate $\dfrac{40 - 4}{4 \times 3}$

Solution

$\frac{40 - 4}{4 \times 3}$ is the same as $\frac{(40 - 4)}{(4 \times 3)}$.

Brackets: $\frac{(40 - 4)}{(4 \times 3)} = \frac{36}{12}$ or $(40 - 4) \div (4 \times 3) = 36 \div 12$
Division: $36 \div 12 = 3$

Example 3.6

Evaluate $22 - 3 \times 5 + 4$

Solution

BODMAS says, 'Multiply before adding or subtracting.'

$22 - 3 \times 5 + 4 = 22 - 15 + 4$
$= 11$

Remember that any sign is always attached to the number that immediately follows it.

Example 3.7

Evaluate $(1 + 2 \times 3)^2$

Solution

BODMAS says, 'Do the operations inside the brackets first,' but BODMAS also applies inside the brackets. So, do the multiplication, then the addition, inside the brackets. Then square the answer.

$$(1 + 2 \times 3)^2 = (1 + 6)^2$$
$$= (7)^2$$
$$= 49$$

*Any **scientific** calculator uses BODMAS. Choose some of the calculations above, and try them out using a calculator. If you enter the numbers and operations in the correct order, you will get the right answer.*

Exercise 3.1

Evaluate the following. See if you get the right answer both with and without a calculator.

1 $16 - 3 \times 5$

2 $6(4 - 1)$

3 3×2^2

4 $(3 + 2 \times 2)^2$

5 $\dfrac{80}{4 + 6}$ (Remember, $80 \div (4 + 6)$. Otherwise the calculator will do $80 \div 4$ first.)

6 $5 + 20 \div 4 - 2$ (You don't need brackets here.)

7 $2^2 - 4$

8 $26 - 2 \times 3^2$

Answers

1 $16 - 15 = 1$ (M then S)

2 $6 \times 3 = 18$ (B then M)

3 $3 \times 4 = 12$ (O then M)

4 $(3 + 4)^2 = 7^2 = 49$ (B first, then A], then O)

5 $80 \div 10 = 8$ (B then D)

6 $5 + 5 - 2 = 8$ (D, A, S)

7 $4 - 4 = 0$ (O, S)

8 $26 - 18 = 9 \times 2 \times 2 - 26 = 8$ (O, M, S)

Substituting numbers into formulae

Candy and Floss are always dreaming up ways of making money. They go along the beach every evening collecting the beach trays that the tourists have left behind, to return them to the café and get the deposit back. They also get paid by the attendant to lug deckchairs back to the stack by the pier. Each day they make a note of what they have earned.

They write t to represent the amount of money they get for returning one tray, and d for the money the attendant gives them for bringing back one deckchair. One evening they find that they have returned four trays and six deckchairs, so they write their results down as $4t + 6d$. Since they get 5p for each tray, and 10p for a deckchair, they work out $4 \times 5 + 6 \times 10 = 80$. (Thanks to BODMAS they remember to multiply before they add.) They have earned 80p. The next evening they work harder and collect 15 trays and 20 deckchairs. They write down $15t + 20d$. Then they work out $15 \times 5 + 20 \times 10 = 275$ and check that they have been paid £2.75.

Candy looks at the calculations and realises that she now understands how to tackle that algebra homework which she has been putting off. All she has to do is to replace the letters by the numerical values which she has been given, and then use BODMAS.

3

Impress your teacher!

$4t + 6d$ and $15t + 20d$ are called **expressions**. The separate parts of an expression (e.g. $6d$, $15t$) are called **terms**. The expression $3a - 2b$ has two terms. The expression $5x + 2y^2 - 10$ has three terms.

Example 3.8

Here is part of Candy's homework.

Find the value of $5x - 4y$ when $x = 3$ and $y = 2$.

Solution

When she thinks about it, Candy realises that if she were to collect five bottles with 3p deposits, she could trade them in for four 2p chews and still be in pocket!

BODMAS says, 'Multiply before you subtract'.

$$5 \times 3 - 4 \times 2 = 15 - 8$$
$$= 7$$

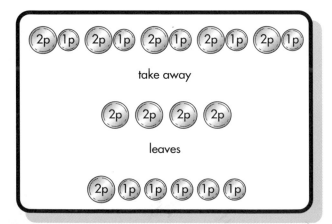

Example 3.9

Evaluate $x^2 + 2xy$ when $x = 8$ and $y = 3$.

Solution

BODMAS says, 'Work out 'to the power of' first, then multiply, then subtract.'

$$8^2 + 2 \times 8 \times 3 = 64 + 2 \times 8 \times 3$$
$$= 64 + 48$$
$$= 112$$

Example 3.10

Evaluate $(a + 3b)^2$ when $a = 3$ and $b = 2$.

Solution

Substituting the numbers in for a and b gives:

$$(3 + 3 \times 2)^2 = (3 + 6)^2$$
$$= 9^2$$
$$= 81$$

Exercise 3.2

Evaluate the following when $a = 4$, $b = 5$, $c = 2$ and $d = {}^-1$.

1 $a + b$ **2** $c - d$

3 $2a - c$ **4** $5b - ab$

5 $a(b + c)$ **6** $(a + c)^2$

7 ab^2 **8** $\dfrac{b + d}{c}$

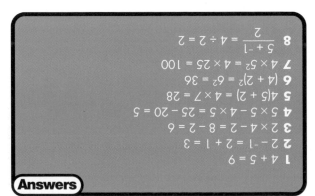

Answers

1 $4 + 5 = 9$
2 $2 - {}^-1 = 2 + 1 = 3$
3 $2 \times 4 - 2 = 8 - 2 = 6$
4 $5 \times 5 - 4 \times 5 = 25 - 20 = 5$
5 $4(5 + 2) = 4 \times 7 = 28$
6 $(4 + 2)^2 = 6^2 = 36$
7 $4 \times 5^2 = 4 \times 25 = 100$
8 $\dfrac{-1 + 5}{2} = 4 \div 2 = 2$

A Quick Dip!

1 Evaluate $11 - 2 \times 4$. **2** Calculate $24 \div 6$.
3 Work out $\frac{1}{2} - \frac{1}{4}$. **4** Simplify $14 : 16$.
5 Calculate $\frac{1}{2} \times \frac{3}{4}$.

Answers

$11-8=3$ **1** 24 **2** $3\frac{1}{4}$ **3** 4 $7:8$ **4** 5 $\frac{3}{8}$

TAKE A BREAK

Collecting and simplifying algebraic expressions

Addition and subtraction

The next evening, Candy and Floss go out separately. Candy collects five trays and lugs back four deckchairs. She writes down $5t + 4d$. Floss only manages three trays, but carts back seven deckchairs altogether. She writes $3t + 7d$. Together they have collected:

$5t + 4d + 3t + 7d$

They will be paid for eight trays and eleven deckchairs, so they write:

$5t + 4d + 3t + 7d = 8t + 11d$

So the items, or terms, with t have been added together:

$5t + 3t = 8t$

and the terms with d have been added together:

$4d + 7d = 11d$

*This is called **simplifying** or **collecting like terms**.*

Next time Candy and Floss go out, they decide to do their bit for the environment and collect up some of the empty crisp bags that they find blowing about. Candy brings back six trays, two deckchairs and ten bags while Floss manages three trays, nine deckchairs – not all in one go, needless to say – and five bags. They won't get any money for the bags, but they still record the number that they collect, just for the 'feel good factor'.

So Candy has $6t + 2d + 10$, while Floss has returned with $3t + 9d + 7$.

Together they have 9 trays, 11 deckchairs and 17 bags.

$6t + 2d + 10 + 3t + 9d + 7 = 9t + 11d + 17$

Now they have added
the terms in t together: $\qquad 6t + 3t = 9t$
the terms in d together: $\qquad 2d + 9d = 11d$
and the number of bags together: $\quad 10 + 7 = 17$

Their answer has three terms, because you can't add tea trays, deckchairs and crisp packets together!

TAKE A BREAK

Whenever you see a letter representing a number, like x or y, written on its own, you can imagine a one in front of it, so in the next examples and exercise, remember x is the same as $1x$, and y is the same as $1y$.

Example 3.11

Simplify the following expression.

$2x + 11 + x - 5$

Solution

'Simplify' just means 'put all the same sort of terms together.'

Since $2x + x = 3x$ (because $x = 1 \times x$), and $11 - 5 = 6$, the answer is:

$2x + 11 + x - 5 = 3x + 6$

You wouldn't confuse tea trays with deckchairs, so don't mix different sorts of terms together.

Example 3.12

Write the following expression in its simplest form.

$6x - 2y - 4 - x + 3y - 3$

Solution

*If it helps, rearrange the expression by putting together all the **like terms** (terms that are alike).*

$6x - x \qquad - 2y + 3y \qquad {}^-4 - 3$

Remember to keep the sign with the number or term that follows it.

$6x - x = 5x$

${}^-2y + 3y = y \qquad$ because ${}^-2 + 3 = 1$

${}^-4 - 3 = {}^-7$

So the answer is:

$6x - 2y - 4 - x + 3y - 3 = 5x + y - 7$

The order in which you write the terms is not important, provided that you remember to keep the sign with the number or term which comes immediately after.

Exercise 3.3

Simplify the following algebraic expressions.

1 $4x + x$ **2** $3x + 2 + 5x + 7$
3 $4x + 6 + 3x + 1$ **4** $9x + 5 - 6x - 2$
5 $7x + 2 - 6x - 3$ **6** $8x + 3y - 4 - 4x - 2y + 3$

Answers

6 $8x - 4x + 3y - 2y - 4 + 3 = 4x + y - 1$
5 $7x - 6x + 2 - 3 = x - 1$ (because $1x = x$)
4 $9x - 6x + 5 - 2 = 3x + 3$
3 $4x + 3x + 6 + 1 = 7x + 7$
2 $3x + 5x + 2 + 7 = 8x + 9$
1 $5x$

Impress your teacher!

$2 + 3$ is the same as $3 + 2$.   We say that addition is **commutative**.

$5 - 2$ is not the same as $2 - 5$.   Subtraction is **not commutative**.

4×3 is the same as 3×4.   Multiplication is **commutative**.

$6 \div 2$ is not the same as $2 \div 6$.   Division is **not commutative**.

TAKE A BREAK

Multiplying algebraic expressions

Impress your teacher!

A **variable** is usually a letter that represents any number, for example in $6x$, x is the variable, in $2y^2$, y is the variable.

If we are asked to simplify $x + x$, the easiest way of writing this is to remember we have $2xs$ or $2 \times x$ or $2x$.

In algebra, we usually leave out the multiplication sign. This stops us from confusing $\times$ with the letter x.

$2 \times x$ is the same as $2x$.

As multiplication is commutative, the numbers or variables that are to be multiplied can be written in any order.

$2 \times x$ could be written as $x \times 2$.

$x + x$ means '2 lots of x', or $2x$.

$2 \times x$ gives the same answer as $x + x$. (Try it. If $x = 3$, then $3 + 3 = 2 \times 3$. Make up more examples for yourself if you're not convinced.)

Example 3.13

Simplify $3x \times 4$.

Solution

$3x \times 4$ can be written as, say, $3 \times x \times 4$ or $4 \times 3 \times x$.

It is often easier to group the numbers together, separately from the variable, x.

$4 \times 3 \times x = 12 \times x$

$\qquad\qquad = 12x$

Example 3.14

Which of the following terms are identical to $n + n + n$?

a) $3 \div n$ **b)** $3n$ **c)** $n \times 3$

d) $n + 3$ **e)** $3 \times n$ **f)** $3 - n$

(**Note:** You may write down more than one possibility.)

Solution

b), c) and e) are all right.

$n + n + n$ is 3 lots of n, or 3 times n, so can be written as b) $3n$ or c) $n \times 3$ or e) $3 \times n$.

Exercise 3.4

Simplify the following expressions.
1 $2x \times 4$ **2** $5x \times 3$
3 $8n \times 2$ **4** $3y \times 3$

Answers

1 $8x$ **2** $15x$ **3** $16n$ **4** $9y$

Multiplying variables

At this stage, you really only need to know that when you are multiplying two variables that are alike (called **like variables**) you get the **square**.

$x \times x = x^2$
x^2 is called 'x squared' or 'x to the power of 2'.

Be careful not to confuse $x + x$ or $2x$ with $x \times x$ or x^2.

x^2 and x are not the same, so you cannot simplify $x^2 + x$.

Example 3.15

Simplify these expressions.

a) $x \times 2x$ **b)** $3y \times 4y$

Solution

a) $x \times 2x = x \times 2 \times x$
$\qquad\qquad = 2 \times x \times x$ because multiplication is commutative
$\qquad\qquad = 2 \times x^2$ because $x \times x = x^2$
$\qquad\qquad = 2x^2$

b) $3y \times 4y = 3 \times y \times 4 \times y$
$\qquad\qquad = 3 \times 4 \times y \times y$ because multiplication is commutative
$\qquad\qquad = 12 \times y^2$ is commutative
$\qquad\qquad = 12y^2$ because $y \times y - y^2$

Exercise 3.5

Simplify these expressions.

1 $3x \times x$ **2** $y \times 4y$
3 $2y \times 2y$ **4** $3x \times 2x$
5 $6x \times 7x$ **6** $8n \times 4n$

Answers

1 $3x^2$ **2** $4y^2$ **3** $4y^2$ **4** $6x^2$ **5** $42x^2$ **6** $32n^2$

Division

Division is not commutative, so it is important to remember the order in which the variables or numbers are written.

'Divide x by 2' can be written as $x \div 2$ or $\dfrac{x}{2}$.

Dividing by 2 is the same as multiplying by a half, so $x \div 2 = \dfrac{x}{1} \times \dfrac{1}{2} = \dfrac{x}{2}$ or $\dfrac{1}{2}x$.

'Divide x by 3' can be written as $x \div 3$ or $\dfrac{x}{3}$.

Dividing by 3 is the same multiplying by a third, so $x \div 3 = \dfrac{x}{1} \times \dfrac{1}{3}$ or $= \dfrac{1}{3}x$.

Exercise 3.6

1 Which of the following are equal to a half of x?
   a) $2x$ **b)** $x - 2$ **c)** $x \div 2$
   d) $\dfrac{x}{2}$ **e)** $\dfrac{1}{2}x$ **f)** x^2

2 Simplify the following expressions.
   a) $10x \div 2$ **b)** $15x \div 5$ **c)** $16y \div 8$
   d) $5x \div 5$ **e)** $\dfrac{6y}{6}$ **f)** $4x^2 \div 2$

1 c) $x \div 2$, d) $\dfrac{x}{2}$ and e) $\dfrac{1}{2}x$
2 In the solutions below, we have grouped the numbers together to make the working easier to understand.
   a) $10x \div 2 = x \times 5 = 5x$
   b) $15x \div 5 = x \times 3 = 3x$
   c) $16y \div 8 = y \times 2 = 2y$
   d) $5x \div 5 = x \times 1 = x$
   e) $6y \div 6 = y \times 1 = y$
   f) $4x^2 \div 2 = x^2 \times 2 = 2x^2$

Answers

A Quick Dip!

1 Calculate 3.45×10.
2 Calculate 3×2^2.
3 Write $2\frac{2}{3}$ as a top-heavy fraction.
4 Calculate $2 + 8 \times 7$.
5 Find the value of $(9 + 6) \div 3$.

Answers

1 34.5 **2** 12 **3** $\frac{8}{3}$ **4** 58 **5** 5

TAKE A BREAK

Buckets and brackets

Candy and Floss have decided on a new money-making venture. The mayor of the scruffy resort of Litter-a-Sea is trying to encourage tidiness by offering to pay a fixed amount for each drinks can which is handed in. Candy and Floss have been down to the beach with their buckets looking for cans – and also for bottles on which they can collect the deposit. Once again they decide to use algebra to record what they collect. As each bottle has the same deposit, they write b to stand for the money which they will get for returning a bottle and c for the amount which they can make on a can. They also decide that they ought to do something about all the bags which people have dropped after eating chips. The first day is wet, and they don't do very well. They each have a bucket containing one bottle and five bags.

Mathematically this can be written as $2 \times (b + 5)$ or $2(b + 5)$.

If both buckets are emptied out, they would have $2 \times b + 2 \times 5$ which is the same as $2b + 10$.

$$2(b + 5) = 2 \times b + 2 \times 5 = 2b + 10$$

The next day they get two bottles and ten cans in each of five buckets. They write this down as $5(2b + 10c)$. Then emptying out the buckets they have

$$5 \times 2b + 5 \times 10c \text{ or } 10b + 50c$$

$$5(2b + 10c) = 10b + 50c$$

Can you see that you need to multiply **each term in the brackets** *by the number outside?*

Example 3.16

Expand $7(x + 2)$

Solution

$$7(x + 2) = 7 \times x + 7 \times 2$$
$$= 7x + 14$$

The 7 multiplies both the x and the $^+2$.

Example 3.17

Expand $2(4y - 6)$

Solution

$$2(4y - 6) = 2 \times 4y + 2 \times {}^-6$$
$$= 8y - 12$$

The 2 multiplies both the $4y$ and the $^-6$.

Example 3.18

Expand $2(x + 3y)$.

Solution

You must multiply each term inside the bracket by 2.

$$2(x + 3y) = 2 \times x + 2 \times 3y$$
$$= 2x + 6y$$

3

Example 3.19

Expand $5(4x + 8y + 1)$

Solution

$$5(4x + 8y + 1) = 5 \times 4x + 5 \times 8y + 5 \times 1$$
$$= 20x + 40y + 5$$

Did you remember that the number before the bracket multiplies everything inside the bracket?

Exercise 3.7

Expand the following expressions.

1 $4(x + 3)$
2 $7(a + 3)$
3 $5(2x + 4)$
4 $3(3y - 1)$
5 $2(x + y)$
6 $3(5y + 2)$
7 $6(x - y)$
8 $2(a + 2b)$
9 $7(6x + 7y + 8)$
10 $8(4x + 6y + 9)$

10 $32x + 48y + 72$	**9** $42x + 49y + 56$
8 $2a + 4b$	**7** $6x - 6y$
6 $15y + 6$	**5** $2x + 2y$
4 $9y - 3$	**3** $10x + 20$
2 $7a + 21$	**1** $4x + 12$

Answers

What do you think of it so far? If you are getting a bit bogged down, have a rest before you come back to meet a new friend on the promenade.

TAKE A BREAK

Solving algebraic equations

You may have come across questions like this: Find x, when $x + 3 = 5$. If you say to yourself, 'I think of a number. I add 3 and the answer is 5. What was the number I thought of?' you should get the answer 2. That one was easy, but sometimes the question is more complicated. You need to know how to solve algebraic equations.

Eva Nanded loves to use the viewers on the side of the promenade to see distant objects. She has to turn the knobs so both sides look the same. For this to work properly, she knows that whatever she does with one hand, she must do with the other. She uses the same method to solve equations.

Eva looks at the problem $x + 3 = 5$.

She wants to get to the situation where she just has '$x =$' on one side of the equation. The problem is the '$+ 3$'. She does not want it on that side. So to get rid of the '$+ 3$', she does the opposite – she subtracts 3 from both sides.

$$\begin{array}{ll} x + 3 = & 5 \\ \underline{- 3 \quad - 3} & \text{(You might have seen this as} \\ & x + 3 - 3 = 5 - 3.) \\ x = 2 & \end{array}$$

Eva has taken 3 from the left-hand side to leave x, and because she is fair, she has taken 3 from the right-hand side to give $5 - 3 = 2$.

Here's another problem for Eva Nanded.

Example 3.20

Find the value of x if $x + 4 = 10$.

Solution

Eva knows she needs to be left with a single x on one side. Therefore she needs to cancel out the '+ 4' from the left-hand side. She realises she has to take 4 from both sides.

$$x + 4 = 10$$
$$\underline{\quad - 4 \quad - 4} \qquad \text{(or } x + 4 - 4 = 10 - 4\text{)}$$
$$x \quad = \quad 6$$

What Eva likes best about algebra is that she can always tell whether she is right. All she does is put her answer, $x = 6$, back in to the original equation of:

$$x + 4 = 10$$
to give: $\quad 6 + 4 = 10 \quad$ ✓

Here's another problem – but it's no problem for Eva!

Example 3.21

Find x if $x - 5 = 3$.

Solution

Again, she wants to end up with an x on its own, so she must do something about the '− 5' on the left-hand side. To get rid of the '− 5', she adds 5. Naturally Eva does this to both sides.

$$x - 5 = \quad 3$$
$$\underline{\quad + 5 \quad + 5} \qquad \text{(or } x - 5 + 5 = 3 + 5\text{)}$$
$$x \quad = \quad 8$$

Checking her answer by putting $x = 8$ into the original equation gives:

$$8 - 5 = 3 \qquad ✓$$

Sometimes Eva finds that her answer is a negative number.

Example 3.22

Solve $x + 5 = 3$.

Solution

Eva realises she must take 5 from both sides.

$$x + 5 = \quad 3$$
$$\underline{\quad - 5 \quad - 5} \qquad \text{(or } x + 5 - 5 = 3 - 5\text{)}$$
$$x \quad = \quad {}^-2$$

Example 3.23

Solve $12 = x + 9$.

Solution

In this equation, the x appears on the right-hand side. Remember, you can swap sides at any stage of your working. This is because if 12 is equal to $x + 9$, then $x + 9$ is equal to 12.

$$12 = x + 9 \qquad\qquad x + 9 = 12 \quad \text{Swap here!}$$
$$\underline{-9 \qquad -9} \text{ (12 − 9} \qquad \underline{\quad -9 \quad -9} \text{ (}x + 9 - 9$$
$$\qquad = x + 9 - 9\text{)} \qquad\qquad = 12 - 9\text{)}$$
$$3 = x \qquad \text{Swap here!} \qquad x = 3$$
$$x = 3$$

Exercise 3.8

Find the value of x in the following equations.

1 $x + 7 = 15$	**2** $x + 9 = 11$
3 $x - 4 = 6$	**4** $x - 2 = 3$
5 $1 = x - 5$	**6** $x + 6 = 1$

Answers

6 $x = {}^-5$	**5** $x = 6$	**4** $x = 5$
3 $x = 10$	**2** $x = 2$	**1** $x = 8$

TAKE A BREAK

Solving equations using multiplication and division

Eva is eager to get her inquisitive eyes on more problems. She has already looked at equations with addition and subtraction. Now she's ready to have a go at problems with multiplication and division.

Example 3.24

Find x when $2x = 6$.

Solution

Eva knows she needs x on one side, but in this question she has $2x$. This is the same as $2 \times x$ or $x \times 2$. The opposite of multiplying by 2 is dividing by 2, so she divides both sides by 2.

$2x = 6$

$\div 2 \quad \div 2$ (or $\dfrac{2x}{2} = \dfrac{6}{2}$)

$\quad x = 3$

Eva has divided both sides by 2, leaving x on the left-hand side and 3 on the right.

Is this the right answer? Putting it into $2x = 6$ gives:

$2 \times 3 = 6 \quad$ ✓

Example 3.25

Solve $5x = 35$.

Solution

To find x, Eva divides both sides by 5.

$5x = 35$

$\div 5 \quad \div 5 \quad$ (or $\dfrac{5x}{5} = \dfrac{35}{5}$)

$\quad x = 7$

Eva checks it: $5 \times 7 = 35 \quad$ ✓

Example 3.26

Solve $\dfrac{x}{8} = 3$.

Solution

Eva sees the 'divided by 8' with the x, so she knows she must multiply both sides by 8 to end up with x on the left-hand side.

$\dfrac{x}{8} = 3$

$\times 8 \quad \times 8 \quad$ (or $\dfrac{x}{8} \times 8 = 3 \times 8$)

$\quad x = 24$

Checking: $\dfrac{24}{8} = 3 \quad$ ✓

Example 3.27

Find x when $\dfrac{x}{6} = 7$.

Solution

This question is the same as 'Solve $\dfrac{x}{6} = 7$'.

$x = 42$

Checking: $42 \div 6 = 7 \quad$ ✓

Exercise 3.9

Find the value of y in the following equations.

1 $3y = 18$ **2** $2y = 22$

3 $32 = 4y$ **4** $5y = 35$

5 $y \div 3 = 2$ **6** $\dfrac{y}{2} = 5$

7 $7 = \dfrac{y}{4}$ **8** $\dfrac{y}{6} = 2$

Answers

1 $y = 6$ **2** $y = 11$ **3** $y = 8$ **4** $y = 7$

5 $y = 6$ **6** $y = 10$ **7** $y = 28$ **8** $y = 12$

A Quick Dip!

1 Simplify $3x \times x$.
2 Which of the numbers is prime? 9, 10, 11, 12
3 Simplify $3x + 4x + 2x^2$.
4 Calculate $3 + 81 \div 9$.
5 What is 10% of £60?

Answers

1 $3x^2$ **2** 11 **3** $7x + 2x^2$ **4** 12 **5** £6

TAKE A BREAK

Solving equations using more than one process

Eva is now eager to try mixing addition and subtraction with multiplication and division.

Example 3.28

Find x when $3x + 1 = 22$.

Solution

Eva knows that she needs to have x on its own on one side, but first she needs to get $3x$ on its own.

$3x + 1 = 22$

$\underline{\quad -1 \quad -1 \quad}$ (or $3x + 1 - 1 = 22 - 1$)
Subtracting 1 cancels out the + 1.

$3x \quad = 21$

$\div 3 \quad \div 3$ (or $\frac{3x}{3} = \frac{21}{3}$, or $x = 21 \div 3$)
Dividing by 3 cancels the × 3.

$x \quad = 7$

Check: $3 \times 7 + 1 = 21 + 1 = 22$ ✓

Example 3.29

Solve $2x - 3 = 17$.

Solution

To get $2x$ on its own, Eva adds 3 to both sides. Then, to get x by itself, she divides by 2.

$2x - 3 = 17$

$\underline{\quad +3 \quad +3 \quad}$ (or $23 - 3 + 3 = 17 + 3$)

$2x \quad = 20$

$\div 2 \quad \div 2$ (or $\frac{2x}{2} = \frac{20}{2}$)

$x \quad = 10$

Check: $2 \times 10 - 3 = 20 - 3 = 17$ ✓

Example 3.30

Solve $\frac{x}{4} - 7 = 1$.

Solution

Eva adds 7, then multiplies by 4.

$\frac{x}{4} - 7 = 1$

$\frac{x}{4} \quad = 8$

$x \quad = 32$

Checking: $\frac{32}{4} - 7 = 8 - 7 = 1$ ✓

Example 3.31

Solve $3x + 9 = 36$.

Solution

Eva takes 9 from both sides, then divides both sides by 3.

$3x + 9 = 36$
$3x \quad = 27$
$x \quad = 9$

Checking: $3 \times 9 + 9 = 27 + 9$
$\qquad\qquad\qquad = 36$ ✓

3

Exercise 3.10

Find the value of x in the following equations.

1 $4x - 1 = 15$ **2** $2x + 5 = 37$

3 $5x + 6 = 41$ **4** $\dfrac{x}{5} - 4 = 3$

5 $9x + 4 = 76$ **6** $\dfrac{x}{3} + 6 = 9$

7 $3x - 7 = 14$ **8** $2x + 11 = 7$

Answers

1 $x = 4$
2 $x = 16$
3 $x = 7$
4 $x = 35$
5 $x = 8$
6 $x = 9$
7 $x = 7$
8 $x = -2$

TAKE A BREAK

Balancing – solving equations with variables on both sides

Eva can even tackle problems such as:

$2x + 3 = x + 9$

All she does is treat the x on the right-hand side just like any other number. She remembers from paddling about in the numbers pool (page 10) that if there is no sign in front of the first number, you have to imagine a plus (+). Therefore, to get rid of the x from that side she subtracts x. She must do the same to both sides of course.

$$\begin{array}{l} 2x + 3 = x + 9 \\ \underline{-x \quad -x} \qquad (\text{or } 2x + 3 - x = x + 9 - x) \\ x + 3 \ = 9 \end{array}$$

Now she knows exactly what to do!

$$\begin{array}{l} x + 3 = 9 \\ \underline{-3 \quad -3} \qquad (\text{or } x + 3 - 3 = 9 - 3) \\ x \ \ = 6 \end{array}$$

Finally, she checks back to the original equation to make sure both sides are equal.

Substituting $x = 6$ into $2x + 3 = x + 9$ gives:

$2 \times 6 + 3 = 6 + 9$

$12 + 3 = 15$ ✓

Example 3.32

Solve $5x - 2 = 2x + 22$.

Solution

Eva starts by taking $2x$ from both sides.

$$\begin{array}{l} 5x - 2 = 2x + 22 \\ 3x - 2 = 22 \\ 3x \ \ = 24 \\ x \ \ = 8 \end{array}$$

Checking: $5 \times 8 - 2 = 2 \times 8 + 22$
becomes $\quad 40 - 2 = 16 + 22$
$\qquad\qquad\qquad\quad = 38$ ✓

Exercise 3.11

Solve the following equations.

1 $3x + 2 = 2x + 9$ **2** $4x - 3 = 3x + 2$
3 $2x + 4 = x + 2$ **4** $5x + 3 = x + 23$
5 $5x - 1 = 3x + 11$ **6** $4x + 2 = x + 11$
7 $3x + 20 = x + 12$ **8** $2x - 4 = 8 - x$

Answers

1 $x = 7$
2 $x = 5$
3 $x = -2$
4 $x = 5$
5 $x = 6$
6 $x = 3$
7 $x = -4$
8 $x = 4$ (**Hint:** First add x to both sides to give $3x - 4 = 8$.)

Function machines

Paul Oosa invents obstacles for crazy golf. He spends hours dreaming them up. He is fascinated by the way the different obstacles change the speed and direction of the ball. He draws out his designs on paper first, using the variable x to represent the ball. Then he notes the effect that each different obstacle has on the ball as it travels through it, by adding, subtracting, multiplying or dividing by a number. He calls his contraptions **function machines**.

Example 3.33

Paul starts with a simple design where he only has to shoot the ball through one machine. The first machine just adds 3 to the ball (variable x), giving an answer of y. Draw his machine.

Solution

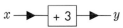

$x \longrightarrow \boxed{+ 3} \longrightarrow y$

Example 3.34

The next machine multiplies the ball by 2. Draw the machine.

Solution

$x \longrightarrow \boxed{\times 2} \longrightarrow y$

Then Paul goes on to more complicated designs using two machines.

Example 3.35

The first machine multiplies by 3, and the second adds 2. Draw a diagram to show these machines.

Solution

If x is the number he puts in, and y is the number that comes out, he gets:

$x \longrightarrow \boxed{\times 3} \longrightarrow \boxed{+ 2} \longrightarrow y$

Formulae from function machines

In the last example, Paul could write an algebraic formula for the function machine, taking x, multiplying by 3 and then adding 2 to give a value of y.

$$y = 3x + 2$$

Sometimes he puts in a number instead of a variable.

Substituting 4 into the previous function machine gives:

$4 \longrightarrow \boxed{\times 3} \longrightarrow \boxed{+ 2} \longrightarrow 14$

because $4 \times 3 = 12$, and $12 + 2 = 14$.

Example 3.36

a) Substitute the following numbers into the function machine below.

   i) $x = 3$ ii) $x = 6$

   iii) $x = 2$

$x \longrightarrow \boxed{- 1} \longrightarrow \boxed{\times 4} \longrightarrow y$

b) Write the function machine as an algebraic formula.

Solution

a)   i) $3 - 1 = 2$, $2 \times 4 = 8$
     ii) $6 - 1 = 5$, $5 \times 4 = 20$
     iii) $2 - 1 = 1$, $1 \times 4 = 4$

b) The function machine says, 'First take away 1, then multiply by 4.'

   BODMAS says, 'Multiply before you subtract,' but the function machine definitely says you have to subtract first.

   So you need to put brackets around the subtraction before the multiplication.

   $y = (x - 1) \times 4$ or $y = 4(x - 1)$.

Example 3.37

Draw the function machines for these formulae.

a) $y = 2x - 5$ **b)** $y = \dfrac{x}{4} + 3$ **c)** $y = 6(x - 1)$

Solution

a) $x \longrightarrow \boxed{\times 2} \longrightarrow \boxed{-5} \longrightarrow y$

b) $x \longrightarrow \boxed{\div 4} \longrightarrow \boxed{+3} \longrightarrow y$

c) $x \longrightarrow \boxed{-1} \longrightarrow \boxed{\times 6} \longrightarrow y$

Exercise 3.12

1 Substitute the following numbers into the function machine below.
   a) i) $x = 2$ **ii)** $x = 0$ **iii)** $x = 3$

$x \longrightarrow \boxed{\times 2} \longrightarrow \boxed{+5} \longrightarrow y$

   b) Write the function machine as an equation involving x and y.
2 Write the following as function machines.
   a) $y = 3x - 4$ **b)** $y = 3(x + 2)$

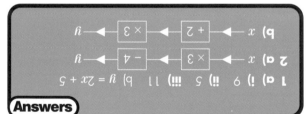

Answers

b) $x \rightarrow \boxed{+2} \rightarrow \boxed{\times 3} \rightarrow y$

2 a) $x \rightarrow \boxed{\times 3} \rightarrow \boxed{-4} \rightarrow y$

1 a) i) 9 ii) 5 iii) 11   b) $y = 2x + 5$

A Quick Dip!

1 $4 - {}^-7$ **2** Solve $\dfrac{x}{5} = 2$.

3 Find the value of 6^2.
4 What is a half of a quarter?
5 The price of a jacket marked £120 is reduced by 25%. What is its reduced price?

Answers

1 11 2 10 3 36 4 $\frac{1}{2} \times \frac{1}{4} = \frac{1}{8}$ 5 £90

TAKE A BREAK

Sequences

Sequences with equal spacing

The town council of New-Mer-a-Sea was planning its illuminations for the next season. One idea was:

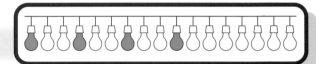

Example 3.38

Colour in the next two bulbs which will be blue, following the pattern above.

Solution

Every third light is blue.

Here is another idea they had.

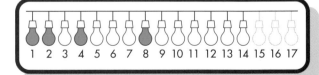

Example 3.39

Write down the numbers of the next two blue bulbs.

Solution

As the pattern formed by the numbers of the blue bulbs is 1, 2, 4, 8, etc., you can see that each number is double the one before. The next blue bulbs would be at 16 and 32.

Now suppose the pattern they use is 1, 4, 9, 16, …

The differences are 3, 5, 7, … and these are increasing by 2 each time.

The next two blue bulbs would be numbers 25 and 36. You may also have noticed that:

$1 \times 1 = 1^2 = 1, 2 \times 2 = 2^2 = 4, 3 \times 3 = 3^2 = 9$

and so on. This is the sequence of **square numbers**.

The main ways of finding the next number
in a sequence are:
- *using a common difference*
- *seeing a pattern in the differences*
- *adding the last two numbers of a sequence to find the next number in the sequence.*

Exercise 3.13

For the following number sequences:
a) work out the rule for finding the next term
b) find the next two terms in each sequence.
1 6, 11, 16, 21, 26, …   **2** 5, 7, 9, 11, 13, …
3 7, 10, 15, 22, 31, …   **4** 1, 1, 2, 3, 5, …

Answers

1 a) Add 5.   **b)** 31, 36
2 a) Add 2.   **b)** 15, 17
3 a) As the differences are 3, 5, 7, 9, etc., add the next odd number.
b) 42, 55 (31 + 11 = 42; 42 + 13 = 55)
4 a) Add the last two terms.
b) 8, 13 (3 + 5 = 8; 5 + 8 = 13)

Finding the *n*th term in sequences with equal spacing

You may be asked to find a rule for finding the *n*th term. This is the method for finding the algebraic rule for sequences. This year, New-Mer-a-Sea has invited their local celebrity, DINO (famous for his annual summer season at the Gaudyville Theatre, if nowhere else), to switch on the illuminations and help with equally-spaced sequences.

Example 3.40

The following numbers form a sequence.

5, 8, 11, 14, …

a) Write down the next two numbers in the sequence.

b) State the rule for finding the next term.

c) Find an expression for the *n*th term.

Solution

a) 17, 20

b) Add 3 to the previous number in the sequence.

c) Here we can use DINO, because the differences are equal.

Draw DINO's microphone by putting a ring in front of the first number:

◯   5, 8, 11, 14, …

What number would go in the ring if there were a number before 5 in the sequence?

Answer: Count back three from 5 to give 2.

②,   5, 8, 11, 14, …

DI stands for the difference (3), N stands for *n* and O stands for the number in the ring (2). DINO gives the formula $3n + 2$.

Check: If you substitute $n = 1$, you should get the first term, $3 \times 1 + 2 = 5$.

$n = 2$ gives the second term, $3 \times 2 + 2 = 8$, etc.

3

In questions involving DINO, you are often asked to find a certain term before finding the *n*th term. It is much easier to find the *n*th term first, then substitute the appropriate number into the formula you have found.

DINO can only help with sequences where the numbers are equally spaced.

Exercise 3.14

For the following sequences, find:
a) the next term
b) the rule for finding the next term
c) the *n*th term
d) the 19th term in the sequence.

1 4, 7, 10, 13, 16, … **2** 3, 5, 7, 9, 11, …
3 5, 12, 19, 26, 33, … **4** 1, 7, 13, 19, 25, …
5 10, 9, 8, 7, 6, … **6** 16, 14, 12, 10, 8, …

Answers

1 a) 19 **b)** Add three to the last term.
c) DI = 3, N = *n*, O = 1 so the *n*th term is 3*n* + 1
d) 3 × 19 + 1 = 58
2 a) 13 **b)** Add 2 to the last term.
c) DI = 2, N = *n*, O = 1 so the *n*th term is 2*n* + 1
d) 2 × 19 + 1 = 39
3 a) 40 **b)** Add 7.
c) DI = 7, N = *n*, O = −2 so the *n*th term is 7*n* − 2
d) 7 × 19 − 2 = 131
4 a) 31 **b)** Add 6.
c) DI = 6, N = *n*, O = −5 so the *n*th term is 6*n* − 5
d) 6 × 19 − 5 = 109
5 a) 5 **b)** Subtract 1.
c) DI = −1, N = *n*, O = 11 so the *n*th term is
−1*n* + 11, or *n* + 11
d) −19 + 11 = −8
6 a) 6 **b)** Subtract 2.
c) DI = −2, N = *n*, O = 18 so the *n*th term is
−2*n* + 18
d) −2 × 19 + 18 = −20

TAKE A BREAK

Making formulae from statements

There is a book in the Town Hall containing the Town Council's bye-laws, which are the rules and regulations made by the Town Council of New-Mer-a-Sea. Below is an extract from the book.

These mean 'add'

- more than
- increased by
- on top of
- added to

Example 3.41

Suppose the number of people on the pier is x, then two more walk onto the pier. Write down an expression for the number of people on the pier now.

Solution

'2 more' is the same as '+ 2'.

Answer = $x + 2$

These mean 'subtract'

- is taken (away) from
- is removed
- less than
- from

However, councillors must be careful when subtracting to get the process the right way round!

Remember: *subtraction* is not *commutative: i.e. 2 − 3 is not the same as 3 − 2 and x − 2 is not the same as 2 − x.*

Even more confusing is converting the wording from English to Mathematics.

'Eight from n' is $n − 8$.

'Taking 7 from y' is written as $y − 7$.

'Five less than x' is $x − 5$.

'Subtracting 3 from n' is $n − 3$.

Exercise 3.15

Write the following as algebraic expressions.
1 5 more than a number b
2 2 less than a number x
3 Increase y by 6
4 Remove 2 from c
5 7 is taken from x

Answers

1 $b + 5$ or $5 + b$
2 $x - 2$ (not $2 - x$)
3 $y + 6$ or $6 + y$
4 $c - 2$ (not $2 - c$)
5 $x - 7$ (not $7 - x$)

Back to the town hall's book.

These mean 'multiply by'

- increased by a factor of
- doubled ($\times 2$)
- tripled ($\times 3$)
- quadrupled ($\times 4$)

Multiplication is commutative: i.e. 4×3 is the same as 3×4 and $x \times 2$ is the same as $2 \times x$. (Remember $2 \times x$ is the same as $2x$.)

These mean 'divide by'

- split between
- shared out
- reduced by a factor of
- halved ($\div 2$)
- quartered ($\div 4$)

Division is not commutative:

$4 \div 2$ *is not the same as* $2 \div 4$.

$\dfrac{4}{5}$ *is not the same as* $\dfrac{5}{4}$.

$x \div 3$ *is not the same as* $3 \div x$.

$\dfrac{y}{4}$ *is not the same as* $\dfrac{4}{y}$.

Example 3.42

Kate O'Ring has p pans in her kitchen, k knives and b bowls.

a) If Kate buys two new pans, write an expression for the number of pans she has now.

b) Kate buys k more knives for the kitchen. Write down and simplify an expression for the number of knives she has now.

c) Kate decides she has too many bowls and gives six away. Write an expression for the number of bowls she has left.

Solution

a) Kate has added 2 to the number of pans, p, so she has $p + 2$.

b) She has added k to the amount she already has so she has $k + k = 2k$.

c) Kate has reduced her number of bowls by 6, so she has $b - 6$.

Exercise 3.16

Write the following as algebraic expressions.
1 I have four lots of x.
2 A prize of y pounds is shared among five people. How many pounds does each receive?
3 I gave my friend a half of b.
4 Fabric measuring x cm is cut into three equal lengths. How long is each piece?

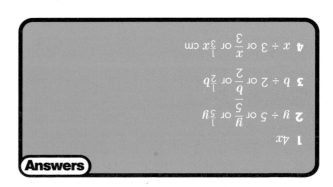

Answers

1 $4x$
2 $y \div 5$ or $\dfrac{y}{5}$ or $\frac{1}{5}y$
3 $b \div 2$ or $\dfrac{b}{2}$ or $\frac{1}{2}b$
4 $x \div 3$ or $\dfrac{x}{3}$ or $\frac{1}{3}x$ cm

These mean 'equals'

- is
- has
- is the same as
- gives the same answer as

Example 3.43

Maria Richman found that if she multiplied the number of pearls she had by 4 and subtracted 1, it was the same as if she added 77 to the number of pearls.

a) If the number of pearls she had was x, write down an equation in x.

b) Solve this equation.

Solution

a) 'is the same as' means = .

If the number of pearls was x, multiplying by 4 and subtracting 1 would give the expression $4x - 1$.

Adding 77 to the number of pearls gives $x + 77$.

Equating these gives:
$4x - 1 = x + 77$

b) $4x - 1 = x + 77$
$\quad\ 4x = x + 78$
$\quad\ 3x = 78$
$\quad\ \ x = 26$

Exercise 3.17

1 Sheila Gree knew that if she took her age, multiplied it by 3 and added 8, the result was the same as if she added 32 years to her age.
   a) If Sheila was x years old, write an equation in x.
   b) Solve this equation.
2 Adam Mupp was counting his money. He knew that if he took the amount of money he has, multiplied it by 4 and added 6 pounds, he would get the same number if he took the

amount of money and added 24 pounds.
a) If he has y pounds, write an equation in y.
b) Solve this equation to find the value of y.

Answers

1 a) $3x + 8 = x + 32$ **b)** $x = 12$
2 a) $4y + 6 = y + 24$ **b)** $y = 6$

A Quick Dip!

1 Calculate $2345 \div 100$.
2 What is the next number in this sequence?
   $1, 7, 13, 19, \ldots$
3 If one pencil costs $x + 2$ pence, write down an expression for the cost of three pencils in terms of x.
4 Write 27% as a decimal.
5 Find x if $x + 6 = 4$.

Answers

1 23.45   **2** 25   **3** $3(x + 2)$ or $3x + 6$ **4** 0.27   **5** $x = -2$

TAKE A BREAK

Trial and improvement

When he is not designing fiendishly complicated machines, Paul Oosa likes to relax on the putting green. He is rather fed up, though, because so far he has never managed to beat anyone. Because his shots are often so wildly off course, he has decided to try a new approach. First he aims in the right general direction. If the ball doesn't go in, he notes how far it was from the hole. Then he retrieves the ball and tries to get it closer to the hole next time.

You can use a similar idea to help you solve problems in algebra.

Example 3.44

There is a solution to the equation $x^2 - x = 7$ between $x = 2$ and $x = 5$. Using trial and improvement, find this solution, correct to 1 d.p.

Solution

Paul tries the values $x = 2, 3, 4, 5$ to find which gets closest to the 'hole' of 7. He writes his results on a scorecard.

x	$x^2 - x$
2	2
3	6
4	12
5	20

His first set of results show him that he shot either side of the hole with $x = 3$ and $x = 4$ (because 6 and 12 lie on either side of the 'hole', 7).

6 is much closer to the 'hole' than 12 is, so the solution is probably closer to $x = 3$. So he now tries a few values close to $x = 3$.

x	$x^2 - x$
3.1	6.51
3.2	7.04

He doesn't need to go any further. He is close enough to the 'hole' to know that his answer is $x = 3.2$. If he went any further, his answers would be getting bigger, further and further away from 7.

Example 3.45

Find the value of x between 4 and 5, correct to 1 decimal place, for which $x^2 - 4x = 2$.

Solution

Paul tries 4 and 5 first, then 4.5.

x	$x^2 - 4x$
4	0
5	5
4.5	2.25

4.5 gives a number a little above 2, so the solution must be between 4 and 4.5.

x	$x^2 - 4x$
4.4	1.76

The solution must be between 4.4 and 4.5, but the outcomes are almost an equal distance away from 2. So Paul tries the number halfway between 4.4 and 4.5.

x	$x^2 - 4x$
4.45	2.0025

This is a little too much, so the true x-value must be just below 4.45. The answer to the question, to 1 decimal place (1 d.p.) is $x = 4.4$.

Exercise 3.18

1 There is a solution to the formula $x^2 - 4x = 17$ near $x = 6$. Using a method of trial and improvement, find this solution, to 1 d.p.
2 Use a trial and improvement method to find the solution of the equation $y^2 - 7y = 22$. Give your answer to 1 d.p. The first trial has been done below.

y	$y^2 - 7y$	
9	18	Too low

Answers

1 $x = 6.6$ 2 $x = 9.4$

check your luggage

HAVE YOU REMEMBERED TO PACK ...

- using the shorthand of algebra
- order of operations (BODMAS)
- simplifying algebraic expressions
- expanding brackets
- solving equations
- function machines
- sequences
- making formulae from statements
- trial and improvement?

A night out – graphs

checklist

Into this chapter we have packed …

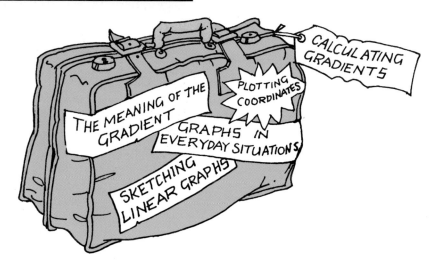

CALCULATING GRADIENTS

PLOTTING COORDINATES

THE MEANING OF THE GRADIENT

GRAPHS IN EVERYDAY SITUATIONS

SKETCHING LINEAR GRAPHS

Basics

In this chapter, we use the words **horizontal** and **vertical**, so you need to be sure that you understand what they mean. It's quite easy to remember, if you realise that 'horizontal' comes from the word 'horizon' which always goes across. Therefore vertical must mean the 'other one' – up or down.

The x-axis is the horizontal axis, and the y-axis is the vertical axis: remember 'y high'.

Plotting coordinates

You write points on a graph as two numbers in brackets. The first number is the **x-value** and the second number is the **y-value**. So the point (3, 5) means a point which has an x-value of 3 and a y-value of 5.

Remember, the x and y values are written alphabetically: x comes before y in coordinates, just as x is before y in the alphabet.

The point (3, 5) is plotted on the graph below.

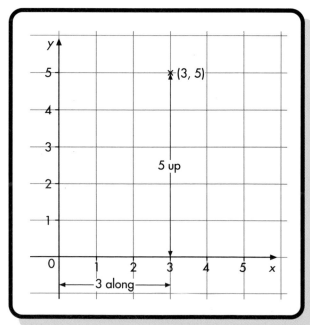

The point (⁻2, 4) is plotted on the graph below. It is 2 units along the x-axis, in the negative x-direction, and 4 units up the y-axis, in the positive y-direction.

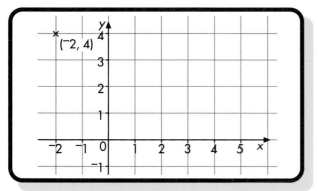

The point (5, ⁻1) is shown on the graph below. It is 5 units along the x-axis in the positive x-direction, and 1 unit down the y-axis, in the negative y-direction.

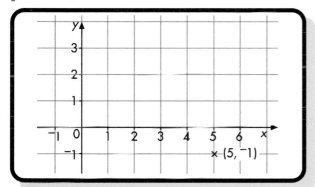

The point (⁻6, ⁻3) is shown on the graph below. It is 6 units along the x-axis, in the negative x-direction, and 3 units down the y-axis, in the negative y-direction.

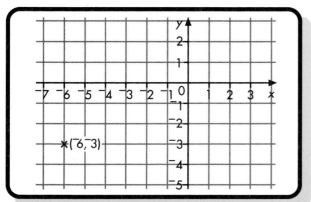

The **origin** is the centre of the graph, where the x- and the y-axes meet. Its coordinates are (0, 0). The origin is often just called O.

Gradients

The **gradient** of a line is the same as its slope.

The gradient measures the slope of a line. The steeper the slope, the bigger the gradient. To calculate the gradient, remember:

Gradients are GRADUAL or Gradients are GROTty

GRADients are Up over ALong, or Gradients are Rise Over Tread.

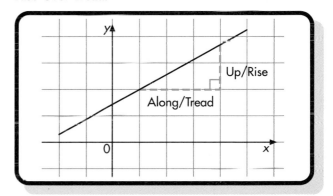

Example 4.1

Find the gradient of this line.

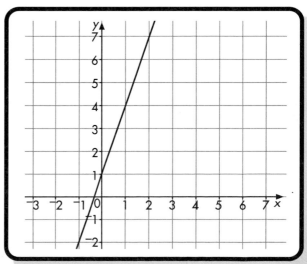

Solution

Using any two points on the line, draw a right-angled triangle. Make sure that the line of the graph is opposite the right angle, i.e. the hypotenuse.

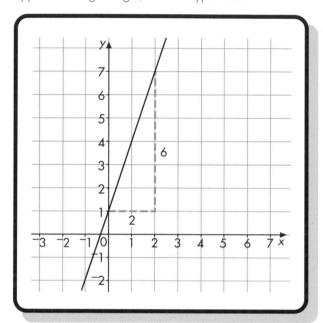

Measure the Up/Rise and the ALong/Tread. Using Gradients are GRADUAL or GROTty:

Gradient = $\frac{6}{2}$ = 3

Solution

Drawing a right-angled triangle and using GRADUAL or GROTty gives:

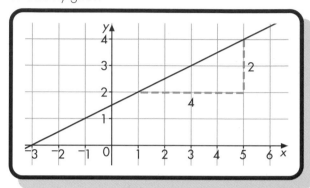

Gradient = $\frac{2}{4}$ = $\frac{1}{2}$ or 0.5

The gradient is a small number because the line is very shallow (not very steep).

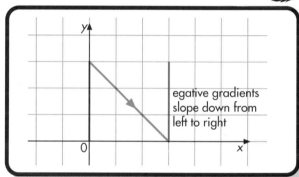

egative gradients slope down from left to right

Example 4.2

Find the gradient of this line.

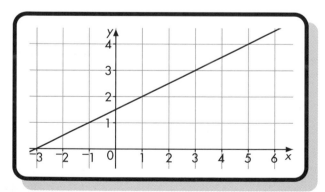

Example 4.3

Evaluate the gradient of this line.

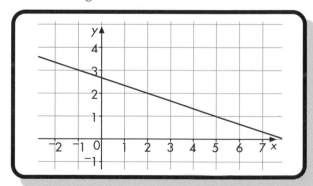

Solution

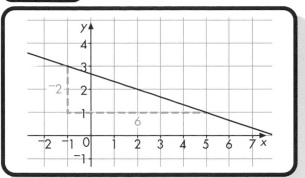

Gradient $= \dfrac{^{-}2}{6} = ^{-}\dfrac{1}{3}$

Exercise 4.1

Find the gradients of the following graphs.

1

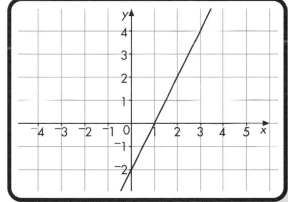

2

3

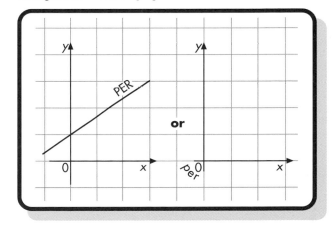

The meaning of the gradient

The gradient means 'y' per 'x'.

If this sounds strange, read on. A few examples should make it clear.

A distance–time graph shows distance travelled (y-axis) against time (x-axis). So for a graph of distance (in metres) against time (in seconds), the gradient means the distance *per* time, or metres *per* second – i.e. the **speed**.

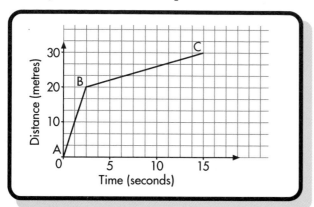

In a graph representing the cost of the telephone bill against the number of units used, the gradient represents the cost (in £) per unit.

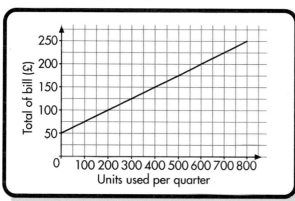

On a **currency conversion** graph which shows dollars on the y-axis and pounds sterling on the x-axis, the gradient is 'dollars per pound' – the **exchange rate**.

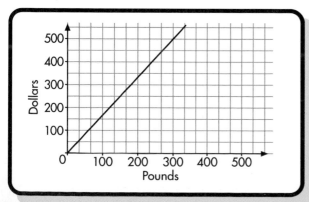

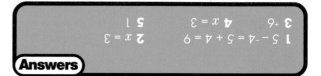
Graphs in everyday situations

Graphs can be used to represent a whole variety of situations, such as:

- distance against time
- speed against time
- the height of a liquid in a container, as it fills up or empties over a period of time
- the total of a telephone, gas or electricity bill, against the number of units that have been used
- the amount of money in one currency that is equivalent to another.

Example 4.4

The graph below shows Dave Isitt's day trip by car from New-Mer-a-Sea to the city of Sunchester.

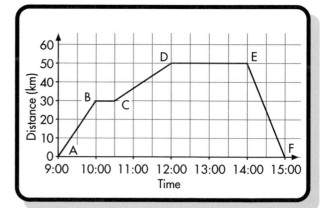

a) How far is Sunchester from New-Mer-a-Sea?

b) On the way to Sunchester, Dave stops at Litter-a-Sea. How long does he stay there?

c) How far is Litter-a-Sea from Sunchester?

d) i) What is the gradient of the line AB?
ii) What does this gradient represent?

e) During which part of his trip does Dave drive fastest? Give a reason for your answer.

Solution

a) 50 km

b) 30 minutes, or half an hour

c) 20 km (This is the vertical distance from point C to point D.)

d) i) Gradient = 30
ii) The distance per hour (km per hour) i.e. the speed

e) On his way back to New-Mer-a-Sea, or from E to F.
The graph is steepest in this part.

Example 4.5

Below is a currency conversion graph for pounds (£) and deutschmarks (DM).

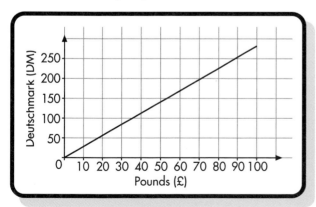

a) Using the graph, estimate the value of:
i) £30 in deutschmarks
ii) 200 deutschmarks in pounds.

b) i) What is the gradient of the graph?
ii) What does the gradient represent?

Solution

a) i) DM84 approximately
ii) £70 approximately

b) i) 280 ÷ 100 = 2.80 (Using the end points of the graph gives the most accurate answer.)
ii) The number of deutschmarks per pound

Exercise 4.2

1 The graph below shows the cost of a household energy bill, depending on the number of units used.

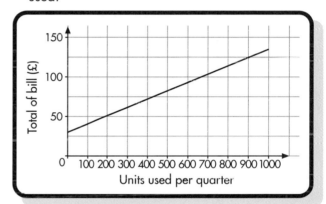

a) What is the total amount of the bill when 800 units are used?
b) If the total cost of the bill was £75, how many units were used?
c) What is the gradient of the line?
d) What does the gradient represent?

2 The graph below shows a journey made by car between two towns.

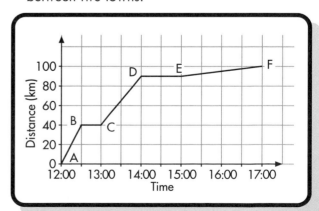

a) How long does the entire journey take?
b) How far do they travel?
c) How many times do they stop?
d) Between which two points on the graph is the car travelling the fastest?
Give a reason for your answer.
e) At what speed is the car travelling between points C and D?

3 The graph below shows what happened last time Paul Oosa had a bath.

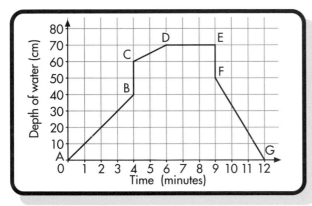

a) How long was the water running before Paul got in?
b) How long did he stay in the bath?
c) At what rate did the bath empty?

A Quick Dip!

1 Flo Wrist has x roses and y carnations. Write an expression for the total number of flowers she has.
2 Simplify $3x + y + x$
3 Which of the following numbers are prime?
12, 13, 14, 15, 17
4 Calculate 100×21.3
5 Write 0.6 as a fraction in its lowest terms.

Answers
1 $x + y$ **2** $4x + y$ **3** 13, 17 **4** 2130 **5** $\frac{3}{5}$

TAKE A BREAK

Sketching linear graphs

Impress your teacher!

The expression **linear graph** is just a fancy name for a graph which is a straight line.

When you need to sketch a linear graph, it is simplest to start with a table. Put in a few values for x, like this.

x	0	1	2	3
y				

To find the values of y, just substitute the values of x into the equation of the line.

When you have completed the table, plot the points as coordinates on a graph and connect them up.

Answers

1 a) £112 approximately
b) 405 approximately
c) 0.1 (Taking the end points of the line and using GRADUAL or GROTIy gives $100 \div 1000 = 0.1$.)
d) The cost per unit (in pounds)
2 a) 5 hours **b)** 100 km **c)** 2
d) Between A and B, because the gradient is higher or because the graph is steeper.
e) Speed = gradient = $50 \div 1 = 50$ kilometres per hour
3 a) 4 minutes (He got in the bath at BC when the graph is vertical and rising.)
b) 5 minutes (He got out at EF, when the graph is vertical and falling.)
c) $50 \div 3 = 16.7$ cm per minute

Example 4.6

For the equation $y = 2x + 1$:

a) complete the table below

x	0	1	2	3
y				

b) draw the graph of the line on a grid.

Solution

a) Work out the values of y by substituting the values of x into the formula for the line, $y = 2x + 1$.

When $x = 0$, $y = 2 \times 0 + 1 = 1$

When $x = 1$, $y = 2 \times 1 + 1 = 3$

When $x = 2$, $y = 2 \times 2 + 1 = 5$

When $x = 3$, $y = 2 \times 3 + 1 = 7$

x	0	1	2	3
y	1	3	5	7

b) Now plot the coordinates (0, 1), (1, 3), (2, 5), (3, 7) on the grid and draw a straight line through them. The line is extended to both edges of the graph.

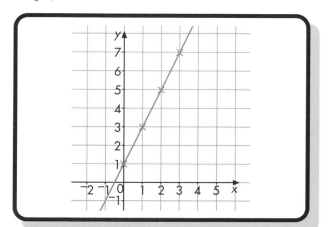

If you have plotted your points, but cannot get a straight line to go through all of them, you have probably got one of the points wrong.

Example 4.7

For the equation $y = 3x - 1$:

a) complete the table below

x	0	1	2	3
y				

b) draw the graph of the line on a grid.

Solution

a) Fill in the y-values in the table by substituting the values of $x = 0, 1, 2, 3$ into $y = 3x - 1$.

When $x = 0$, $y = 3 \times 0 - 1 = {}^-1$

When $x = 1$, $y = 3 \times 1 - 1 = 2$

When $x = 2$, $y = 3 \times 2 - 1 = 5$

When $x = 3$, $y = 3 \times 3 - 1 = 8$

x	0	1	2	3
y	${}^-1$	2	5	8

b) Now plot the coordinates and join them up with a straight line. Extend the line to the edges of the graph.

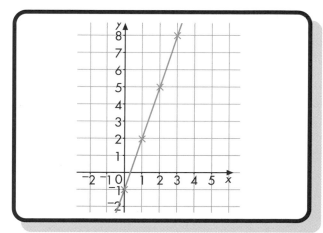

4

Exercise 4.3

For each of the following equations, complete the table of values and draw the graph.

1 $y = 2x - 3$

x	0	1	2	3
y				

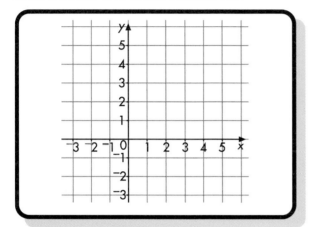

2 $y = x - 1$

x	0	1	2	3
y				

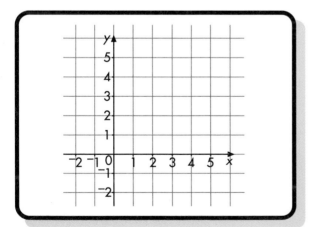

3 $y = 4 - 2x$

x	0	1	2	3
y				

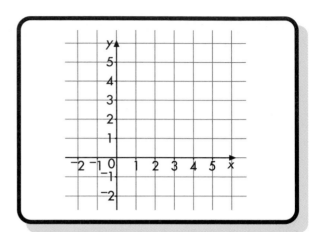

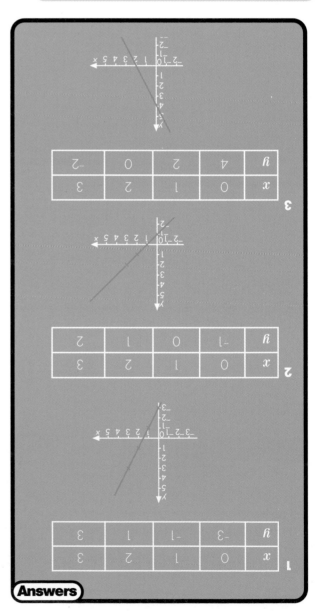

Answers

3

x	0	1	2	3
y	4	2	0	-2

2

x	0	1	2	3
y	-1	0	1	2

1

x	0	1	2	3
y	-3	-1	1	3

A Quick Dip!

1 Expand $3(x + 1)$
2 What is the gradient of the graph $y = 1 + 5x$?
3 Calculate $3\,400\,000 \div 100$
4 Which is the larger fraction: $\frac{4}{5}$ or $\frac{2}{3}$?
5 Solve $x - 2 = {}^-9$

Answers

5 $x = {}^-9 + 2 = {}^-7$
4 $\frac{4}{5}$ ($\frac{4}{5} = \frac{12}{15}$, $\frac{2}{3}$ is $\frac{10}{15}$)
3 $34\,000$
2 5
1 $3x + 3$

check your luggage

HAVE YOU REMEMBERED TO PACK ...

● plotting coordinates

● calculating gradients

● the meaning of the gradient

● graphs in everyday situations

● sketching linear graphs?

Ready for more? Turn to page 139 for:
• solving simultaneous equations graphically.

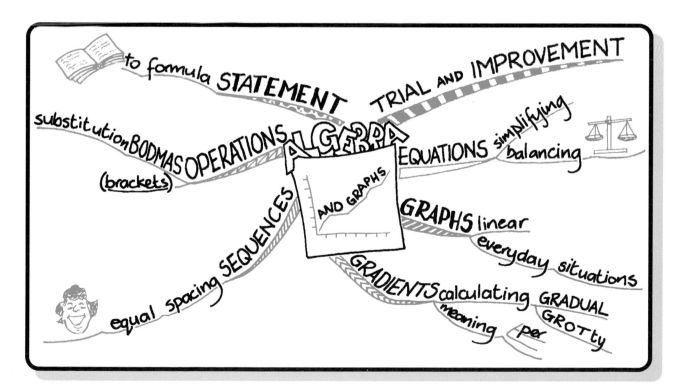

Algebra review

1 Betty Normaslee and Lou Syashirt went into the crazy golf course. They each hired a club. Betty hired two boxes of balls and Lou hired one box of balls. All the boxes contained x balls.

a) How many balls did Betty start off with?

b) Betty was a very poor player and lost 11 balls during the game. Write an expression for the number of balls Betty had left at the end of the game.

c) Lou lost three balls. Write an expression for the number of balls he had left at the end of the game.

d) Both players returned with the same number of balls at the end of the game. Write an equation to show this.

e) Solve this equation to find the value of x.

2 Some algebraic expressions are written next to the letters a) to k) below.

a) $2x$ **b)** x^2 **c)** $\frac{1}{2}x$ **d)** x^3

e) $3x - 2x$ **f)** $x - 1$ **g)** $1 \times x$

h) $1 + x$ **i)** $x \times 2$ **j)** $x + x$ **k)** $\frac{x}{2}$

  i) One of the above expressions is the same as $x + 1$. Which one is it?

  ii) Two of the above expressions are the same as $x \div 2$. Which are they?

  iii) Two of the above expressions may be simplified to x. Which are they?

  iv) Which expression is the same as $x \times x$?

3 Here is a number sequence.

1, 4, 7, 10, 13, ...

a) Find the next two terms in the sequence.

b) Find the nth term in the sequence.

c) Find the 31st term in the sequence.

4 Here is a number sequence.

3, 4, 5, 6, 7, 8, ...

The rule for finding the next term is: add 1 to the last term.

  i) Some more number sequences are shown below. For each of them, write down the rule for finding the next term.

   a) 1, 3, 5, 7, 9, 11, ...
      Rule: _____

   b) 3, 6, 12, 24, 48, 96, ...
      Rule: _____

  ii) Here is the start of a different number sequence.
      2, 4, ... , ... , ...

Find three different ways of continuing the number sequence. For each of them, find the next three numbers and state the rule for finding the next term in the sequence.

a) 2, 4, ... , ... , ...
  Rule for finding the next term:

  _____

b) 2, 4, ... , ... , ...
  Rule for finding the next term:

  _____

c) 2, 4, ... , ... , ...
  Rule for finding the next term:

  _____

5 On the diagrams below, each line is found by adding the two expressions to the left of it. For example,

x

$\underline{x + y}$

y

a) Write an expression for the line below. Express your answer as simply as possible.

$a + 2b$

  _____

$b + c$

b) Fill in the missing expressions on the lines below. Write your answers in their simplest form.

$d + 2$

  _____

$2d - 1$

                              $\underline{5d - 2}$

$3d - 4$

  _____

$^-d + 1$

c) Complete the diagram below.

$3e - 1$

  _____

$-2f$

                              $\underline{6e - f + 4}$

$2e + 5$

              $\underline{3e + f + 5}$

  _____

6 Evaluate the following expressions when $p = 2$, $q = 6$, $r = 7$ and $s = 4$.

a) $p(q + s)$ **b)** $\dfrac{q + s}{p}$ **c)** $\dfrac{qr}{p + s}$

d) pq^2 **e)** $qr - ps$

7 Expand the following expressions, giving your answer in its simplest form.
   a) $3(p + q)$ **b)** $4(2x - y)$
   c) $5(1 - 3x)$ **d)** $10(3c - 2d)$

8 Solve the following equations for x.
   a) $8 = x + 3$ **b)** $4x = 36$
   c) $5 = \dfrac{x}{3}$ **d)** $2x + 1 = x + 8$
   e) $3x - 2 = 10 - x$

9 Dan Chures has y sweets in a bag.
   a) He shares the sweets equally among three people. Write an expression for the number of sweets each person receives.
   b) Dan has x gobstoppers in his pocket. He eats two. Write an expression for the number of gobstoppers he has left in his pocket.

10 This distance–time graph shows two car journeys made by Vera Cross and Carly Sing. Vera sets off first.

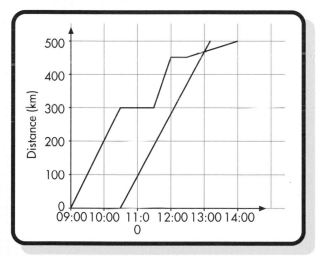

   a) How far away is their destination?
   b) What time does Carly set off?
   c) How many times does Vera stop?
   d) How many times does Carly stop?
   e) At what time does Carly overtake Vera?
   f) At what time does Vera arrive at their destination?

11 Plot the following points on the graph below.
   A(2, 1), B(⁻4, 3), C(⁻5, ⁻2), D(4, ⁻5)

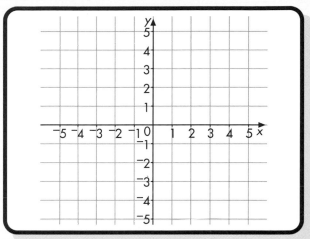

12 Find the gradients of the graphs below.
   a)

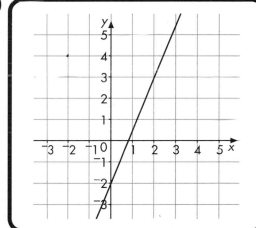

   b)

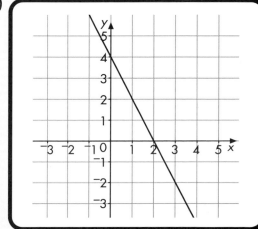

13 A company charged for car hire according to the amount of miles driven per day. The charges are shown in the graph below.

a) From the graph, estimate the daily charge for a car driven 80 miles.

b) If the charge per day was £60, approximately how many miles were driven per day?

c) What is the gradient of the graph?

d) What does the gradient represent?

14 a) Complete the table for the equation $y = 2x - 3$.

x	0	1	2	3
y	-3			

b) Hence, or otherwise, draw the graph of the line $y = 2x - 3$ on the grid below.

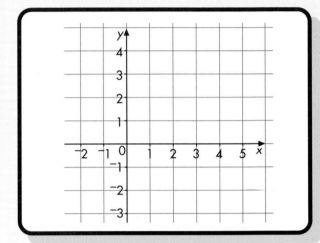

c) What is the gradient of the graph?

Answers

1 a) $2 \times x = 2x$ **b)** $2x - 11$ **c)** $x - 3$ **d)** $2x - 11 = x - 3$
 e) $2x - 11 = x - 3,\ x - 11 = -3,\ x = 8$

2 i) h), because addition is commutative.
 ii) c) and k)
 iii) e) and g)
 iv) b)

3 a) 16, 19
 b) Using DINO, DI = 3, N = n, O = -2, so the nth term is $3n - 2$.
 c) $3 \times 31 - 2 = 91$

4 i) a) Add 2 to the last term.
   b) Multiply the last term by 2.
 ii) Three possibilities are:
   a) 2, 4, 6, 8, 10, ... (Add 2 to the last term.)
   b) 2, 4, 8, 16, 32, ... (Multiply the last term by 2.)
   c) 2, 4, 6, 10, 16, ... (Add the last two terms together.)

5 a) $a + 3b + c$
 b) $3d + 1$
   $2d - 3$ (Check your results by making sure that they add to $5d - 2$.)
 c) $3e - 2f - 1$ or $3e - 1 - 2f$
   $e + f$

6 a) 20 **b)** $10 \div 2 = 5$ **c)** $42 \div 6 = 7$ (Remember to put brackets around the $p + q$.)
 d) $2 \times 36 = 72$ (O then M) **e)** $42 - 8 = 34$ (M then D)

7 a) $3p + 3q$ **b)** $8x - 4y$ **c)** $5 - 15x$
 d) $30c - 20d$

8 a) $x = 5$ **b)** $x = 9$ **c)** $x = 15$
 d) $x = 7$ **e)** $x = 3$

9 a) $y \div 3$ or $\frac{y}{3}$ or $\frac{1}{3}y$ **b)** $x - 2$

10 a) 500 km **b)** 10:30 **c)** 2 **d)** 0 **e)** 13:00 **f)** 14:00

11

12 a) 2.5 or $2\frac{1}{2}$ **b)** -2

13 a) £50 approximately **b)** 140 **c)** 0.17
 d) The cost per mile in pounds

14 a)

x	-3	0	1	2	3
y	3	-1	-1	1	3

b)

c) 2

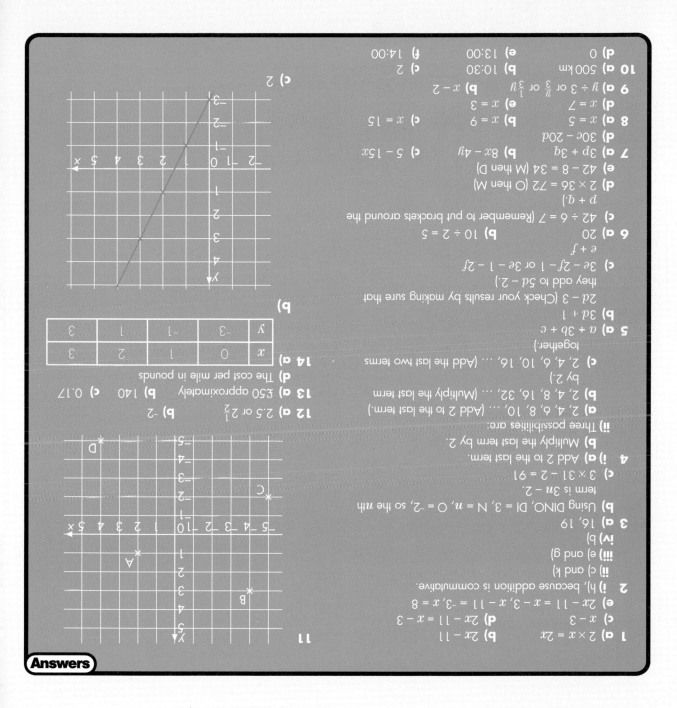

Lazing around the beach – measurement

checklist
Into this chapter we have packed ...

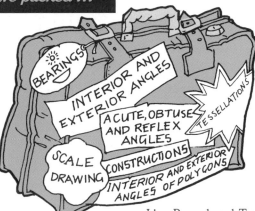

BEARINGS
INTERIOR AND EXTERIOR ANGLES
ACUTE, OBTUSE AND REFLEX ANGLES
TESSELLATIONS
SCALE DRAWING
CONSTRUCTIONS
INTERIOR AND EXTERIOR ANGLES OF POLYGONS

Basics

Angles

Liza Round and Tanya Leggz like lazing around on the beach. Sometimes they stir themselves enough to go and watch the Punch and Judy show. Recently, however they've got acutely bored with the show, because it's not violent enough. One of their complaints is that the crocodile only opens its mouth this far.

Acute!

Angles which are **less than 90°** are called **acute angles**.

Liza Round and Tanya Leggz have decided to sunbathe instead. Liza Round adjusts her sun lounger like this.

Angles which are **greater than 90° but less than 180°** are **obtuse angles.**

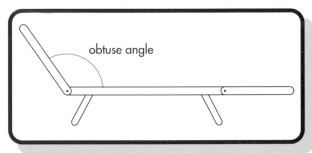

obtuse angle

Tanya Leggz wants to give the sun a chance to get to her knees, so she adjusts her lounger like this.

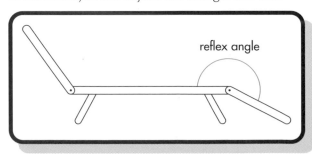

reflex angle

Angles which are **greater than 180° but less than 360°** are **reflex angles**.

Angles which are **exactly 90°** are **right angles**.

Putting acute, obtuse and reflex in alphabetical order also puts them in order of size, smallest to largest.

Using a protractor

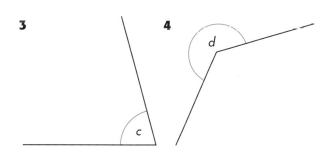

Exercise 5.1

Try these for size! Measure each angle.

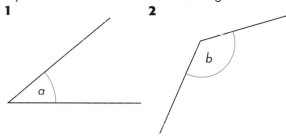

1

2

3

4

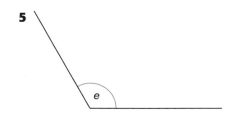

5

How did you get on?

All of them right?

Well done! You can skip the next section and move on to bearings on page 82.

Any mistakes?

Don't worry. Everyone has to learn how to do this at some stage. You'll soon get the idea.

Many people don't know how to put the protractor in the right place. You need to have the central cross piece right in the corner of the angle, and one of the base lines lying along the line of the angle. If you don't know which scale to read, look at the position of the zero along the bottom of the angle. If it's on the inside scale, read the inside figures, and if it's on the outside, use the outside scale. If your base line isn't horizontal, try turning the page round until it is.

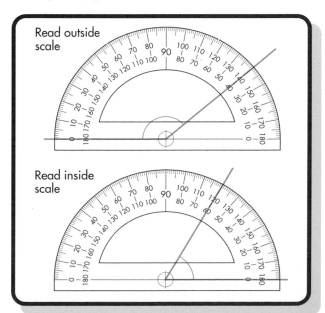

Read outside scale

Read inside scale

Don't lose your bearings!

Bearings: You always measure bearings in a clockwise direction starting from the north, and you always write the answer using three figures.

Exercise 5.2

Measure these angles. Write them as bearings.

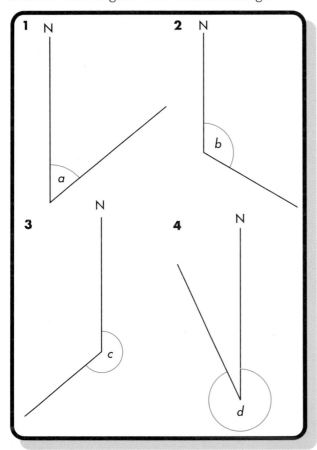

Always start by putting your protractor on the angle so that the nought points to the north.

Answers   1 050°   2 120°   3 230°   4 340°

Identifying angles

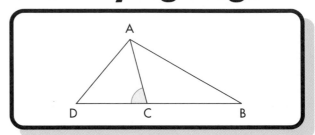

The angle marked at C may be called angle ACD or angle DCA. In some books this is written as ∠ACD, ∠DCA, AĈD or DĈA.

The marked angle at C is made up of two lines, AC and CD. To name the angle, follow the line from A to C to D, or from D to C to A. This avoids confusing it with the other angle at C, which runs from A to C to B, or from B to C to A, which is called ∠ACB or ∠BCA. The important letter is the middle one.

Exercise 5.3

Mark the required angles on the diagram below.

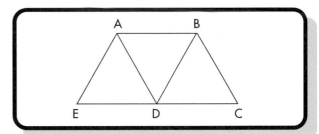

1 Angle ADB
2 Angle BCD
3 Angle EAD

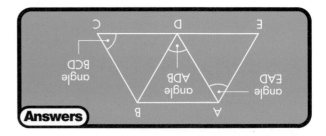

Answers

A Quick Dip!

1 9×7
2 $y + 3 = 10$. Find y.
3 How many minutes make half an hour?
4 How many degrees make a right angle?
5 10% of £36.00

Answers
1 63 2 7 3 30 minutes 4 90° 5 £3.60

Seeing things from a new angle!

Diagrams marked like this show lines that are parallel.

Diagrams marked like this show sides that are equal.

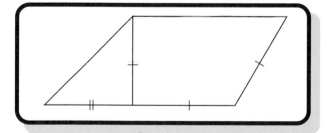

Diagrams marked like this show angles that are equal.

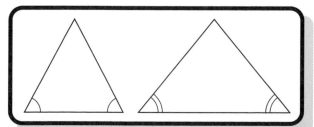

Howard Eye-No has been working closely with Con Survaishun to take a completely new look at the COAST. Here are their latest findings.

C – Corresponding angles are equal.

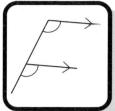

If you write to your Friends, and they write back, (Ⅎ), you **correspond** with them.

O – Opposite angles are equal. Think of noughts and crosses.

A – Alternate angles are equal.

Impress your teacher!
You may know these angles as **Z angles**, but the correct term is **alternate**.

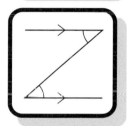

S – straight line. Remember, angles at a common point on a straight line add up to 180°.

T – triangles.
 1 The angles of a triangle always add up to 180°.
 2 Triangles with all three sides equal and all three angles equal are called **equilateral triangles**. Each angle is 180° ÷ 3 = 60°.
 3 Triangles with two sides equal and two angles equal are called **isosceles triangles**.
 4 Triangles with all three sides and angles of a different size are called scalene triangles.

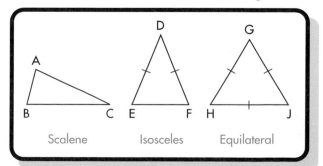

Scalene · Isosceles · Equilateral

Example 5.1

In the diagram below, which is not accurately drawn, find the values of x, y and z. Give reasons for your answers.

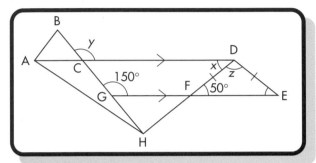

Solution

$x = 50°$ alternate angles

$y = 150°$ corresponding angles

$z = 80°$ $180° - 2 × 50°$

Test your knowledge of the COAST with Howard Eye-No and Con Survaishun

Just to recap
You need to know these special angles formed by intersecting lines.

Exercise 5.4

Study this diagram, then underline the correct answers in the brackets.

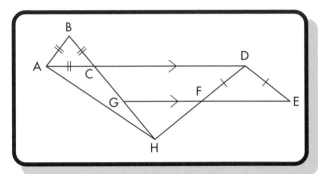

1 a) Angles BCD and CGE are
(alternate   corresponding   opposite).
 b) Angles CDF and DFE are
(alternate   corresponding   opposite).
 c) Angles DFE and GFH are
(alternate   corresponding   opposite).

2 a) Triangle GFH is
(scalene   isosceles   equilateral).
 b) Triangle ABC is
(scalene   isosceles   equilateral).
 c) Triangle DFE is
(scalene   isosceles   equilateral).

Now look at these angles.

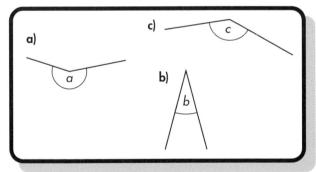

3 a) Angle a is (acute   obtuse   reflex).
 b) Angle b is (acute   obtuse   reflex).
 c) Angle c is (acute   obtuse   reflex).

A Quick Dip!

1 20% of 60
2 Two angles of a triangle are 90° and 40°.
   What is the third?
3 $z - 10 = 15$. What does z stand for?
4 6×7
5 What do we call angles which are larger than
   90° but smaller than 180°?

TAKE A BREAK

Constructions

Amy Tirstik has to complete a Maths investigation comparing the old town with the modern New-Mer-a-Sea. She needs to learn how to include diagrams of some of the landmarks.

Drawing shapes

Example 5.2

Using a ruler and compasses only, construct triangle ABC such that AB = 3 cm, AC = 4 cm and BC = 5 cm. Measure angle BAC.

Solution

1 Start by drawing any one line, e.g. AB, and label this.

2 Open your compasses to 4 cm and, putting the point on A, draw an arc as shown on the right.

Hold the compasses carefully at the top, or they will wobble and your construction will be inaccurate.

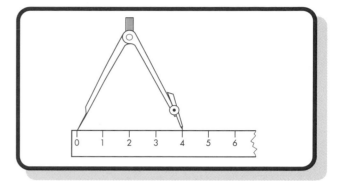

3 Open your compasses to 5 cm and draw an arc from B as shown below.

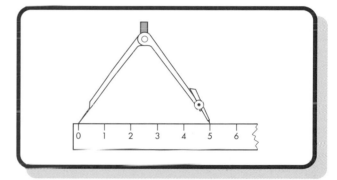

4 Join A and B to the point where the arcs cross to make triangle ABC.

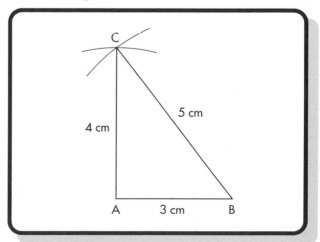

If you have drawn the triangle accurately, angle BAC should be a right angle, i.e. 90°.

Always leave your construction lines on a diagram to show your working.

Example 5.3

Draw a line 5 cm long, and label it PQ. Using your protractor, draw an angle from P and an angle from Q of 60° each. Mark the point where they cross as R. Measure PR and QR. What is the special name given to the triangle which you have drawn?

Solution

Draw the base line. Mark on it the point P, then use compasses, radius 5 cm, to mark point Q.

Put the cross piece of your protractor at each point P and Q of the base line in turn, and draw a line from it at the required angle.

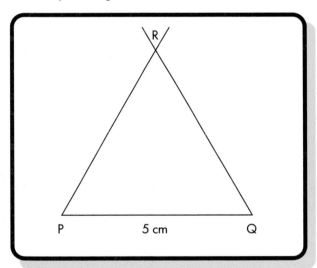

The crossing point of the two construction lines completes the triangle.

Since angles RPQ and RQP are each 60°, angle PRQ should also be 60°.

(60° + 60° = 120°. 180° − 120° = 60°)

The triangle is therefore equilateral.

Don't rub out the construction lines.

Of course, you can draw shapes other than triangles.

Exercise 5.5

Using the measurements as given on the sketch below, make an accurate drawing. Then measure AD to the nearest 0.5 cm.

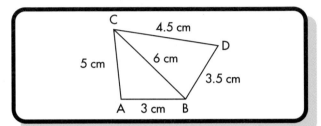

AD = 5 cm

Answers

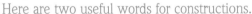

Impress your teacher!

Here are two useful words for constructions.

- When two lines meet at right angles, they are **perpendicuLar**.
- To **bisect** is to cut in half.

Putting those two pieces of information together gives you the **perpendicular bisector**, i.e. a line which cuts another line in half at right angles.

Drawing the perpendicular bisector

Example 5.4

The First Aid Post and Victoria Spunj's beach café are **equidistant** (i.e. the same distance) from a breakwater. Draw the position of the breakwater.

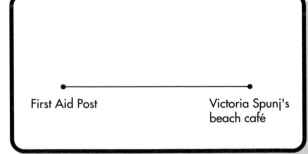

First Aid Post   Victoria Spunj's beach café

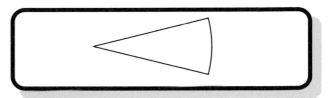

Solution

1   Put the point of your compasses on one end of the line between the First Aid Post and the café. Open the compasses to a radius that is more than half the length of the line.

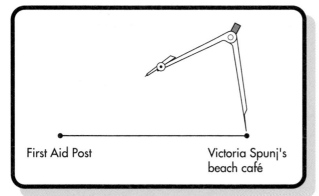

First Aid Post   Victoria Spunj's
                              beach café

2   Using light pressure, draw an arc on either side of the line.

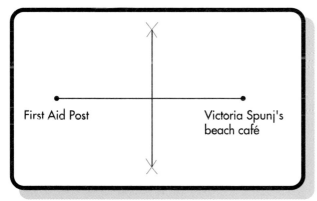

First Aid Post   Victoria Spunj's
                              beach café

3   Without changing the radius, draw arcs from the other end of the line, to cut the first two arcs. Join the points where the arcs cross.

Bisecting an angle

Example 5.5

There is a disputed piece of land between Millie-Anne Eyre's grounds and those of Iona Manshion. The Planning Department at the Town Hall has decided that the only fair solution is to divide it down the middle.

Solution

1   Put the point of the compasses on the point of the angle and make an arc at each arm, at A and B.

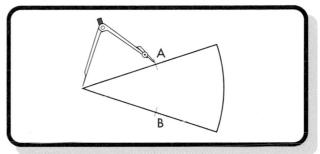

2   Move the point of the compasses to A and draw another arc, further away from the point of the angle. Keeping the radius of the compasses the same, repeat at B.

3   Join the point where the arcs cross to the point of the angle, to make the bisector of the angle.

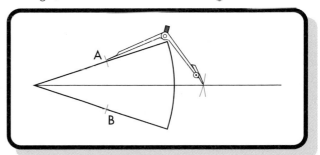

A Quick Dip!

1   How many chocolate bars at 25p each could you buy for £2.00?
2   If $6t = 42$, find $4t$.
3   One night the temperature is 2°C. Over the next hour it falls by 3 degrees. What temperature is it then?
4   Seven people share 30 sweets equally among them. How many would be left over?
5   $x^2 = 81$. Give one possible value of x.

Answers 1 8 2 28 3 -1°C 4 2 5 9 or -9

....

TAKE A BREAK

....

Using metric measurements

How much do you remember about decimals?

Exercise 5.6

Answer these without using a calculator.

1	5.76×100	**2**	43×10
3	$164 \div 100$	**4**	4.7×1000
5	$160 \div 1000$	**6**	$75 \div 10$
7	1.3×100		

Answers 1 576 2 430 3 1.64 4 4700 5 0.16 6 7.5 7 130

How did you get on?

All or most of them right?

Good. You are obviously ready to tackle the next section.

Don't even ask?

The bad news is that you need to be able to multiply and divide by powers of ten in order to work with metric units. The good news is that it's not that difficult once you get the hang of it. Look back to pages 2 and 5 to refresh your memory, then try the exercise again.

Scale drawing

Amy Tirstik has to draw plans of some parts of the town to scale. Her teacher has given her the following list.

$10\,mm = 1\,cm$
$100\,cm = 1\,m$
$1000\,m = 1\,km$

Some of the old maps that Amy has found use yards, feet and inches, but fortunately Esther Mait has already converted them to their approximate metric equivalents. (She will share her know-how with you in the next chapter.)

Example 5.6

As part of her project, Amy Tirstik wants to draw a plan of the rectangular garden of Ma Jinn's guest house. Esther Mait has worked out the metric measurements as being 10 m wide and 25 m long. Choose a suitable scale and draw a plan of the garden.

Solution

It's a good idea to start by drawing a rough sketch and marking in the measurements.

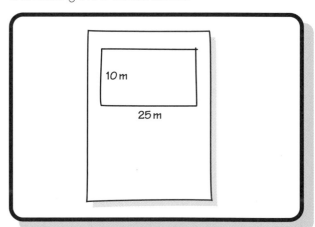

You need to choose a scale so that your diagram is big enough to be read easily, and small enough to fit comfortably on to your page. In this case, let 1 cm represent 1 m. Draw a rectangle 10 cm wide, and 25 cm long.

Example 5.7

Ma Jinn is very impressed by Amy's diagram, and has decided that she would like her own copy. However, she only has small scraps of paper, and Esther suggests that Amy draws a plan half the size. Draw Ma Jinn's rectangle.

Solution

1 cm represents 2 m

5 cm represent 10 m (or, for every 2 m, Amy draws 1 cm, and 10 ÷ 2 = 5)

12.5 cm represent 25 m (25 ÷ 2 = 12.5 or 12$\frac{1}{2}$)

Example 5.8

Iona Manshion has bought a field on which to build a holiday home. Amy is drawing a scale diagram to help Iona to plan the layout of her house and garden. The plot is 40 m wide at the front. Amy draws this to scale and labels it AB. AD is at right angles to AB and is 70 m and BC is at right angles to AB and is 100 m. Draw the field to scale and measure CD. What length does this represent?

Solution

Start by making a rough sketch to give you an idea of the shape.

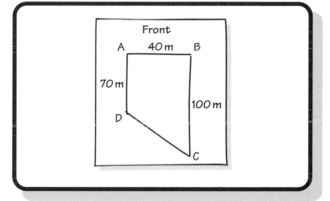

Let 1 cm represent 10 m. AB will be 4 cm, BC will be 10 cm, AD will be 7 cm. Draw the lines and measure CD. You should have a line 5 cm long.

CD = 5 × 10 = 50 m

Working with metric units is really easy – as long as you remember that:

milli – means 'a thousandth'
  1 ml = $\frac{1}{1000}$ l

centi – means 'a hundredth'
  1 cm = $\frac{1}{100}$ m

kilo – means 'a thousand'
  1 kg = 1000 g

5

Exercise 5.7

Amy Tirstik's rough sketch of a rectangular floor plan is shown below. Taking 1 cm to represent 5 m, make an accurate scale drawing from her sketch.

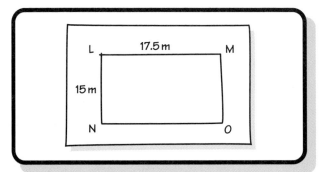

1 How long is LM on your plan?
2 How long is it in reality?

Answers

ʍ S˙ZL **Z**   ɯɔ S˙E L **1**

A Quick Dip!

1 Change 1.5 m to centimetres.
2 How many pence in £3.20?
3 How many 5p pieces could you exchange for £1.00?
4 $x = 2y$. If $y = 7$, find x.
5 How many centimetres are the same as 120 mm?

Answers

ɯɔ ZL **S**   ⅁L **4**
OZ **E**   dOZE **Z**   ɯɔ OSL **1**

Polygons

A polygon is the mathematical name for any flat, straight-sided shape. If all the sides of a polygon are equal, all the angles are also equal, and the shape is called a **regular polygon**.

Some important polygons

A **quadrilateral** is a flat, or two-dimensional, four-sided shape. ('Quad' usually involves four of something. Think of 'quadruplets' or 'quadrangle'.) There are six quadrilaterals which you will often meet in Maths.

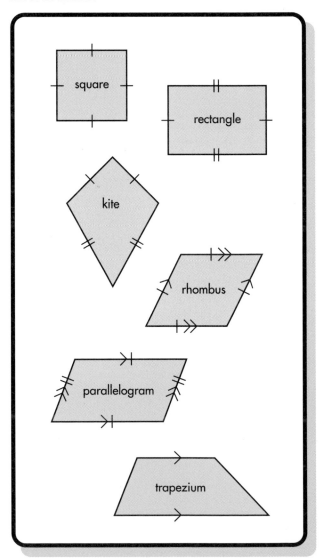

A **pentagon** has five sides.

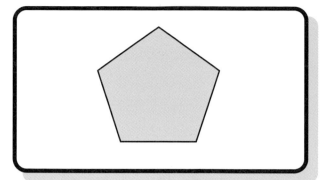

A **hexagon** has six sides. (Remember he**x**agon and si**x**.)

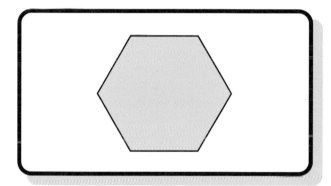

An **octagon** has 8 sides. (Think of **oct**opus.)

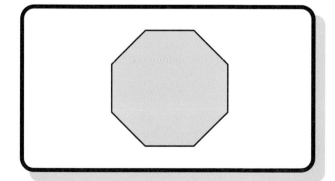

Impress your teacher!

Other polygons you might meet are **heptagons** (seven sides), **nonagons** (nine sides) and **decagons** (ten sides). If you look carefully at your coins, you will see that 20p and 50p coins have seven sides. The proper name for the shape of these coins is **equicurvilinear heptagon**.

Interior and exterior angles

Interior angles are the inside angles at the corners of the polygon. **Exterior angles** are formed by extending the sides, as shown.

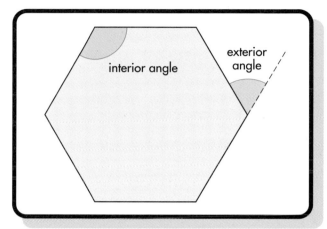

Exercise 5.8

1 What size is the interior angle of a regular pentagon?
2 The exterior angle of a regular polygon is 45°. How many sides does the polygon have?
3 Find the size of an exterior angle of a regular hexagon.

Answers 1 108° 2 8 3 60°

How did you get on?

All right?

Well done. You can skip the next section and move on to Tessellation on page 92.

Some problems?

Don't worry. This is easily put right. Read the next section, then try the previous exercise again.

5

Finding an exterior angle

There are several different ways of doing this, but don't worry; we shall only show you one. If you walk all the way round a shape and get back to where you started, you will turn through 360°. In any regular n-sided polygon (i.e. all sides and angles are equal):

$360° \div n$ = exterior angle

Finding an interior angle

Looking at the diagram in column 2 on page 91, you can see that the exterior and interior angles lie on a straight line.

180° − exterior angle = interior angle

In the diagram:

$360° \div 6 = 60°$ The exterior angle = 60°
$180° − 60° = 120°$ The interior angle = 120°

Tessellation

Fitting it all together with Tessa Laishen

Tessa Laishen's company specialises in laying tiled floors. The Council wants to replace the floor in the kitchen of the Town Hall and Tessa Laishen has brought along some of her designs (below).

Shapes which fit together without a gap are said to **tessellate**.

How can you tell which shapes will tessellate?

Angles round a point add up to 360°. If the interior angles of the shape which you are using is a factor of 360°, the shape will tessellate. If you are using different shapes, their interior angles must add up to 360°.

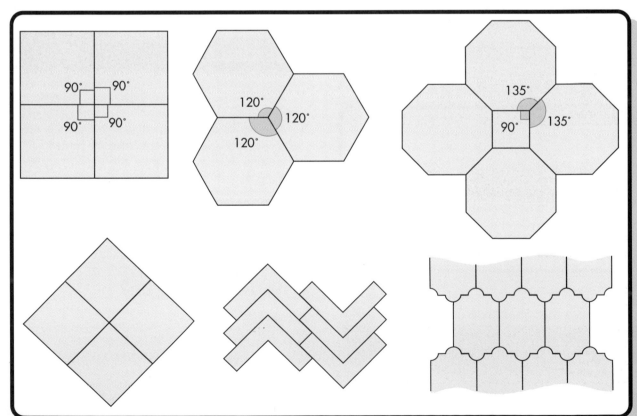

Exercise 5.9

1 How many sides does an octagon have?
2 What size is the exterior angle of a regular octagon?
3 What size is the interior angle of a regular octagon?
4 What is the largest number of regular octagons which you could fit round a point?
5 Will octagons tessellate? Give a reason for your answer.
6 What shape could you combine with regular octagons to make them tessellate?

 Ready for more? Turn to page 147 for:
• loci.

Answers

1 8
2 $360° \div 8 = 45°$
3 $180° - 45° = 135°$
4 2 ($135° \times 2 = 270°$. Another octagon would take the total over 360°.)
5 No. They do not tessellate, because 135 is not a factor of 360. Or, $360 \div 135$ always leaves a remainder.
6 If the octagon is regular, you will have a square. You always have a four-sided space between the octagons. 2 octagons joined together use $135° \times 2 = 270°$. $360° - 270° = 90°$ which is the angle at each corner of a square.

check your luggage

HAVE YOU REMEMBERED TO PACK …

● interior and exterior angles

● acute, obtuse and reflex angles

● corresponding and alternate angles

● bearings

● constructions

● scale drawing

● interior and exterior angles of polygons

● tessellation?

A Quick Dip!

1 9×6
2 $56 \div 8$
3 Is an angle of 89° acute, obtuse, reflex or a right angle?
4 $z \div 3 = 12$. Find z.
5 $a + b = 10$. If $b = 6$, find a.

Answers

1 54 2 7 3 acute 4 36 (Not 4!) 5 4

6

Beach attractions
– length, area and volume

checklist

Into this chapter we have packed ...

METRIC AND IMPERIAL MEASURES

LENGTH PERIMETER AND CIRCUMFERENCE

AREA OF TRIANGLES QUADRILATERALS AND CIRCLES

VOLUME OF CUBES AND CUBOIDS

Length

Amy Tirstik uses the metric system to measure length.

10 mm = 1 cm   100 cm = 1 m   1000 m = 1 km

The old maps of the town, however, use the imperial system.

12 inches = 1 foot   3 feet = 1 yard
1760 yards = 1 mile

Amy calls in her friend Esther Mait to give her a rough idea of their metric equivalents.

Esther points out that rulers marked with inches and centimetres can help you remember that 30 cm is approximately 12 inches.

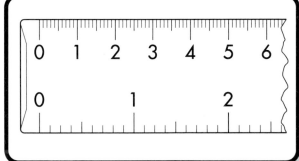

12 inches = 1 foot   36 inches = 3 feet = 1 yard

You also might need to know that 1 m is approximately 39 inches.

If you have to convert metres to yards without a calculator, take 1 m = 1 yard.

Example 6.1

When the pier at New-Mer-a-Sea was built in the nineteenth century, its length was given as 450 yards. Taking 1 m = 39 inches, how many metres is that approximately? Give your answer to the nearest metre.

Solution

450 yards = 1350 feet   (450 × 3)

1350 × 12 = 16 200 inches

16 200 ÷ 39 = 415 m to the nearest metre.

Exercise 6.1

1 How many inches are there in 6 feet?
2 Approximately how many centimetres are equal to 4 feet?
3 Approximately how many centimetres are there in 60 feet?

Answers

(Answers printed upside down:)
1 6 × 12 = 72
2 30 cm = 1 foot, 4 × 30 = 120
3 1800 cm (1 foot is approximately 30 cm.)

Perimeter

The **perimeter** is the distance all round a shape.

Example 6.2

A rectangle has sides of length 20 cm and 18 cm. Find its perimeter.

Solution

Choose whichever way you find easiest.

20 + 18 + 20 + 18 = 76 cm

20 × 2 + 18 × 2 = 76 cm

2(20 + 18) = 76 cm

Exercise 6.2

Find the perimeters of the following shapes.

1

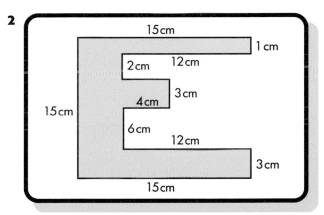

2

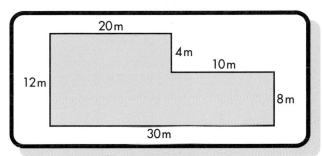

Answers

(Answers printed upside down:) 1 84 m   2 92 cm

A Quick Dip!

1 How many centimetres are there in 1.56 m?
2 7 − ☀ = ⁻2
3 What is the perimeter of a square with sides of 6 cm?
4 How many yards are equal to 30 feet? (1 yard = 3 feet)
5 3 − ⁻5

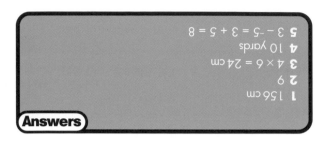

TAKE A BREAK

Parts of a circle

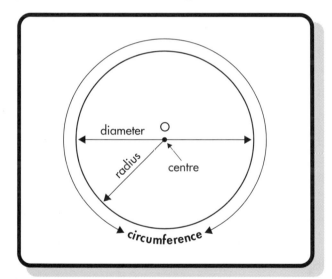

The perimeter of a circle is called the **circumference**. To calculate this you will need to use your calculator's π button.

When you press the π button, your calculator should show a number with a very long decimal tail, i.e. 3.14159... . If you have to use π without using a calculator, use 3 as an approximation.

Calculators differ. π on one model is not necessarily in the same place as π on another. You need to become familiar with yours.

Finding the circumference of a circle

Circumference = $2\pi r$ or πd

Example 6.3

Wat Annoys conducts New-Mer-a-Sea's brass band in their summer concerts in the park. The bandstand is in the shape of a circle with radius 6.25 m.

a) Find the circumference of the bandstand, to the nearest metre.

b) Chairs for the players are to be placed $\frac{2}{3}$ of the way round the circumference. If each chair requires a total width of 80 cm, how many chairs can be placed?

Solution

a) Circumference = $2\pi r$ or πd

Circumference = $C = 2 \times \pi \times 6.25$ or $\pi \times 12.5$ (diameter = 2 × radius = 12.5)

$C = 39.27$ m

b) Converting 39.27 m to centimetres, $C = 3927$ cm.

$\frac{2}{3} \times 3927 = 2618$ cm (or 3927 ÷ 3 × 2)

$2618 \div 80 = 32.725$

Although you would usually round up with this value, you cannot squeeze in an extra chair, so the answer is 32.

A Quick Dip!

1 Solve $8x = 32$. 2 Calculate $\frac{26 - 8}{3}$.

3 Solve $2x = -12$. 4 Solve $x + 6 = 11$.

5 Find the next term of the sequence 10, 12, 14, 16, ...

Finding the diameter of a circle when you have the circumference

$C = \pi d$ so $d = \dfrac{C}{\pi}$

Example 6.4

The circular boating lake at New-Mer-a-Sea has a circumference of 110 m. Rhoda Weigh steered her boat from one side of the lake to the other, going through the middle. How far did she travel?

Solution

You need to find the diameter.

$d = \dfrac{C}{\pi} = 110 \div \pi = 35\text{m}$

A Quick Dip!

1 A circle has a radius of 7 cm. What is its circumference, approximately?
2 ⁻6 – 2
3 The diameter of a circle is 12 cm. What is its radius?
4 $2x = 10$. Find the value of x.
5 0.4×0.2

Answers

1 $2 \times 7 \times 3 = 42\,\text{cm}$
2 ⁻8
3 $12 \div 2 = 6\,\text{cm}$
4 $x = 5$
5 0.08 (Look back to page 32 if you thought the answer was 0.8.)

TAKE A BREAK

Area

If the lengths are measured in cm, the area is measured in cm².
If the lengths are measured in m, the area is measured in m².

The area of a square or a rectangle

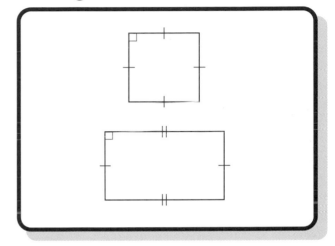

Area = length × width

The area of a parallelogram

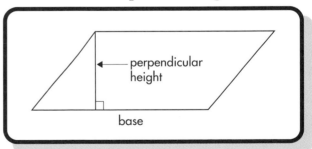

Area = length × perpendicular height

Remember, perpendicular lines cross at right angles to each other.

The area of a triangle

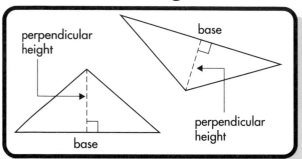

Either:

area = $\frac{1}{2}$ base × perpendicular height, or

area = $\dfrac{\text{base} \times \text{perpendicular height}}{2}$

*Be careful always to use the **perpendiculaR** height.*

Exercise 6.3

Find the areas of the following shapes. (**Hint:** Split the shapes into rectangles or triangles before you start. Then add together the separate parts.) Remember, these are only sketches, so do not try to answer the questions by measuring.

Example 6.5

a) Millie-Anne Eyre has a rectangular lawn 20 m by 15 m. Find the area of the lawn.

b) She plans to plant a rectangular rose bed inside the lawn, leaving a path 1 m wide around its edge. What are the length and width of the rose bed?

c) What is the area of the rose bed?

d) What area of the plot will the path take up?

Solution

a) 20 × 15 = 300 m²

b) 18 m long and 13 m wide

Not 19 m by 14 m! Remember to take one metre off each end.

c) 18 × 13 = 234 m²

d) 300 − 234 = 66 m²

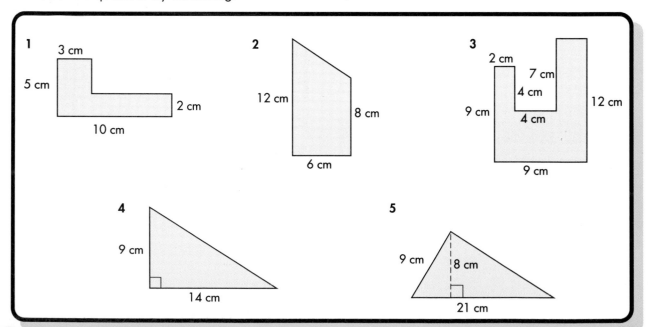

The area of a circle

Remember, 'πr squarea gives you the area.'

Example 6.6

When Terry Bulldinn plays trumpet solos, the noise can be heard within a radius of 50 m. What area of the park should people avoid if they do not wish to hear his performance? Round off your answer to a sensible degree of accuracy. Give a reason for your choice.

Solution

'πr squarea gives you the area'

Area of a circle = πr^2

$\pi \times 50^2 = 7853.98$ m^2

A sensible rounding would be 7850 m^2. The larger the quantity you are measuring the more difficult, and the less important, it gets to be accurate in every detail. In this situation, a few metres or centimetres would not make much difference to the overall answer.

Exercise 6.4

The Town Council of New-Mer-a-Sea is planning its schemes for the flower beds in the park.

1 The largest bed is circular, with a radius of 5.4 m. Find its area.
2 The head gardener remembers from last year that one of the circular beds had a circumference of 14.45 m. What is its diameter?
3 Part of the park in the shape of a rectangle 20 m by 30 m, is to be fenced off for a new playground.
   a) Letting 1 cm represent 5 m, make an accurate scale drawing.
   b) What is the area of the playground?
   c) If they allow 3m for a gate, how much fencing will they need?

4 The diagram shows a circular flower bed in the middle of a lawn. Calculate the area of the lawn. (The diagram is not drawn to scale.)

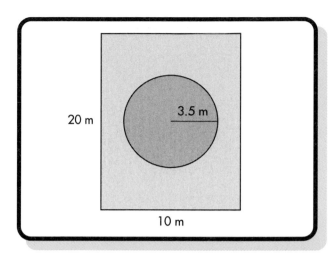

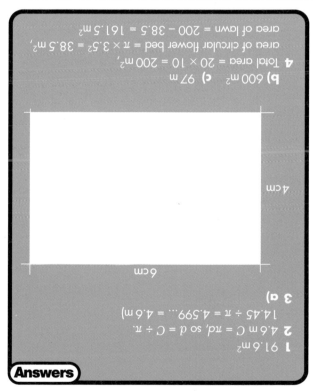

Answers

1 91.6 m^2

2 4.6 m $C = \pi d$, so $d = C \div \pi$.
($14.45 \div \pi = 4.599... = 4.6$ m)

3 a)

6 cm
4 cm

b) 600 m^2 c) 97 m

4 Total area = 20 × 10 = 200 m^2,
area of circular flower bed = $\pi \times 3.5^2 = 38.5$ m^2,
area of lawn = 200 − 38.5 = 161.5 m^2

A Quick Dip!

1 Find the approximate area of a circle with radius 10 cm.
2 What is the circumference of the same circle, approximately?
3 2 − ⁻3
4 15% of 60
5 Give 23.195 to 2 decimal places.

99

TAKE A BREAK

Weight or mass

Although weight and mass are slightly different, at Key Stage 3 you can treat both terms in the same way. Nowadays quantities are usually weighed in grams and kilograms.

1000 grams = 1 kilogram
1000 kilograms = 1 tonne

Example 6.7

a) Express 1565 grams in kilograms.

b) Change 4.6 kilograms to grams.

c) How many grams are the same as 2.4 tonnes?

Make sure that you have remembered how to multiply and divide decimals using powers of ten. A quick visit to the rock pool on page 29 should refresh your memory.

Solution

a) 1.565 kg
(1565 ÷ 1000)

b) 4600 g
(4.6 × 1000)

c) 2400 kg
(1 tonne = 1000 kg, 2.4 × 1000 = 2400)

2 400 000 g
(1 kg = 1000 g, 2400 × 1000 = 2 400 000)

(If you prefer, you can carry out one calculation only, i.e.

2.4 × 1 000 000 = 2 400 000)

Imperial measures

You will sometimes find quantities given in stones (st), pounds (lb) and ounces (oz).

16 oz = 1 lb   14 lb = 1 st

If you have to change these to the metric system, and have use of a calculator, use 1 kg = 2.2 lb. If you have to work without a calculator, use 1 kg = 2 lb.

Example 6.8

Esther Mait is making some cakes from a recipe that she has found in an old book. Here are some of the ingredients.

8 oz flour	10 oz dried fruit
6 oz butter	2 oz ground almonds
4 oz sugar	2 large eggs

Esther's scales use the metric system. Change the recipe so that she can weigh out the ingredients.

Solution

You need DIM to answer this question. Look back to page 41 if you have forgotten.

2.2 lb = 1 kg   2.2 lb = 2.2 × 16 = 35.2 oz

Using DIM: 35.2 oz = 1000 g   D

$1 \text{ oz} = \frac{1000}{35.2} \text{ g}$ I

$8 \text{ oz} = \frac{1000}{35.2} \times 8 = 227.2727 \dots$ M

Kitchen scales do not need to be that accurate, so a sensible approximation would be 8 oz = 230 g.

using DIM again:

$$8\,oz = 230\,g \qquad\qquad D$$
$$1\,oz = \frac{230}{8}\,g \qquad\qquad I$$
$$6\,oz = \frac{230}{8} \times 6 = 172.5\,g \qquad M$$

(There are faster ways of reaching this result. If you can spot one, by all means use it.)

A weight of 172.5 g is more accurate than you need for cooking. You would probably use 170 g.

8 oz = 230 g (approximately)

4 oz = 230 ÷ 2 = 115 g   Round this up to 120 g.

To find 10 oz you can either use DIM again, or add together the metric equivalents of 6 oz and 4 oz.

172.5 + 115 = 287.5 g

A sensible approximation would be 290 g or 300 g.

2 oz = 115 ÷ 2 = 57.5 g. Round this to 60 g.

Esther's recipe now looks like this.

230 g flour	300 g dried fruit
170 g butter	60 g ground almonds
120 g sugar	2 large eggs

A Quick Dip!

1 6 × 7
2 56 ÷ 8
3 How many grams are there in 1.5 kg?
4 A temperature of ⁻5°C falls by 7 degrees. What temperature is it now?
5 When a number is doubled, the answer is 16. What was the original number?

TAKE A BREAK

Volume

Volume is a measure of the amount of space a solid shape takes up, or the amount of something which a container will hold.

A **cube** is like a three-dimensional square. All sides are the same length, and all the angles are right angles.

A **cuboid** is like a three-dimensional rectangle. Its opposite sides are the same length and all its angles are right angles.

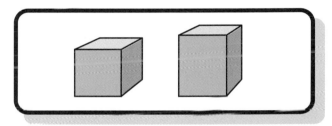

The volume of a cube or cuboid is length × width × height.

Volume is usually given in cubed or cubic units.

Example 6.9

Find the volume of the cuboid sketched below.

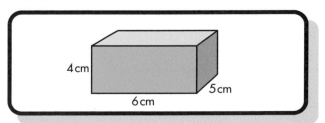

Solution

Volume = 6 × 4 × 5 cm³ = 120 cm³

Exercise 6.5

Find the volume of the following shapes.
1 A cube with each side 3 m
2 A cuboid with sides 20 cm, 1 m and 1.5 m
   Give your answer in:
   a) cubic centimetres
   b) cubic metres.
3 A cuboid with sides of length 3.2 m, 4.6 m and 5.4 m
   Give your answer to 2 d.p.

Answers

3 $79.488 = 79.49 \, m^3$ to 2 d.p.
2 a) $300\,000 \, cm^3$ b) $0.3 \, m^3$
1 $27 \, m^3$

Capacity

If the container holds a liquid, the word **capacity** is often used to describe the volume, and the measurement is given in millilitres (ml) and litres (l).

$1 \, cm^3 = 1 \, ml$ $1000 \, cm^3 = 1000 \, ml = 1$ litre

Example 6.10

Phil Yerbuckitt has bought a vase in the shape of a cuboid.

If the dimensions are $6 \, cm \times 8 \, cm \times 30 \, cm$, how much water will it hold? Give your answer to the nearest half-litre.

Solution

$6 \times 8 \times 30 = 1440 \, cm^3 = 1440 \, ml$

$1440 \div 1000 = 1.44$ litres $= 1.5$ litres to the nearest half litre

Exercise 6.6

1 A cuboid has sides of lengths 20 cm, 30 cm and 15 cm. How many litres does it hold?
2 One of the Sand Witches has a sore throat. Cherie Towtt has a half-litre bottle of Kwickure syrup. How many $5 \, ml$ doses is that?

Answers

2 Half a litre $= 500 \, ml$, $500 \div 5 = 100$ doses
1 $9000 \, cm^3 = 9$ litres

check your luggage

HAVE YOU REMEMBERED TO PACK ...

● metric and imperial measures of length, capacity and weight

● length, perimeter and circumference

● area of triangles, quadrilaterals and circles

● volume of cubes and cuboids?

Ready for more? Turn to Chapter 10 for:
• Pythagoras' theorem
• volume of a prism
• distance, speed and time
• amount, rate and time.

7

Boat trips around the bay – transformations

checklist

Into this chapter we have packed ...

Basics

Remember that horizontal lines go the same way as the horizon; vertical lines therefore go straight up and down.

Hand signals

Sam O'Forr signals to the ships at sea, from the top of Decimal Point. He uses a flag to warn them of any danger.

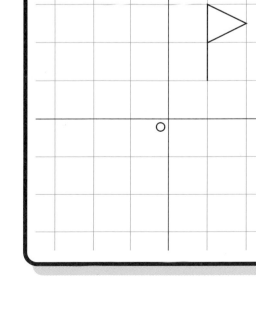

He likes there to be a sensible rule or pattern to the way he moves the flag. In the next sections are all the ways he likes to move the flag. Today he has decided to start with his flag at this position.

Reflections

Reflections are like mirror images. When you look in the mirror, everything on the right of your face looks as if it is on the left, The most common reflections he makes are in the *y*-axis, like this:

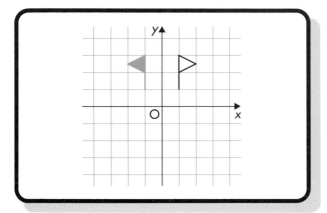

and in the *x*-axis, like this.

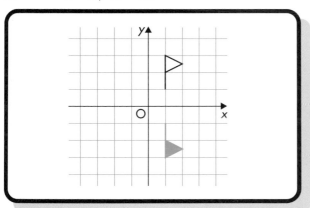

Sometimes he makes a reflection in the line $y = x$:

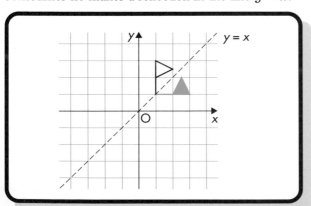

or a reflection in the line $y = {}^-x$, like this.

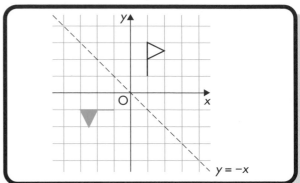

Rotations

Sam can make rotations by holding the flag in his hand and moving his arm around, in a curve centred on his shoulder. Below are the most common rotations he makes. Again, he always starts with the flag in the position on page 103.

This is a rotation of 90° clockwise about the origin, O(0, 0) – or Sam's shoulder.

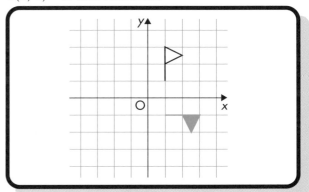

Here is a rotation of 90° anticlockwise about O:

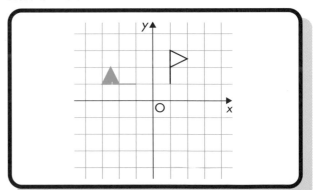

and here is a rotation of 180° about O.

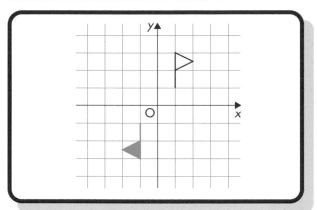

A rotation of 180° about O does need to have its direction described as clockwise or anticlockwise because whichever way it is rotated, the object still ends up at the same place.

Enlargements

Sometimes, if visibility is poor, Sam uses a special flag. It is exactly the same shape as his usual one, but larger. The increase in the length of his flag is called the **scale factor**.

If the scale factor of the enlargement is 2, then all the lengths on his flag have doubled.

This is an enlargement, scale factor 2, centred at O.

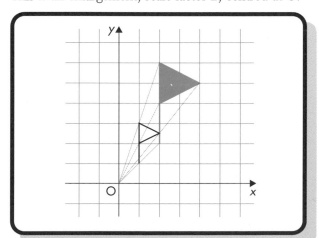

If the scale factor of the enlargement is 3, then all the lengths have tripled.

Here is an enlargement of the flag, scale factor 3, centred at O.

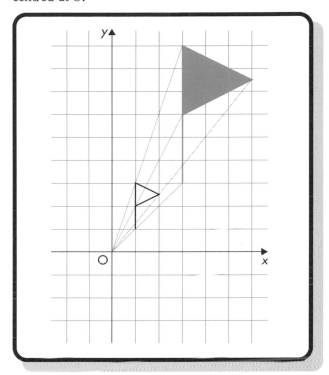

A scale factor of 1 means that the lengths have not changed at all.

Further enlargements

If the scale factor is between 0 and 1, such as $\frac{1}{2}$, the object gets smaller – but it is still called an enlargement!

Here is an enlargement of the flag, scale factor $\frac{1}{2}$, centred at O.

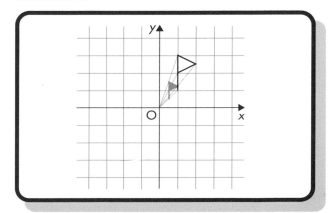

Example 7.1

Draw the position of this triangle after is has been reflected in the *y*-axis, then rotated 90° anticlockwise about the origin O(0, 0).

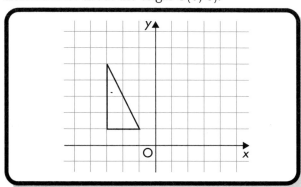

Solution

Imagine the shape flipping over the **y**-axis, then draw its final position.

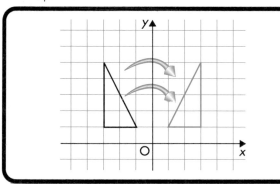

Now rotate the shape by 90° anticlockwise around the origin. To picture this, it may help to turn the whole page around through 90° in an anticlockwise direction.

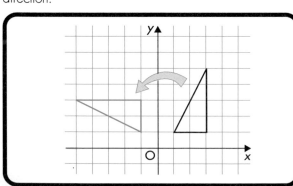

Example 7.2

Enlarge the shape P on the diagram below, by a scale factor of 2, centre O and label it as Q. Then reflect Q in the *y*-axis and label the image R.

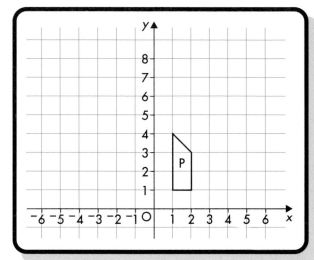

Solution

To enlarge the shape by a scale factor of 2, first draw lines from O to its vertices (corners).

Now extend these lines, from O through the vertices, doubling their lengths. Join up to end points of the lines you have just drawn, to make the image Q after the enlargement.

Then reflect the object in the **y**-axis to get the final image. Label it R.

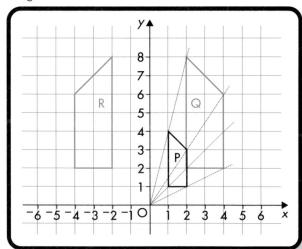

Example 7.3

Reflect this triangle in the line $y = {}^-x$.

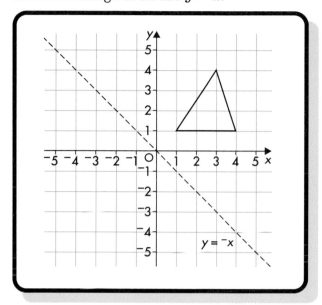

Solution

To make life a bit easier, take some tracing paper and trace over the shape and the line $y = {}^-x$. Now carefully fold the tracing paper along the line of reflection, $y = {}^-x$, so that the back of your tracing is lying in the bottom left quadrant (quarter) of the axes. You should now be able to see where the image of the shape will be after the reflection.

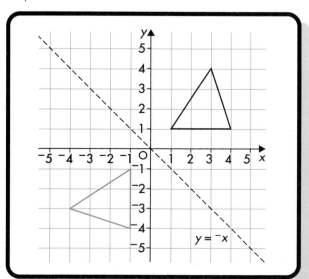

Exercise 7.1

1 Abel Macintosh has written a computer program to transform pictures of shapes. It has two instructions: the first is to reflect the shape in the x-axis, the second is to rotate it through 90° anticlockwise about the origin. Draw the images of the following objects after the above two transformations.

a)

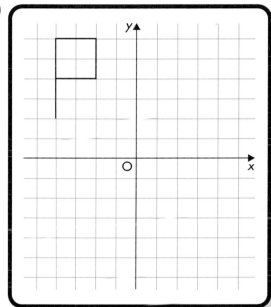

b)

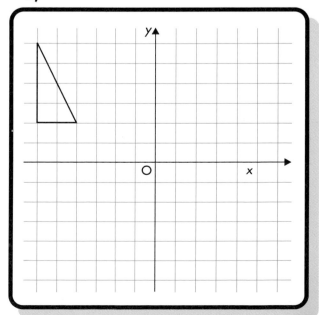

2 Enlarge the following shape by a scale factor of 2, centre O.

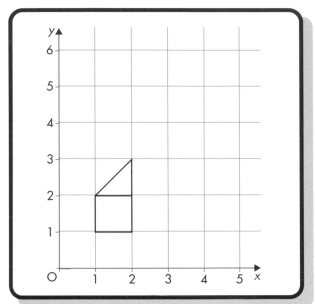

3 a) Reflect the figure P below in the line $y = x$. Label the image Q.

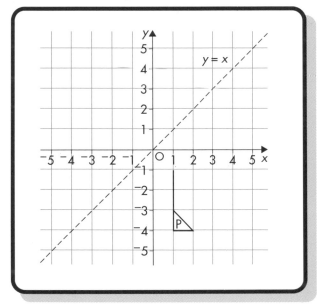

b) Rotate Q 90° clockwise about O. Label the image R.

c) What single transformation would transform P onto R?

4 The shape P is transformed onto the image P′ by an enlargement. What is the scale factor of this enlargement?

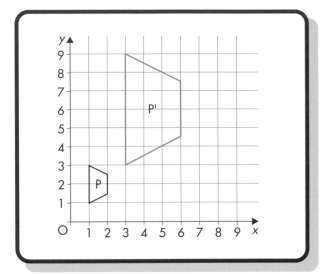

5 The shape Q is transformed onto the image Q′ by an enlargement. What is the scale factor of this enlargement?

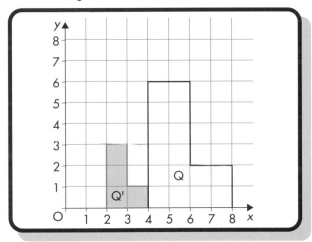

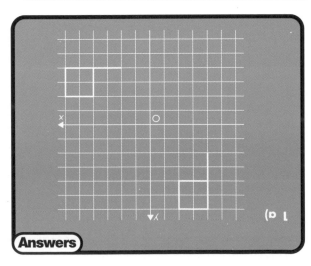

Answers

1 d)

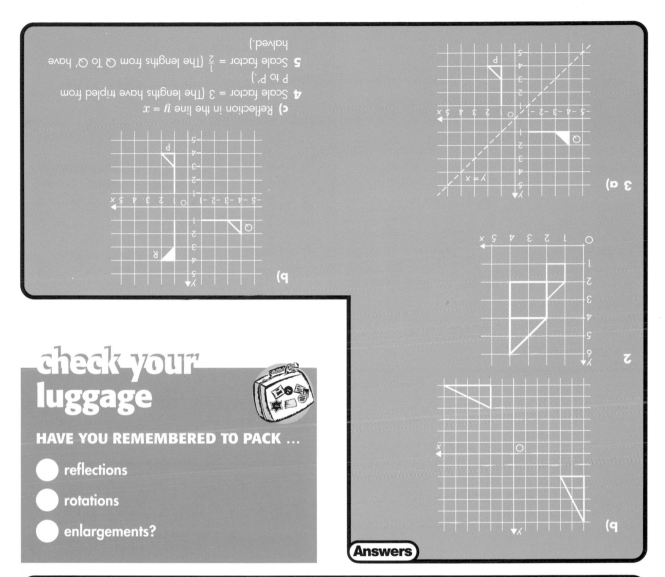

Answers

b) Reflection in the line $y = x$

4 Scale factor = 3 (The lengths have tripled from P to P'.)

5 Scale factor = $\frac{1}{2}$ (The lengths from Q to Q' have halved.)

check your luggage

HAVE YOU REMEMBERED TO PACK ...

- reflections
- rotations
- enlargements?

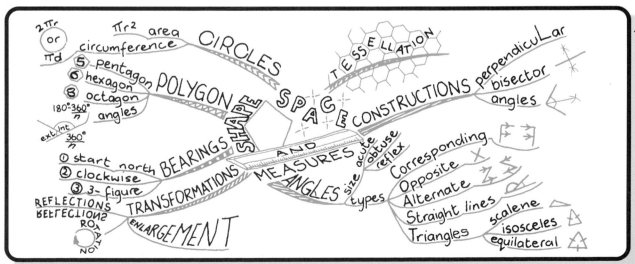

Shape and space review

1 Millie-Anne Eyre's lounge is in the shape of a rectangle 8.5 m long and 4.25 m wide. Find its area.

2 She wants to buy a new carpet for it, but the carpet is sold by the square metre. How many square metres must she buy?

3 Lil Eepond is planning to put a water feature in her garden. She has to dig a circular hole with radius 4 m.
   a) What area of the garden will this cover?
   b) She wants to lay a border of ornamental tiles round the edge. Find the circumference of the hole.

4 Two angles of a triangle are 75° and 30°. How can you tell that the triangle is isosceles?

5 Use the diagram below to find:
   a) angle ACB   b) angle ACD.
   c) How can you tell from your answers that AC is not parallel to DE?

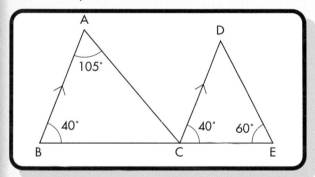

6 The perimeter of a rectangle is 80 cm and the length of one of its sides is 15 cm.
   a) Find the length of its other side.
   b) Find its area.

7 The diagram below is not accurately drawn. Use it to calculate a, b and x. Give reasons for your answers.

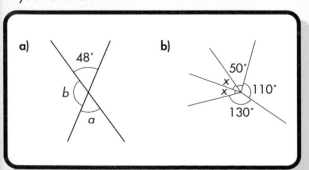

8 A nonagon has nine sides.
   a) Find the exterior angle of a regular nonagon.
   b) Find the interior angle of a regular nonagon.
   c) Do nonagons tessellate? Give a reason for your answer.

9 Find the area of a parallelogram with base 16 cm and a perpendicular height of 5 cm.

10 a) Cherie Towtt has a large box in the shape of a cuboid 60 cm long, 20 cm wide and 10 cm high. Find its volume in cubic centimetres.
   b) She is filling it with packets of biscuits of length 10 cm, width 5 cm and height 6 cm. What is the greatest number of packets that she can fit into the box and still be able to shut the lid?

Answers

1 36.125 m²
2 37 m²
3 a) 50.3 m² to 1 d.p.
  b) 25.13 m
4 75 + 30 = 105
  The third angle = 180° − 105° = 75°
  You have two identical angles.
5 a) 35°   b) 105°
  c) If AC and DE were parallel, angle DEC would equal angle ACB.
6 a) 25 cm (15 × 2 = 30.
     80 − 30 = 50. 50 ÷ 2 = 25)
  b) 15 × 25 = 375 cm²
7 $a = 48°$, $b = 132°$, $x = 35°$
8 a) 360 ÷ 9 = 40°
  b) 180 − 40 = 140°
  c) No. 360 is not a multiple of 140.
     (2 × 140 = 280. This is too small.
     3 × 140 = 420. This is too big.)
9 80 cm²
10 a) 12 000 cm³   b) 40

110

The vi−w from th− pier − statistics

checklist

Into this chapter we have packed ...

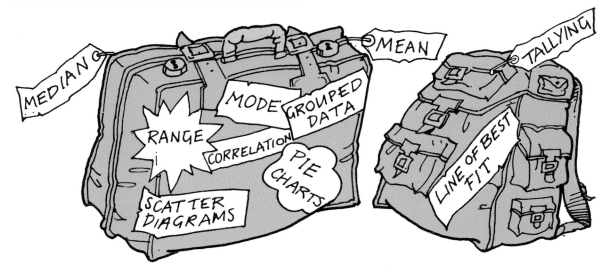

MEDIAN · MEAN · MODE · GROUPED DATA · RANGE · CORRELATION · PIE CHARTS · SCATTER DIAGRAMS · TALLYING · LINE OF BEST FIT

Basics

Statistics is all about collecting information and studying it. Sometimes, statisticians can make predictions about what is likely to happen, based on what they work out from the information they have already.

New-Mer-a-Sea's main amusement arcade, Luzytt Hall, is owned by four partners: Ava Ridge, Sam Pull, Kez Chunnair and Sir Vaye. They are constantly keeping records about the number of people who visit the arcade, how much money is taken and how many prizes are won. In this chapter, we are going to look over the partners' shoulders as they try to keep track of their punters and their profits.

Averages

Five people go into an amusement arcade to play a stock car video game called 'Bumped off'. The object of the game is to avoid obstacles to get the highest score. The five friends' scores are 10, 34, 23, 54 and 54.

Sam Pull's job is to study the day's average scores. He uses three kinds of average:

- the **mean**
- the **median**
- the **mode**.

Let's see what he does with the five scores above.

The mean

To find the mean of the data, Sam must add up all the scores (or values) and then divide the result by the total number of values. For the five scores above:

$$\text{average} = \frac{10 + 34 + 23 + 54 + 54}{5} = \frac{175}{5} = 35$$

The median

The median of a set of data is the middle value when the data are arranged in order of size.
The scores are 10, 34, 23, 54 and 54. Arranging then according to size:

10, 23, 34, 54, 54

To find the median value, take the number of values, add one and divide the result by 2. In this example, the median is the $\frac{1}{2}(5 + 1)$ or 3rd value.

So the median, the 3rd value, is 34.

The median is the middle value.

M$^{\text{E}}_{\text{I}}$D$^{\text{IAN}}_{\text{DLE}}$

The mode

The mode is the most common value, in this case, 54.

MO$^{\text{DE}}_{\text{ST COMMON}}$

The three averages are:
- *the **mean**: add all the values together and divide by the number of values*
- *the **median**: the middle value when the values are arranged from smallest to largest*
- *the **mode**: the most common.*

MO$^{\text{DE}}_{\text{ST}}$

Don't be modest about the mode.

Range

The **range** is a measure of how far the data are spread.

Range = biggest value − smallest value

The range is a measure of the spread of the data. It is not a measure of the average.

Example 8.1

Kez Chunnair interviewed eleven people as they were leaving the arcade. He asked, 'How much have you just spent at the arcade?' He recorded the following amounts, in pounds.

4, 4, 7, 8, 3, 1, 4, 9, 23, 5, 9

Find the mean, median, mode and range of the data.

Solution

To find the mean, add up all the amounts, then divide by the number of amounts.

Mean

$$= \frac{4 + 4 + 7 + 8 + 3 + 1 + 4 + 9 + 23 + 5 + 9}{11}$$

$$= \frac{77}{11}$$

$$= 7$$

To find the median, first arrange the values in order:

1, 3, 4, 4, 4, 5, 7, 8, 9, 9, 23

then take the middle, or $\frac{1}{2}(n + 1)$th value.

This is the $\frac{1}{2}(n + 1)$th = 6th value

When the amounts are all arranged in order, the sixth value is 5.

The median is 5.

The mode is the value which occurs most often.

Looking again at the amounts, arranged in order, it is easy to see which value occurs the most.

1, 3, 4, 4, 4, 5, 7, 8, 9, 9, 23

The mode is 4.

The range is a measure of how spaced out the data are.

Range = biggest value − smallest value
    = 23 − 1
    = 22

Example 8.2

The data collected in a survey were 4, 5, 11, 16.

a) Find the median of the data.
b) Find the mean of the data.
c) If another value is added to the data and the mean remains unchanged, what is this value?

Solution

a) The median value is the $\frac{1}{2}(4 + 1)$th = 2.5th

Therefore the median is the number that lies halfway between the 2nd and 3rd values.

The number halfway between 5 and 11 (or the mean of 5 and 11) is 8.

b) Mean = $\dfrac{4 + 5 + 11 + 16}{4}$

$= \dfrac{36}{4}$

$= 9$

c) For the mean to remain unchanged, the new value must be the same as the mean. So the new value is 9.

Example 8.3

Kez and Sam have one final game on 'Shoot and Scoot'. Their scores have a mean of 7 and a range of 6. Kez wins the match. What do Kez and Sam score?

Solution

If the mean of their scores is 7, the two scores must be centred around the number 7. That is, the scores could be 7 and 7, or 6 and 8, or 5 and 9, etc. To have a range of 6, the scores must be 4 and 10.

So Kez scored 10 and Sam scored 4.

Example 8.4

a) Find the mean of the data 5, 7, 11, 17.

b) What number should be added to the data to give a mean of 11?

Solution

a) Mean = $\dfrac{5 + 7 + 11 + 17}{4} = \dfrac{40}{4} = 10$

b) If five numbers have a mean of 11, then they must add up to $11 \times 5 = 55$.
If the first four numbers have a total of 40, then the extra number must be 15.

The total of a sample of data using the mean

Frequency is how many times something happens or occurs.

The total of all the values in a set of data = total frequency × mean. This is the same as the number of items of data × the mean. So for example, if there are five items of data, with a mean of 6, then the total of the values of the data will be $5 \times 6 = 30$.

If there are 7 items of data with a mean of 10, then the total of the values of the data will be $7 \times 10 = 70$.

Example 8.5

a) Find the mean of the following numbers.

3, 6, 8, 9, 14

b) Another number is added to the set of data, and the mean rises by 2. What is this number?

Solution

a) Mean = $\dfrac{3 + 6 + 8 + 9 + 14}{5} = \dfrac{40}{5} = 8$

b) If the mean rises by 2, then the new mean will be 10.

The sum of all the data will be $6 \times 10 = 60$.

The sum of all the data is currently 40, so the number that must be added is

$60 - 40 = 20$

Example 8.6

Five numbers have a mean of 7. Another number is added to lower the mean to 6.

What is this number?

Solution

The sum of five values with a mean of 7 is
$5 \times 7 = 35$.

The sum of six values with a mean of 6 is
$6 \times 6 = 36$.

The total has risen by 1, so 1 must be the new number added to the data.

Exercise 8.1

1 For the data 19, 3, 7, 12, 17, find:
 a) the mean
 b) the median
 c) the range.
2 Find the mean, median and mode of this sample.
 16, 18, 16, 11, 33, 14, 25
3 Find the mean, median, mode and range of these data.
 3, 15, 1, 7, 11, 11
4 a) Find the mean of these data.
 25, 33, 40, 52, 60
 b) If a sixth number is added to the data, but the mean remains unchanged, what is this number?
5 a) What is the mean of these data?
 14, 17, 18, 21, 25
 b) A number is added to the data, and its mean rises by 2.
 What is this number?

Answers

1 a) 11.6
 b) 12 (Remember to arrange the values before choosing the middle value.)
 c) 16
2 Mean = 19, median = 16, mode = 16
3 Mean = 8, median = 3.5th value = 9, mode = 11, range = 14
4 a) 42   **b)** 42
5 a) 19
 b) The mean of the six numbers must be $19 + 2 = 21$
 The total of six numbers with a mean of 21 is $21 \times 6 = 126$.
 The numbers currently total 95, so the new number must be $126 - 95 = 31$.

A Quick Dip!

1 A rectangle has sides of length x and y. What is its perimeter?
2 Expand $2(x + y)$.
3 A rectangle has a height of 9 cm and an area of 72 cm². What is its width?
4 Two angles of a triangle are 70° and 30°. What is the third angle?
5 Which of the following always has four equal sides?
 rhombus, trapezium, parallelogram, kite

Answers

1 $2x + 2y$ or $2(x + y)$
2 $2x + 2y$
3 $72 \div 9 = 8$ cm
4 80° (The angles of a triangle add up to 180°.)
5 rhombus

TAKE A BREAK

Grouped data

Mean, median, mode and range of grouped data

Sometimes data are not collected in separate items, but they are presented in groups or classes. Instead of being presented as individual numbers, the data are presented in some form of graph or table. This method of presenting statistical information is more commonly used when there is a large quantity of data.

Let's see how Ava Ridge deals with grouped data.

Ava has had a busy day expelling disruptive children from the arcade. She recorded the ages of the children she expelled. She threw out:

- 12 ten-year-olds

- 15 eleven-year-olds

- 18 twelve-year-olds

- 15 thirteen-year-olds but

- 0 fourteen-year-olds.

She presented her data in a table.

Age	10	11	12	13	14
Frequency	12	15	18	15	0

Then she made it into a bar chart.

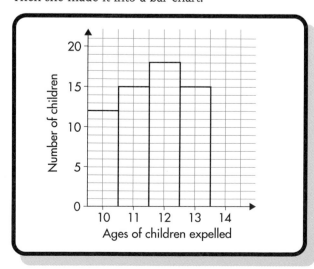

Mean

To find the mean, a new row needs to be set up in the table. This should show $f \times x$, or the frequency times the ages.

Age	10	11	12	13	14
Frequency	12	15	18	15	0
$f \times x$	120	165	216	195	0

To calculate the mean, add all the $f \times x$ values together, and divide this by the total of the frequencies.

$$\text{Mean} = \frac{\text{sum of } f \times x}{\text{sum of } f}$$

$$= \frac{120 + 165 + 216 + 195 + 0}{12 + 15 + 18 + 15 + 0} = \frac{696}{60} = 11.6$$

The mean age of the offenders is 11.6 years.

Remember, 11.6 years is $11\frac{6}{10}$ years, not 11 years 6 months; $11\frac{6}{10}$ years is nearer 11 years 7 months.

Remember, Sam often asks Ava to fax over the frequencies $\left(\frac{f \times x}{f}\right)$.

Median

To find the median, we must first work out which value would be the middle value.

As there are 60 values in the data, the middle would be the $\frac{1}{2}(60 + 1)$th value, or the 30.5th value, or the 30.5th youngest offender. Starting from the bottom group and working up, the youngest 12 are aged ten, the 13th to 27th youngest are aged eleven, and the 28th to 45th youngest are aged twelve. Therefore the 30.5th youngest is aged twelve.

The median age of the offenders is 12.

Mode

The mode is the age that occurs the most often, or the x-value with the highest frequency. This is easy to spot from the table.

The mode is 12.

Impress your teacher!

In grouped data, the mode, or the modal value, occurs in one of the groups of data. This is called the **modal class**. The data are put into groups according to their value. So the value of the data in one group, or class, is called the **class value**.

It is important to look at the frequencies first, to find the modal class, then to write down the class value (in this case 12), not the frequency (which is 18 here) as the answer.

Range

The range of grouped data is still the difference between the highest and the lowest values of data in the set.

Range = 13 − 10 = 3

Although 14 is written in the table, it should not be included as part of the range because no fourteen-year-olds were expelled.

Example 8.7

Sam Pull worked for 25 days during July. He recorded the hours he worked on each day on this bar chart.

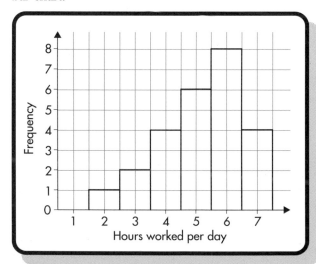

Sir Vaye asked him to complete the following table.

Hours worked	1	2	3	4	5	6	7
Frequency							

Then he was asked to work out the mean, median, mode and range of his hours worked during these 25 days in July.

Solution

Hours worked	1	2	3	4	5	6	7
Frequency	0	1	2	4	6	8	4

Mean
Sam added the row $f \times x$ to his graph.

$f \times x$	0	2	6	16	30	48	28

Using 'fax over frequencies' gives:

$$\text{mean} = \frac{0 + 2 + 6 + 16 + 30 + 48 + 28}{0 + 1 + 2 + 4 + 6 + 8 + 4}$$

$$= \frac{130}{25} = 5.2$$

Median
The middle value is the $\frac{1}{2}(25 + 1)$th value, which is the 13th value. The first value lies in the 2-hour class, the second and third lie in the 3-hour class, the fourth to seventh lie in the 4-hour class, the eighth to thirteenth lie in the 5-hour class. Therefore the median is 5 hours.

Mode
The highest frequency is in the 6-hour class.

The mode is 6.

Range
The range is $7 - 2 = 5$.

Do not include 1 hour in the range as Sam does not work a 1-hour shift during July (it has a frequency of 0).

Exercise 8.2

2, 3, 5, 5, 5, 6, 4, 3, 3, 2, 2, 1, 1, 2, 1, 3, 8, 8, 8, 6, 5, 4, 3, 3, 3

Complete this table for the data listed above.

Value	1	2	3	4	5	6	7	8
Frequency								

Find the mean, median, mode and range of the data.

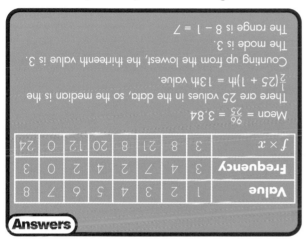

(Answers — shown inverted)

Value	1	2	3	4	5	6	7	8
Frequency	3	4	7	2	4	2	0	3
$f \times x$	3	8	21	8	20	12	0	24

Mean $= \frac{96}{25} = 3.84$

There are 25 values in the data, so the median is the $\frac{1}{2}(25 + 1)$th $= 13$th value.

Counting up from the lowest, the thirteenth value is 3.

The mode is 3.

The range is $8 - 1 = 7$.

Tallying

In the arcade there is always lots of information to record, and it often needs to be written down quickly. They have found that **tallying** is a very useful way of collecting and recording data. A tally mark is made each time an entry has to be recorded. When four marks have been written in any one class, the fifth mark is made as a line through the first four. The process is then repeated. The numbers 1 to 10 would be recorded as

\, \\, \\\, \\\\, ⧸⧸⧸⧸, ⧸⧸⧸⧸ \, ⧸⧸⧸⧸ \\, ⧸⧸⧸⧸ \\\, ⧸⧸⧸⧸ \\\\, ⧸⧸⧸⧸ ⧸⧸⧸⧸

Example 8.8

In the games machine called 'Cranial Overload', a metal claw is lowered into a pile of prizes. It grabs one and deposits it into a chute. Kez always has the task of recording the different prizes that are drawn. Last Thursday, the following prizes were drawn.

teddy, teddy, watch, parrot, teddy, watch, parrot, parrot, parrot, game, game, parrot, teddy, watch, watch, teddy, watch, game, game, watch, teddy, teddy, parrot, money, watch, money, watch, game, game, game, teddy, teddy, watch, teddy, teddy, money

Complete the tally chart below, to show the different numbers of prizes.

	Tally	Frequency
Teddy		
Watch		
Parrot		
Game		
Money		

Solution

	Tally	Frequency
Teddy	⧸⧸⧸⧸ ⧸⧸⧸⧸ \	11
Watch	⧸⧸⧸⧸ \\\\	9
Parrot	⧸⧸⧸⧸ \	6
Game	⧸⧸⧸⧸ \\	7
Money	\\\	3

A Quick Dip!

1 Calculate $2340 \div 100$
2 What size is each angle of an equilateral triangle?
3 Calculate 8×7
4 How many centimetres are there in a kilometre?
5 What is the mean of 7 and 11?

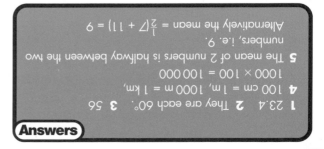

(Answers — shown inverted)

1 23.4 **2** They are each 60°. **3** 56
4 100 cm = 1 m, 1000 m = 1 km,
$1000 \times 100 = 100\,000$
5 The mean of 2 numbers is halfway between the two numbers, i.e. 9.
Alternatively the mean $= \frac{1}{2}(11 + 7) = 9$

Methods of representing data

Pie charts

The Gaudyville Theatre management is trying to find out about audience numbers and preferences. It intends to display some of its findings on pie charts.

As its name suggests, a pie chart looks a bit like a pie, cut into slices. Each slice represents one of the groups of data.

The tricky bit about using pie charts is working out the size of the slices. The next example shows how the management at the Gaudyville Theatre tackled their last bit of audience research.

Example 8.9

A recent audience was asked about the show. Here is one of the questions they were asked, and the results.

How good did you think tonight's show was?

Very good	Quite good	Not very good	Awful
30	56	75	139

Display the results on a pie chart.

Solution

Number of people = 30 + 56 + 75 + 139 = 300.

Now use DIM to find out the sizes of the slices. You need to work out the angles at the centre. (Look back to page 41 if you need to remind yourself about DIM.)

People	Degrees (°)	
300	360	D
1	$\frac{360}{300} = 1.2$	I
30	$30 \times 1.2 = 36$	M

Now that you know that 1.2° (degrees) represent 1 person, you can easily work out the size of the other angles, and draw them to the nearest degree.

$1.2 \times 56 = 67.2° = 67°$

$1.2 \times 75 = 90°$

$1.2 \times 139 = 166.8 = 167°$

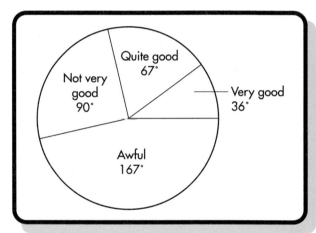

You may find that your total will not always equal exactly 360° because of rounding to the nearest degree.

Example 8.10

From another pie chart, the Council noticed that the number of people visiting Ma Jinn's guest house during July the previous year was represented by 30°. If there had been 16 visitors, how many people altogether did the pie chart represent?

Solution

	People	Degrees
D	16	30
I	$\frac{16}{30}$	1
M	$\frac{16}{30} \times 360 = 192$	360

The pie chart represents 192 people.

Example 8.11

The Gaudyville Town Council was planning the colour scheme for the summer bedding plants in the park. They decided that 50% of the flowers this year should be red, 30% white, 15% blue and the rest yellow.

a) Draw a pie chart to show this.

b) How many degrees represent the yellow flowers?

c) What percentage of the flowers were to be yellow?

Solution

a) Start by working out how many degrees you need to allow for each section.
50% of 360° = 180°
30% of 360° = 108°
15% of 360° = 54°
180° + 108° + 54° = 342°

b) 360° − 342° = 18°

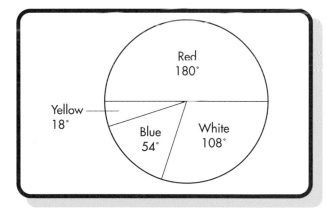

c) The easiest way is to add the percentages.
50% + 30% + 15% = 95% so 100% − 95% = 5%

Example 8.12

Represent the results of Kez's 'Cranial Overload' tally chart on a pie chart.

Solution

Firstly he added the frequencies to find the size of his sample. This gave a total of 36.

So the entire circle – or 360° – represents 36 prizes. He knows the number of prizes in each column, so he needs to work out the number of degrees per prize.

Number of degrees per prize is 360° ÷ 36 = 10°

	Frequency	Degrees
Teddy	11	11 × 10° = 110°
Watch	9	9 × 10° = 90°
Parrot	6	6 × 10° = 60°
Game	7	7 × 10° = 70°
Money	3	3 × 10° = 30°

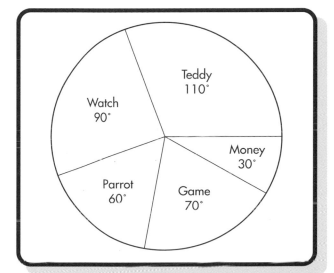

Exercise 8.3

Dave Isitt worked out how he had spent his money when he called in briefly at New-Mer-a-Sea recently. Out of the £60.00 which he spent, £10.00 went on lunch at Victoria Spunj's cafe, £7.50 on a ticket for a Cherie Towtt concert, £5.00 on a present for his sister Maeve and the rest on clothes which he bought in a sale.

1 What angles on a pie chart would represent his purchases?

2 How much did he spend on clothes?

Answers

1 lunch = 60°, concert ticket = 45°, present = 30°, clothes = 225°

2 360° = £60.00, 225° = $\frac{60}{360} \times 225$ = £37.50

Scatter diagrams

Scatter graphs are used to see whether there is a relationship between two sets of data, such as colour of eyes and colour of hair.

Impress your teacher!

The statistical term for relationship between two sets of data is **correlation between paired data**.

The pairs of values in the data are plotted on a graph. The closer the points are to forming a line, the stronger the correlation.

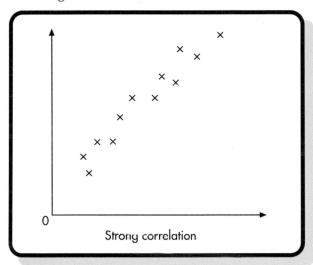

The more scattered they are, the weaker the correlation.

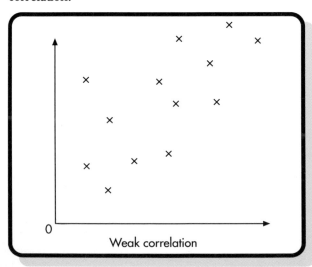

If the points are going up from left to right, they have **positive correlation**.

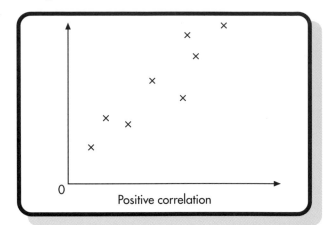

If they are going downward from left to right, they have **negative correlation**.

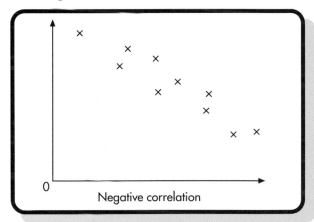

If they do not appear to be grouped around any sort of line, they have **no correlation**.

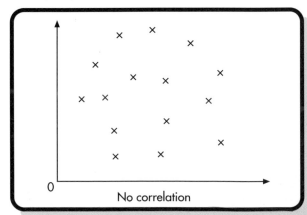

Line of best fit

The line of best fit is a line drawn on a scatter diagram which is closest to the data. When drawing this, a useful rule of thumb is to have the same number of points above the line as are below the line.

Ready for more? Turn to page 151 for:
*   frequency polygons
*   questionnaires.

Exercise 8.4

Ava Ridge was given the task of recording the scores of 12 people who played the pinball game 'Flipper Rover', and one of the motor racing games 'Speed Up'.

Flipper Rover	160	140	110	220	90	200	170	220	170	130	140	210
Speed up	4	6	4	10	3	8	6	8	5	5	4	9

She used the following graph to show the results.

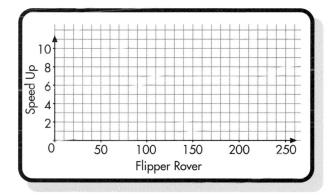

Plot the points on the graph, then draw the line of best fit on it.

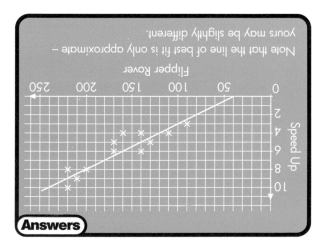

Note that the line of best fit is only approximate – yours may be slightly different.

Answers

check your luggage

HAVE YOU REMEMBERED TO PACK ...

*   mean
*   median
*   mode
*   range
*   grouped data
*   pie charts
*   scatter diagrams
*   correlation

and from Level 7:

*   tallying
*   line of best fit?

Having a flutter – probability

checklist

Into this chapter we have packed ...

THE PROBABILITY SCALE

CALCULATING PROBABILITIES

PROBABILITY OF AN EVENT NOT HAPPENING

PRESENTING OUTCOMES

Basics

At the entrance to the arcade, there is a machine called 'Adore'.

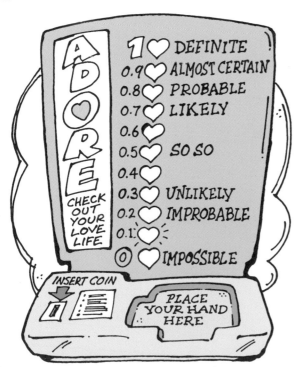

When someone inserts £1 and puts their palm on the front of the machine, it tests their love life. Then it gives an estimate of the likelihood of that person finding love in the next year.

'Adore' has a scale of numbers ranging from 0 to 1.

0 means NO Way.

1 means certa1n or def1n1te.

If you look closely, you can see that there are words written next to the scale. The words 'unlikely' and 'improbable' are next to fairly low numbers (0.3 or 0.2), while the words 'probable' and 'likely' are next to high numbers (0.8 or 0.7).

Probability and certainties

On a scale from 0 to 1 ...

The closer the probability is to 1, the more likely the event is to happen.

The closer the probability is to 0, the less likely it is to happen.

If an event has a probability of 1, it will definitely happen.

If it has a probability of 0, it cannot happen.

Example 9.1

Draw lines to match the word with the numerical probability.

Impossible	1
Certain to happen	0.92
Probably will not occur	0
Almost certain to happen	0.25

Solution

Impossible	1
Certain to happen	0.92
Probably will not occur	0
Almost certain to happen	0.25

Looking back at the probabilities in the last example, if they were put on a number line, the words and the numbers would look like this.

Impossible	Probably will not occur	Almost certain to happen	Certain to happen	
0	0.25		0.92	1

Probability of an event not happening – an impossibility

Abel's brother Ivor Macintosh wants to go for a walk along the promenade, but he thinks it might rain.

Ivor knows that either it will rain, or it won't. His problem is that there are two possible outcomes – 'rain' or 'no rain'. One of them is bound to happen, but which one?

The probability of there being either 'rain' or 'no rain' is 1 (a certainty).

The probability of 'rain' + the probability of 'no rain' = 1.

The probability of an event not happening = 1 – the probability of the event happening.

Example 9.2

If there is a 0.2 chance of it raining tomorrow, then what is the probability that it will not rain tomorrow?

Solution

$1 - 0.2 = 0.8$

Exercise 9.1

1 Match the following words to the probabilities.
  i) probable
  ii) impossible
  iii) certain
  iv) unlikely
  a) 1
  b) 0.85
  c) 0
  d) 0.31
2 If the probability of winning a game is 0.45, what is the probability of not winning the game?
3 If the likelihood of a football match not being rained off tomorrow is 0.77, what is the probability of it being rained off?

Answers

1 i) and b), ii) and c), iii) and a), iv) and d)
2 $1 - 0.45 = 0.55$
3 $1 - 0.77 = 0.23$

1 What is the range of the data below?
6, 7, 19, 11, 10
2 Simplify $x + 2y - 4x$
3 What is 50% of 16?
4 Write 0.75 as a fraction in its lowest terms.
5 What is the lowest common multiple of 6 and 8?

Answers

5 24
4 $\frac{3}{4}$
3 50% of 16 is the same as a half of 16, which is 8.
2 $-3x + 2y$ or $2y - 3x$
1 $19 - 6 = 13$

TAKE A BREAK

Working out probabilities

The probability of a particular outcome of an event occurring

$$= \frac{\text{number of ways the outcome can occur}}{\text{total number of possible outcomes}}$$

Presenting outcomes

Example 9.3

A coin is tossed, and a die is thrown. The results of each are noted.

a) Write down all the different possible results.

b) What is the probability of the result being a head on the coin with an even number on the die?

Solution

a) Using H for head and T for tail:

H, 1	H, 2	H, 3	H, 4	H, 5	H, 6
T, 1	T, 2	T, 3	T, 4	T, 5	T, 6

b) There are three different possible ways of getting a head and an even number. The total number of possible outcomes is 12.

The probability of getting a head on the coin with an even number on the die is $\frac{3}{12} = \frac{1}{4}$.

Example 9.4

At the 'Golden Fleecing' Casino at New-Mer-a-Sea, a game is played using two sets of identical cards, like those below. A card is drawn from each pack. The result of the game is found by adding the numbers on the cards together.

The possible results are shown on this table of outcomes.

		Card 1			
		3	4	5	6
	3	6	7	8	9
Card 2	4	7	8	9	10
	5	8	9	10	11
	6	9	10	11	12

Each entry is found by adding the numbers at the end of the row and column: for example, the numbers shown as 7 in the table were found by adding 4 and 3.

a) How many different outcomes are there?

b) What is the probability of an outcome of 11?

c) What is the probability of the result being less than 20?

d) What is the probability of the result being less than 8?

Solution

a) 16

b) $\frac{2}{16} = \frac{1}{8}$

c) All results are less than 20, so the answer is 1.

d) $\frac{3}{16}$

Impress your teacher!

The method of showing all the possible outcomes of two events, as in the example above, is called a **possibility space diagram**.

Example 9.5

A similar game was played using the same two packs, the difference being that the score was found by multiplying the numbers on the cards.

a) Complete the table below. Some of the entries have already been made.

		Card 1			
		3	4	5	6
Card 2	3	9			
	4				24
	5		20		
	6			30	

b) What is the probability that the player scores 24 or more?

c) What is the probability of scoring less than 24?

Solution

a)

		Card 1			
		3	4	5	6
Card 2	3	9	12	15	18
	4	12	16	20	24
	5	15	20	25	30
	6	18	24	30	36

b) As there are six different ways of scoring 24 or more, out of a total number of 16 outcomes, the probability is $\frac{6}{16} = \frac{3}{8}$.

c) This can be worked out in two ways.
Either: counting the number of entries in the table gives $\frac{10}{16} = \frac{5}{8}$

Or: 1 − probability of scoring 24 or more
$= 1 - \frac{3}{8} = \frac{5}{8}$

Exercise 9.2

1 Two fair dice are thrown. The numbers shown on the dice are added, and the results are entered into a table. The table has been started.

		Die 1					
		1	2	3	4	5	6
Die 2	1	2			5		
	2		4				
	3						
	4			7			
	5						
	6					11	

a) Complete the table of outcomes.

b) How many different possible outcomes are there?

c) What is the probability that both dice show the same number?

d) What is the probability that the dice total at least 9?

e) What is the probability that the total is an even number?

f) What is the probability that the outcome is 1?

2 Two fair dice are thrown, and the numbers on the dice are multiplied together.

a) Complete this table of results.

		Die 1					
		1	2	3	4	5	6
Die 2	1					5	
	2						
	3						
	4				12		
	5	5					
	6						24

b) What is the probability that the numbers on the two dice multiply to 12?

125

c) What is the probability that the numbers on the two dice multiply to give an odd number?
d) What is the probability that the outcome is an even number?

3 Three red marbles, four blue marbles and nine green marbles are placed in a bag. A marble is drawn from the bag. What is the probability that it is:
a) blue **b)** green **c)** yellow?

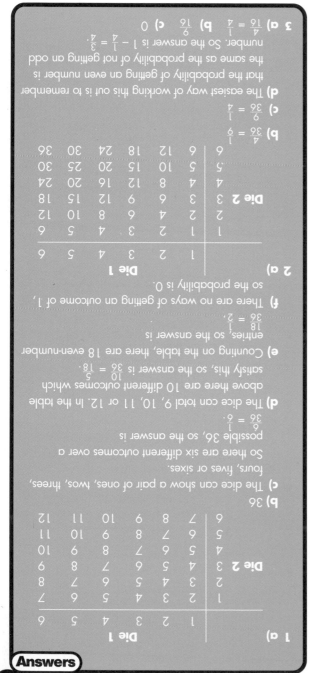

Answers

1 a)

	Die 1					
	1	2	3	4	5	6
Die 2 1	2	3	4	5	6	7
2	3	4	5	6	7	8
3	4	5	6	7	8	9
4	5	6	7	8	9	10
5	6	7	8	9	10	11
6	7	8	9	10	11	12

b) 36
c) The dice can show a pair of ones, twos, threes, fours, fives or sixes. So there are six different outcomes over a possible 36, so the answer is $\frac{6}{36} = \frac{1}{6}$.
d) The dice can total 9, 10, 11 or 12. In the table above there are 10 different outcomes which satisfy this, so the answer is $\frac{10}{36} = \frac{5}{18}$.
e) Counting on the table, there are 18 even-number entries, so the answer is $\frac{18}{36} = \frac{1}{2}$.
f) There are no ways of getting an outcome of 1, so the probability is 0.

2 a)

	Die 1					
	1	2	3	4	5	6
Die 2 1	1	2	3	4	5	6
2	2	4	6	8	10	12
3	3	6	9	12	15	18
4	4	8	12	16	20	24
5	5	10	15	20	25	30
6	6	12	18	24	30	36

b) $\frac{4}{36} = \frac{1}{9}$
c) $\frac{9}{36} = \frac{1}{4}$
d) The easiest way of working this out is to remember that the probability of getting an even number is the same as the probability of not getting an odd number. So the answer is $1 - \frac{1}{4} = \frac{3}{4}$.

3 a) $\frac{4}{16} = \frac{1}{4}$ **b)** $\frac{9}{16}$ **c)** 0

A Quick Dip!

1 What is $\frac{3}{4}$ of £40?
2 Which of the following shapes does not have two pairs of equal opposite angles?
rhombus, parallelogram, kite, trapezium
3 Simplify $x(x + 2)$
4 Write 17.5% as a decimal.
5 Find y when $y = x^2$ and $x = 5$.

Answers

1 A quarter of £40 is £10, so three-quarters of £40 is £30.
2 trapezium, kite
3 $x^2 + 2x$
4 0.175
5 $y = 5^2 = 25$

TAKE A BREAK

Calculating probabilities with replacement

Example 9.6

One very wet afternoon, Delia Cardswright tried to invent a new card game. She shuffled half a full pack then cut it and picked a card at random. She tried to guess the suit, then checked if she was right before she put the card back in the pack. She recorded the suits of the cards she picked in a tally chart, like this.

Suit	Tally
♣	\\
♠	卌
♡	\
♢	

a) Delia says that from her results she concludes that there are no diamonds in her pack. Why is she wrong?

b) What is the smallest possible number of spades in her pack?

Solution

a) There may be a diamond in the pack, but she may have missed it each time she picked a card.

b) 1 (She may have picked the same spade five times.)

Exercise 9.3

Al Finch works as a waiter at Victoria Spunj's café. He puts all his tips – and sometimes other people's – in his pocket. Last week he had ten coins in his pocket. He took one out, wrote down its value and put it back. He did this ten times, and found he had pulled out 50p five times, 20p twice and 10p three times.

1 What is the minimum number of 50p coins he could have had in his pocket? Give a reason for your answer.

2 Can Al be sure that there were no £1 coins in his pocket? Explain your answer.

3 Can Al be sure that the probability of picking a 10p coin is $\frac{3}{10}$?

check your luggage

HAVE YOU REMEMBERED TO PACK ...

- the probability scale
- calculating probabilities
- the probability of an event not happening
- presenting outcomes
- probabilities without replacement?

Ready for more? Turn to page 154 for:
- estimating probabilities using relative frequency.

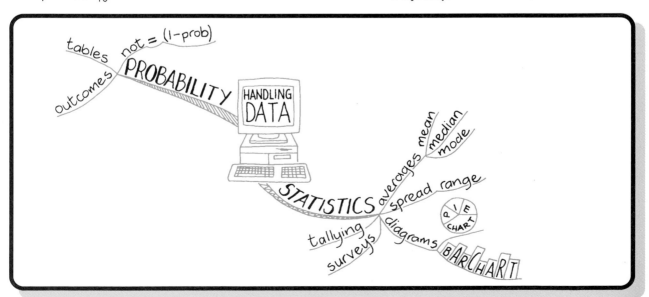

Handling data review

1 Find the mean, median, mode and range of the following set of numbers.

14, 17, 20, 16, 25, 35, 20

2 What is the number written on the fifth card if the numbers on these five cards have a mean of 7?

| 4 | 5 | 9 | 6 | ☀ |

3 What two numbers have a mean of 12 and a range of 6?

4 a) Draw a line of best fit on the scatter graph below.

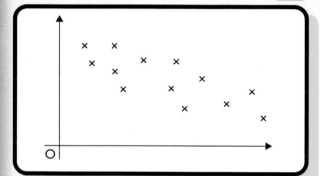

b) How would you describe the correlation?

5 The pie chart below represents 72 homes in a road. Write down the number of homes which are flats, bungalows, terraced, semi-detached and detached houses.

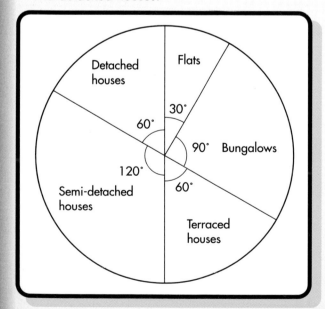

6 Cards were picked at random and the suits were noted.

♣ ◇ ◇ ♠ ♣ ♣ ◇ ♡ ♣ ♡ ♡ ♡ ♡ ♠ ♣ ♡ ♠ ♠ ♣ ◇
♠ ♣ ♡ ♠ ♡ ♠ ♣ ♣ ♡ ♠ ♣ ♣ ◇ ♡ ♠

a) Complete the tally chart below.

Suit	Tally	Frequency
Clubs (♣)		
Diamonds (◇)		
Hearts (♡)		
Spades (♠)		

b) Show the results on the bar chart below.

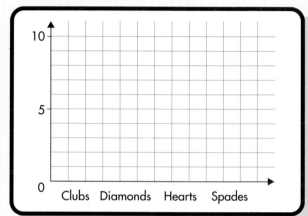

7 Maeve and Dave Isitt are each holding three cards, numbered 6, 7 and 8.

a) They each pick one card at random from their own hands. The numbers on the cards are then added together. The results recorded on a table, like the one started below.

i) Complete the table.

		Maeve's card		
		6	7	8
	6	12	13	....
Dave's card	7	....	....	....
	8	....	....	16

ii) What is the probability that their answer is 14?

iii) Complete the following sentence. The probability that the answer will be more than _____ is $\frac{8}{9}$.

b) They then play a similar game with the same cards, but they multiply the numbers on the cards they have picked.

i) Complete the table.

		Maeve's card		
		6	7	8
Dave's card	6	36	42	....
	7	....	....	....
	8	....	....	64

ii) What is the probability that their answer will be greater than 60?

8 A hand contains the following cards.

8♣ 4♢ 3♡ 2♣ 5♣ 8♡ 9♣ 7♣ 3♣

A card is chosen at random.

Fill in the missing spaces with one of the following words or phrases.

certain   impossible   not likely   likely

a) It is _____ that the card will be a club (♣).

b) It is _____ that the number on the card will be 2.

c) It is _____ that the card will be a spade (♠).

d) It is _____ that the number on the card will be greater than 1.

9 If a person has a 0.35 chance of winning a game, what is the probability that he does not win the game?

10 At a fairground stall, prizes are won by getting a table tennis ball into a bowl. In the first hour, 150 balls are thrown and 60 prizes are won.

a) What would you estimate the probability to be of getting a ball into a bowl?

b) In the second hour, 90 balls are thrown. How many prizes would you expect to be won?

11 A bag contains ten marbles. A marble is drawn, its colour is noted and then it is replaced in the bag. The process is repeated ten times. The results are shown below.

Green   6
Red   3
Yellow   1

a) What is the minimum possible number of green marbles in the bag? Explain your answer.

b) Can you be sure that there are no blue marbles in the bag? Give a reason for your answer.

Answers

1 mean = 21, mode = 20, median = 20, range = 21

2 The numbers on the five cards should have a sum of $7 \times 5 = 35$.
The first four cards have a total of 24, so the missing number is $35 - 24 = 11$.

3 If they have a mean of 12, then they must be centred around 12. They could be 12 and 12, or 11 and 13, or 10 and 14, etc. The pair that has a range of 6 is 9 and 15.

4 a) The line should be through the centre of the points, sloping down from left to right, with the same number of points on each side.

b)

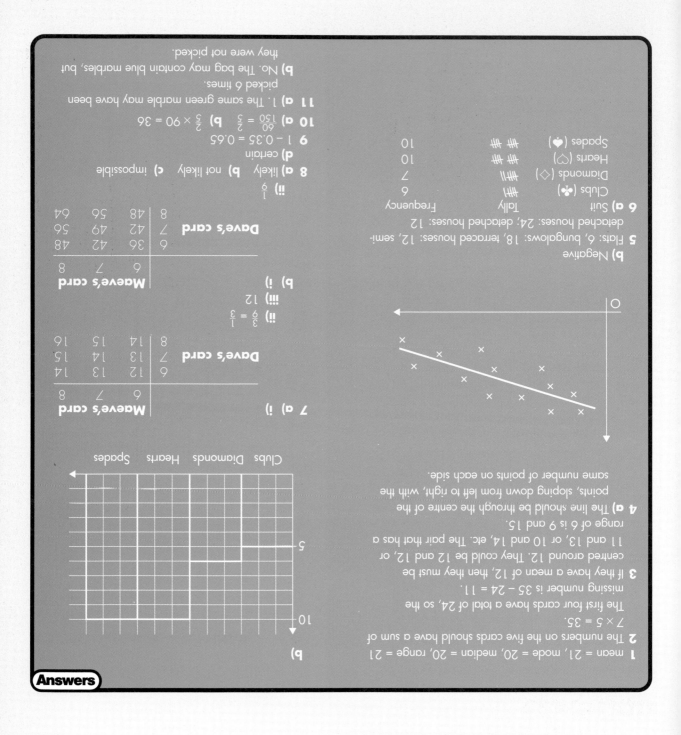

5 Flats: 6, bungalows: 18, terraced houses: 12, semi-detached houses: 24, detached houses: 12

6 a)

Suit	Tally	Frequency
Clubs (♣)	|||||	6
Diamonds (◇)	||||| ||	7
Hearts (♡)	||||| |||||	10
Spades (♠)	||||| |||||	10

b) Negative

7 a) i)

	Maeve's card		
Dave's card	6	7	8
6	12	13	14
7	13	14	15
8	14	15	16

ii) $\frac{3}{9} = \frac{1}{3}$

iii) 12

b) i)

	Maeve's card		
Dave's card	6	7	8
6	36	42	48
7	42	49	56
8	48	56	64

ii) $\frac{1}{9}$

8 a) likely **b)** not likely **c)** impossible **d)** certain

9 $1 - 0.35 = 0.65$

10 a) $\frac{60}{150} = \frac{2}{5}$ **b)** $\frac{2}{5} \times 90 = 36$

11 a) 1. The same green marble may have been picked 6 times.
b) No. The bag may contain blue marbles, but they were not picked.

130

10

checklist

If you are on Level 7 you are allowed some extra baggage

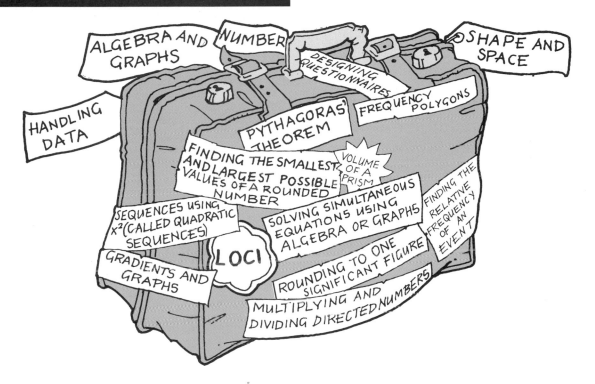

ALGEBRA AND GRAPHS

NUMBER

DESIGNING QUESTIONNAIRES

SHAPE AND SPACE

HANDLING DATA

PYTHAGORAS' THEOREM

FREQUENCY POLYGONS

FINDING THE SMALLEST AND LARGEST POSSIBLE VALUES OF A ROUNDED NUMBER

VOLUME OF A PRISM

SEQUENCES USING x^2 (CALLED QUADRATIC SEQUENCES)

SOLVING SIMULTANEOUS EQUATIONS USING ALGEBRA OR GRAPHS

FINDING THE RELATIVE FREQUENCY OF AN EVENT

LOCI

GRADIENTS AND GRAPHS

ROUNDING TO ONE SIGNIFICANT FIGURE

MULTIPLYING AND DIVIDING DIRECTED NUMBERS

Number

Multiplying and dividing directed numbers

You studied directed numbers on pages 8–10. Now that you are familiar with **same/plus** and **different/minus**, this work is a piece of (fish)cake!

*When you multiply or divide two directed numbers, if the signs are the **same** you end up with a **plus**, but if they're **different**, you **don't**.*

Example 10.1

$2 \times 5 = 10$ (2 and 5 are the **same**. They are both **positive**.)

$^-2 \times {}^-5 = 10$ (2 and 5 are the **same**. They are both **negative**.)

$2 \times {}^-5 = {}^-10$ (2 and 5 are **different**. 2 is **positive** and 5 is **negative**.)

$^-2 \times 5 = {}^-10$ (2 and 5 are **different**. 2 is **negative** and 5 is **positive**.)

Exercise 10.1

Work these out without using a calculator.

1 $^-2 \times 7$ **2** $5 \times ^-10$ **3** $8 \times ^-9$ **4** $^-7 \times ^-8$

Answers

1 $^-14$ 2 $^-50$ 3 $^-72$ 4 56

Rounding

Eva Nanded gives the smallest and largest values of a rounded number

Example 10.2

The audience for the Punch and Judy show on the beach was given as 70, rounded to the nearest 10.

a) What was the smallest number which could have been present?

b) What was the largest possible audience?

Solution

Eva Nanded uses the breakwater to help her. She marks a post with the number she has been given – in this case 70 – and labels the posts next to it as shown below.

Then she marks the midpoints between the pairs of posts.

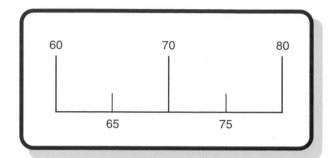

a) The smallest number of people that could have been in the audience is 65.

b) The largest number of people that could have been in the audience is 75.

Example 10.3

Buster Spaid caught a crab 8 cm long, to the nearest centimetre. Give its smallest and largest possible lengths.

Solution

Eva Nanded marks out 7, 8, 9.

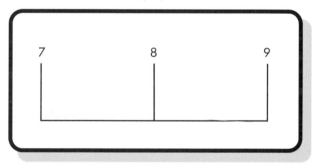

She then finds the midpoints.

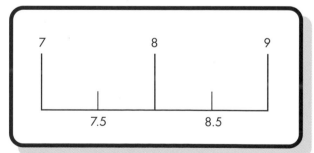

The crab could have been as small as 7.5 cm or as large as 8.5 cm.

Exercise 10.2

Give
a) the smallest, b) the largest
values of these numbers.
1 90, rounded to the nearest 10
2 300, rounded to the nearest 100
3 10.1, rounded to the nearest 0.1

Answers

3 a) 10.05 b) 10.15
1 a) 85 b) 95 2 a) 250 b) 350

Rounding to one significant figure

Example 10.4

Write the following numbers correct to one significant figure.

3.14   4. 8   0.0014   5.009   0.000 75

Solution

The first significant figure is the first non-zero digit starting from the left. To round a number to one significant figure (sig. fig. or s.f.) look at the digit that comes immediately after the first non-zero digit, i.e. next to it to the right. The usual rules for rounding then apply.

3.14 = 3 to 1 s.f.

4.8 = 5 to 1 s.f.

5.009 = 5 to 1 s.f.

0.0014 = 0.001 to 1 s.f. (1 is the first non zero digit.)

0.000 75 = 0.0008 to 1 s.f. (7 is the first non-zero digit, and 5 is big enough to make it become an 8.)

Do not confuse decimal places with significant figures. Decimal places only involve the digits placed after the decimal point. Significant figures involve all the digits starting with the first non-zero digit from the left.

4.006 has been given to 3 decimal places or 4 significant figures.

0.07 has been given to 2 d.p. or 1 sig. fig.

Algebra and graphs

Simultaneous equations – an offer you can't refuse!

Costas à Bombe is worried. Despite the undoubted attractions of DINO, The Great Barry O'Reefe, Cherie Towtt and the Sand Witches and a whole host of other stars, audience numbers at the Gaudyville have been falling alarmingly. Costas has decided to try to pull the visitors in by a series of special offers. He sticks a poster up outside the theatre.

Special offer!

For one night only!
Treat the family!
3 adults and 5 children only £31.00
2 adults and 5 children only £24.00

Winnie de Braik decides that a night at the theatre is just what she and the family need after all those picnics on the beach in the freezing cold. First, though, she works out the cost, writing out the details in the form of two equations.

Using a to represent the price of an adult ticket and c to represent the price of a child's ticket, she writes:

$3a + 5c = 31$
$2a + 5c = 24$

Looking at the left-hand side of each equation, she sees that the only difference between them is a, or one adult ticket. On the right-hand side, the difference is 7, so from this she can tell that an adult's ticket costs £7.00. Now she works out the cost of a child's ticket.

$3a + 5c = 31$

But if $a = 7$, $3a = 21$

$21 + 5c = 31$
$5c = 10$
$c = 2$

A ticket for a child costs £2.00. To check her working out, she puts the values she has found into the other equation.

$2a + 5c = 24$
$2 \times 7 + 5 \times 2 = 24$ ✓

Costas is so delighted with the increased numbers for that night, that he tries another special offer.

Special offer!

For this Saturday's matinee only!
Don't miss it!
4 adults and 3 children can see today's spectacular for only £52.00
2 adults and 3 children a mere £32.00

Winnie de Braik writes down:

$4a + 3c = 52$ **1**
$2a + 3c = 32$ **2**

From these equations, she works out the cost of two adult tickets.

Equation **1** minus equation **2** gives:

$2a = 20$
$a = 10$

From equation **1**:

$40 + 3c = 52$
$3c = 12$
$c = 4$

Checking in equation **2**:

$2 \times 10 + 3 \times 4 = 32$

An adult's ticket costs £10.00 and a child's costs £4.00.

Costas' special offers are examples of **simultaneous equations**. Winnie de Braik solved them using the process of **elimination**, i.e. she eliminated or got rid of one quantity at a time. This is the most common method of solving simultaneous equations using algebra. Simultaneous equations usually involve two equations and two variables (often x and y).

For example:

1 Solve the equations:
$2x - y = 7$
$x + y = 5$

2 Find x and y where:
$3x + 2y = 10$
$y = x - 1$

There are three different ways of solving simultaneous equations: two are algebraic, the other uses graphs.

The two algebraic methods of solving simultaneous equations are:

- elimination
- substitution.

*Remember, the letters in algebra, such as x and y, are called **variables**, because they represent numbers – but they can vary in value.*

Impress your teacher!

Here's another word to impress your teacher. A **coefficient** is a number that multiplies a variable. For example, in the equation $2x + 3y = 6$, the coefficient of x is 2 and the coefficient of y is 3. In the equation $x - y = 4$, the coefficient of x is 1 (because $1 \times x$ is x), and the coefficient of y is $^-1$ (because $^-1 \times y$ is ^-y).

Solving simultaneous equations by elimination

This method involves making the coefficients of either x or y the same in both equations.

Example 10.5

Solve these simultaneous equations.

$3x + y = 17$
$x + y = 7$

Solution

1 Start by looking at the x-coefficients, 3 and 1, then at the y-coefficients, 1 and 1. The y-coefficients are the same, which makes life very easy! Box the y-terms in the two equations: these are going to cancel out.
2 Look at the signs of the terms which are the same (in this case, the y-terms).

*Now STOP. This stands for **S**ame **T**ake, **O**pposite **P**lus. In other words, if the signs in front of the number which you wish to eliminate are the **s**ame – both plus or both minus – you take one equation away from the other. If you have **o**pposite signs – one plus, one minus – you add (**p**lus) the equations. **S**ame **T**ake **O**pposite **P**lus.*

$$3x \boxed{+\ y} = 17$$
$$x \boxed{+\ y} = 7$$
$$2x = 10$$
$$x = 5$$

3 Now take one of the equations (in this example, make life easy and choose the second one, which is simpler), and substitute the value you have just found to find the value of the other variable. Now there is an equation in just one variable to solve.

Substituting $x = 5$ into $x + y = 7$ gives:

$5 + y = 7$
$y = 2$

So the solution is $x = 5$, $y = 2$.

4 Check in the other equation: substituting the values you have found into $3x + y = 17$ gives:
$3 \times 5 + 2 = 17$ ✓

Example 10.6

Find values of x and y which satisfy the following equations.

$x + 2y = 2$
$x - 2y = 6$

Solution

1 Firstly, look at the x-coefficients (1 in both equations) and the y-coefficients (2 and $^-2$).

Ignoring the signs, the coefficients are both the same, so we have the choice of cancelling out the x-terms or the y-terms. Both methods are shown below.

Two for the price of one! Cancelling out the x-terms

2 Box the x-terms in the two equations.

$$\boxed{x} + 2y = 2$$
$$\boxed{x} - 2y = 6$$

Using STOP (Same Take, Opposite Plus), the coefficients of the x-terms are the same, so we must take away the second equation from the first.

$$\boxed{x} + 2y = 2$$
$$\boxed{x} - 2y = 6$$
$$4y = {}^-4$$

$2y - {}^-2y = 2y + 2y = 4y$ (Remember directed numbers.)

3 Now there is an equation in just one variable to solve.

$4y = {}^-4$
$y = {}^-1$

4 Don't forget to solve for the second variable. Substitute the value of y back in to one of the equations to find x.

Using $x + 2y = 2$:

$x + 2 \times {}^-1 = 2$
$x - 2 = 2$
$x = 4$

Cancelling out the y-terms

2 The signs of the y-terms are different so, using Same Take, Opposite Plus (STOP), as the signs are opposite, we must add (plus) the two equations.

$$x \boxed{+ 2y} = 2$$
$$x \boxed{- 2y} = 6$$
$$2x = 8$$

3 Now there is an equation in just one variable and we can solve for x.

$$2x = 8$$
$$x = 4$$

4 Now substitute $x = 4$ into one of the original equations to find y.

Using $x + 2y = 2$:

$$4 + 2y = 2$$
$$2y = {}^-2$$
$$y = {}^-1$$

Using either method, $x = 4$ and $y = {}^-1$.

5 Check in the equation not used in part **4**, to confirm these values for x and y.

$x - 2y = 6$ becomes $4 - 2 \times {}^-1 = 4 + 2 = 6$ ✓

Example 10.7

Solve these simultaneous equations.

$$2x + 3y = 29$$
$$x + 2y = 18$$

Solution

1 The coefficients of the x-terms are 2 and 1, and the coefficients of the y-terms are 3 and 2. Neither the x-term nor the y-term has the same coefficient in both equations. One or both of the equations must be multiplied by a whole number to make the coefficients of one variable the same. It is easier to make the x-terms the same, because you just have to multiply the second equation by 2 to make x into $2x$.

Multiplying $x + 2y = 18$ by 2 gives $2x + 4y = 36$, so the two equations are now:

$$\boxed{2x} + 3y = 29$$
$$\boxed{2x} + 4y = 36$$

The whole of the second equation is being multiplied by 2, so everything on both sides of the equation must be multiplied by 2. (Don't forget to multiply the right-hand side by 2.)

2 Using STOP (Same Take, Opposite Plus), the signs of the x-terms are the same, so we must take one equation away from the other.

The numbers in the second equation are bigger than those in the first, so it makes the working easier to follow if you write the equations the other way round.

$$\boxed{2x} + 4y = 36$$
$$\boxed{2x} + 3y = 29$$
$$y = 7$$

3 Substitute back into one of the original equations to find x.

Using $x + 2y = 18$:

$$x + 2 \times 7 = 18$$
$$x + 14 = 18$$
$$x = 4$$

4 Checking in the other equation, $2x + 3y = 29$, gives:

$$2 \times 4 + 3 \times 7 = 29$$
$$8 + 21 = 29 \qquad ✓$$

Exercise 10.3

Using the elimination method, find the values of x and y in the following simultaneous equations.

1 $3x + y = 16$
  $x + y = 6$

2 $5x - 2y = 31$
  $x + 2y = 11$

3 $3x + 4y = 44$
  $3x + 2y = 34$

4 $4x + 7y = 61$
  $4x - 2y = 34$

5 $9x + 2y = 49$
  $x + y = 14$

6 $3x + 4y = 17$
  $5x - 2y = 37$

Solving simultaneous equations by substitution

Ricky Tea is having a bad season. Fewer people than ever are booking coach trips with him, and things are getting desperate. He sees the success that Costas is having with his special offers, and decides to try out something along the same lines.

Special offer!

Treat the family to a Ricky Tea Mystery Coach Tour this evening!

2 adults and 3 children travel for £57.00

1 adult only £6.00 more than a child

Winnie de Braik is feeling even more exhausted after enduring two sessions at the Gaudyville Theatre so, against her better judgement, she decides to give the Ricky Tea coach trip the benefit of the doubt. First she needs to work out the cost. As before, she writes two equations.

$$2a + 3c = 57 \qquad \mathbf{1}$$
$$a = c + 6 \qquad \mathbf{2}$$

Since $a = c + 6$, she replaces $2a$ in equation **1** with $2(c + 6)$.

The brackets are important.
$2(c + 6) = 2c + 12$,
not $2c + 6$.

$$2(c + 6) + 3c = 57 \qquad \mathbf{3} \quad \text{Multiply out the brackets.}$$
$$2c + 12 + 3c = 57$$
$$5c + 12 = 57 \qquad \text{Simplify.}$$
$$5c = 45 \qquad \text{Divide both sides of the equation by 5.}$$
$$c = 9$$

Using the second equation, because it's easier, she gets:

$$a = 9 + 6 = 15$$

She checks in equation **1**.

$$2 \times 15 + 3 \times 9 = 57 \qquad ✓$$

An adult's ticket costs £15.00 and a child's ticket costs £9.00.

Finding few people attracted by this offer, Ricky Tea tries again.

---

4 adults and 2 children travel
for £104.00

Child's fare: £8 less than adult's ticket.

Winnie de Braik turns this into two equations.

$$4a + 2c = 104 \qquad \mathbf{1}$$
$$c = a - 8 \qquad \mathbf{2}$$

She can then replace $2c$ in equation **1** by $2(a - 8)$.

Her new equation is:

$$4a + 2(a - 8) = 104 \qquad \mathbf{3}$$

Expanding the brackets gives:

$$4a + 2a - 16 = 104$$
$$6a - 16 = 104 \qquad \text{Simplifying.}$$
$$6a = 120$$
$$a = 20$$

So $c = 20 - 8 = 12$.

An adult's ticket costs £20 and a child's costs £12.

Winnie de Braik solved these simultaneous equations using the method of **substitution**. This method works well in examples where one of the variables is on its own, e.g. '$x = $' or '$y = $'.

Example 10.8

Solve these equations.

$$3x + y = 22 \qquad \mathbf{1}$$
$$y = 2x + 7 \qquad \mathbf{2}$$

Solution

Replace y in equation 1 with $2x + 7$.

Equation 1 becomes:

$$3x + 2x + 7 = 22 \qquad \mathbf{3}$$

This simplifies to:

$$5x + 7 = 22$$
$$\text{So } 5x = 15$$
$$x = 3$$

To find y, use the second equation.

$$y = 2x + 7$$
$$y = 2 \times 3 + 7$$
$$y = 13$$

Now try the following examples.

Use brackets where necessary, and be careful with the signs.

Example 10.9

Solve these equations for x and y.

$$2x - y = 7$$
$$x = y + 1$$

Solution

Because $x = y + 1$, you can replace x in the first equation with $y + 1$ (but put the expression $y + 1$ in brackets).

$$2(y + 1) - y = 7$$
$$2y + 2 - y = 7$$
$$y + 2 = 7 \qquad \text{because } 2y - y = y$$
$$y = 5$$

Using $x = y + 1$, you can now replace y by its value, 5.

$$x = 5 + 1$$
$$x = 6$$

Checking in $2x - y = 7$:

$$2 \times 6 - 5 = 7$$
$$12 - 5 = 7 \qquad \checkmark$$

So $x = 6$ and $y = 5$.

Example 10.10

Solve these simultaneous equations.

$$3x - y = 3$$
$$y = 2x - 5$$

Solution

Substitution is the best method to use here because the second equation gives y in terms of x.

When substituting, remember to put the expression you are substituting in brackets.

Substituting $y = 2x - 5$ into $3x - y = 3$ gives:

$$3x - (2x - 5) = 3$$
$$3x - 1(2x - 5) = 3$$
$$3x - 2x + 5 = 3 \qquad \text{because } -1 \times 2x = {}^-2x,$$
$$\qquad\qquad\qquad\qquad\quad \text{and } {}^-1 \times {}^-5 = 5$$
$$x + 5 = 3$$
$$x = {}^-2$$

Using $y = 2x - 5$:

$$y = 2 \times {}^-2 - 5$$
$$y = {}^-4 - 5$$
$$y = {}^-9$$

Checking in $3x - y = 3$:

$$3 \times {}^-2 - {}^-9 = {}^-6 + 9$$
$$= 3 \qquad \checkmark$$

Now try the following exercise.

Use brackets where necessary, and be careful with the signs.

Exercise 10.4

Solve the following simultaneous equations using the substitution method.

1 $5x + 2y = 36$
$x = y + 3$

2 $3x + 2y = 31$
$y = 2x - 2$

3 $4y - 5x = 16$
$y = x + 5$

4 $7y - 2x = 51$
$x = y - 3$

5 $y - 2x = 10$
$y = x + 7$

6 $3x - y = 15$
$y = x + 1$

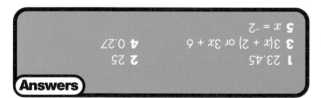

Answers

6 $x = 8, y = 9$ **5** $x = -3, y = 4$
4 $x = 6, y = 9$ **3** $y = 4, x = 9$
2 $x = 5, y = 8$ **1** $x = 6, y = 3$

A Quick Dip!

1 Calculate $2345 \div 100$.
2 What is the next number in the sequence below?
1, 7, 13, 19, …
3 If one pencil costs $x + 2$ pence, write down an expression for the cost of three pencils in terms of x.
4 Write 27% as a decimal.
5 Find x if $x + 6 = 4$.

5 $x = -2$
3 $3(x + 2)$ or $3x + 6$ **4** 0.27
2 25 **1** 23.45

Answers

TAKE A BREAK

Solving simultaneous equations using graphs

Candy and Floss are reviewing their finances. The beach kiosk has changed hands, and Costas à Bombe now has control of the deckchair trade. Candy and Floss are trying to work out the new rates.

As before, they write d to stand for the amount of money they get for returning a deckchair, and t for the amount they get for a tray.

Candy knows from her takings that she gets the same for returning two trays as she does for every one deckchair. Floss has worked out that she only had 40p when she returned four trays and two deckchairs.

$$d = 2t$$
$$4t + 2d = 40$$

Winnie de Braik bossily offers to show them how to solve simultaneous equations by algebra, but they decide that *that* could take for ever, so they try to work out another method of their own. They decide to draw a graph.

First, they work out some possible values for t and d, and set them out in a table like this. They start with a few values for t. Then they multiply the t-values by 2 to get the second line of the table.

t	0	1	2	3	4
d	0	2	4	6	8

The method they use for the equation $4t + 2d = 40$ is a bit more complicated. Pay attention!

$t = 0$ $4 \times 0 + 2d = 40$ $2d = 40$ $d = 20$
$t = 1$ $4 \times 1 + 2d = 40$ $2d = 36$ $d = 18$
$t = 2$ $4 \times 2 + 2d = 40$ $2d = 32$ $d = 16$

and so on. (Try to work out d for yourself when $t = 3$ and $t = 4$.)

They summarise their results on a table like this.

t	0	1	2	3	4
d	20	18	16	14	12

They then draw each equation on a graph, as shown.

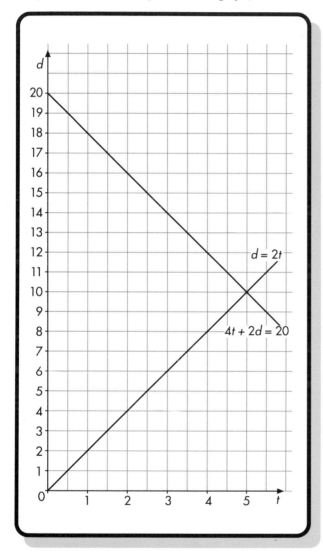

The lines cross at $t = 5$, $d = 10$, so they know that they are being paid 5p for every tray and 10p for every deckchair. This is the **graphical** method of solving simultaneous equations.

To solve simultaneous equations graphically, draw the lines given on a graph. The x- and y-values where the lines cross give the solution of the simultaneous equations.

Example 10.11

The graph below shows the equation $3x + 2y = 18$.

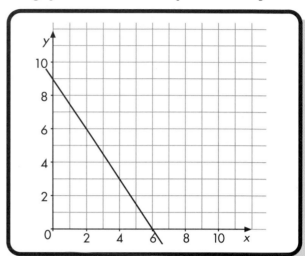

By drawing a suitable line on the grid, solve these simultaneous equations.

$$3x + 2y = 18$$
$$y = 2x + 2$$

Solution

Draw the graph of the line $y = 2x + 2$ on the grid.

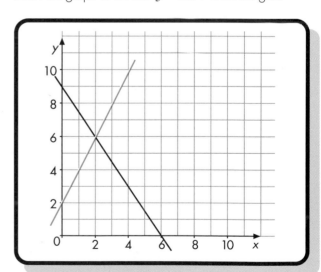

The solution to the simultaneous equations, read from the coordinates of the point where the lines cross, is $x = 2$, $y = 6$.

Gradients and graphs

Cliff and Walter Sedge have fallen out. Walter is stomping along the beach, sulking, whilst his brother is making his way up the straight path which leads to the top of the cliff. Every now and again they stop to shout insults at each other. To gain the maximum advantage from his position of superiority, Cliff makes sure that he is standing directly above Walter. As you can see from this diagram (obtainable for a modest charge from the tourist information office), for every horizontal metre which Walter covers, Cliff covers two vertically. Cliff is gaining height twice as fast as Walter is going along horizontally. This means that the gradient of the path is 2.

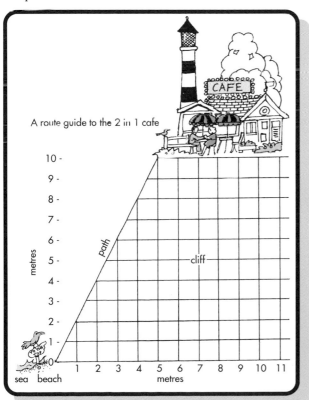

A route guide to the 2 in 1 cafe

The **gradient** of a line tells you the steepness of the line. It measures the rate at which things change. Knowing the gradient of a line helps you to work out the equation of a straight line on a graph.

Equations of lines using $y = mx + c$

Let's examine the line $y = 2x + 1$. Here is a table of values. The graph of the line is shown below it.

x	0	1	2	3
y	1	3	5	7

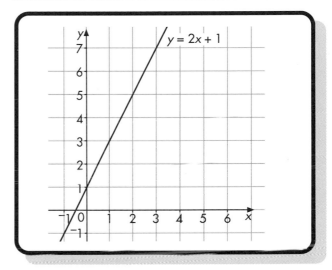

Now here is a table of values for $y = 3x - 1$. Again, the graph is shown below it.

x	0	1	2	3
y	-1	2	5	8

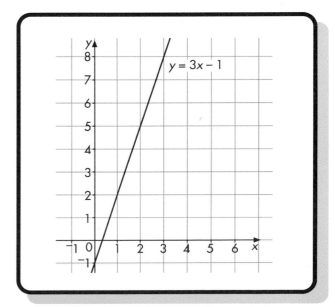

Similarly for $y = x + 2$:

x	0	1	2	3
y	2	3	4	5

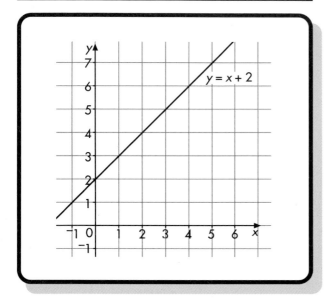

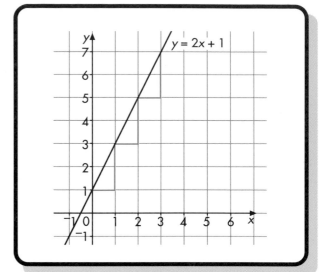

Whenever $x = 0$ is substituted into the equation of the line, the value of y is the same as the term without x in the equation. When the graph is drawn, this is the point where the graph cuts the y-axis. It is known as the **y-intercept.**

In the equation $y = 2x + 1$, when $x = 0$, y is 1, so the graph cuts the y-axis at (0, 1).

In the equation $y = 3x - 1$, when $x = 0$, y is ⁻1, so the graph cuts the y-axis at (0, ⁻1).

Similarly, the graph of the line $y = x + 2$ has a y-intercept at (0, 2).

By examining the formula of the equation of the line, it is possible to find its gradient. Look at the tables of the three lines $y = 2x + 1$, $y = 3x - 1$ and $y = x + 2$. Can you see a pattern?

In the table of $y = 2x + 1$:

x	0	1	2	3
y	1	3	5	7

each time x increases by 1, y increases by 2.

This is shown as triangles on the graph.

For $y = 3x - 1$:

x	0	1	2	3
y	⁻1	2	5	8

Each time x increases by 1, y increases by 3.

This is shown on the graph below.

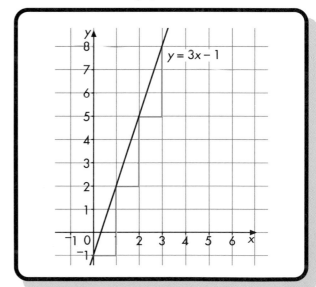

For $y = x + 2$:

x	0	1	2	3
y	2	3	4	5

Each time x increases by 1, y increases by 1.

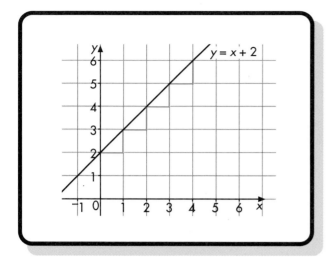

The triangles on the graph show the gradients of each graph. By using GRADUAL or GROTty, the gradient of $y = 2x + 1$ is 2, the gradient of $y = 3x - 1$ is 3 and the gradient of $y = x + 2$ is 1. Can you see the connection?

If you need to remind yourself about GRADUAL and GROTty, look back to page 67.

When the equation of a line is written in the form '$y = \ldots$' the gradient of its graph is the coefficient of x. This is m in the form $y = mx + c$.

Remember, the coefficient is the number that multiplies the term.

For example the coefficient of x in:

a) $y = 3x - 4$ is 3 **b)** $y = x - 1$ is 1

c) $y = 1 - 2x$ is $^-2$ **d)** $y = 3 - x$ is $^-1$.

Example 10.12

Write down the gradients and the y-intercepts of the following lines.

a) $y = 4x + 3$ **b)** $y = x - 2$

c) $y = 5 - 2x$ **d)** $y = 1 - x$

Solution

The coordinate of the y-intercept of a line is most easily found by substituting $x = 0$ into the equation and finding the y-value. The gradient is the coefficient of x.

a) Gradient = 4, y-intercept is 3.

b) The coefficient of x here is 1 because $1 \times x = 1x = x$.

So the gradient is 1 and the y-intercept is $^-2$.

c) The equation of this line is written confusingly as the x term is written after the constant. This equation may be rewritten as $y = ^-2x + 5$. The gradient (or coefficient of x) is $^-2$ and the y-intercept is 5.

d) This is similar to part (c) and can be rewritten as $y = ^-x + 1$. The gradient (or coefficient of x) is $^-1$ and the y-intercept is 1.

Example 10.13

a) Draw the graph of $y = 2x - 1$ on a grid.

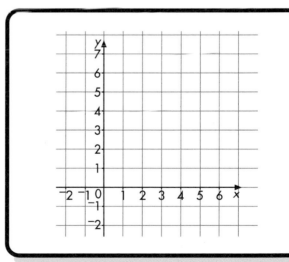

b) Write the equation of a different linear graph which passes through the point $(0, ^-1)$.

c) Write down the equation of the line parallel to $y = 2x - 1$ which passes through the point $(0, 2)$.

Solution

a) Either tabulate values, or use the fact that the line has gradient 2 and y-intercept of 1.

For $y = 2x - 1$:

x	0	1	2	3	4
y	$^-1$	1	3	5	7

Remember to draw the line of the graph to the ends of the grid.

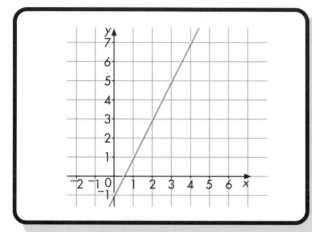

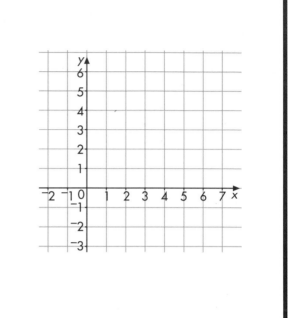

b) The line should be in the form $y = mx - 1$, so the answer could be

$y = x - 1$, or $y = 3x - 1$, or $y = 4x - 1$, or even $y = ^-1$.

c) If two lines are parallel, they have the same gradient. Therefore, all that is needed to find the equation of the line is the y-intercept. This is given in the question as the point $(0, 2)$. So the equation of the line is $y = 2x + 2$.

Exercise 10.5

1 Write down the gradient and y-intercept of each of the following graphs.

   a) $y = 4x + 1$ **b)** $y = 5x - 2$
   c) $y = 1 - x$ **d)** $y = 2 + 3x$
   e) $y = 3 - 5x$ **f)** $y = x$
   g) $y = 2x$

2 a) On the grid provided, draw and label the line $y = x - 3$.

   b) i) On the same grid, draw the line parallel to $y = x - 3$ through the coordinates $(2, 3)$.

      ii) Write down an equation for this line.

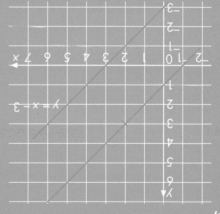

Sequences involving x^2 and x^3

As well as managing the Gaudyville Theatre, Costas à Bombe runs the Odious Cinema. Unfortunately, he can't get hold of the latest releases. It has taken until now for the 1933 black and white epic, *The Sinking of the Quadratic*, to receive its first showing in New-Mer-a-Sea. Not surprisingly, despite keeping 75% of all the takings, he is still losing money.

To encourage larger audiences and to advertise the attractions of the Odious Cinema, Costas has come up with the idea of lucky numbers on the programmes. He puts a numbered programme on each seat. In the intermission, a number is flashed up on screen and anyone with a programme bearing that number can claim a free ice cream.

As usual, his generosity is not all it seems! Costas always numbers his programmes according to a formula. His children work out the formula in advance, so that they know where to sit to get the free ice cream. Costas is a winner twice over. He doesn't have to fork out on ice cream for the kids, and larger audiences mean a larger rake-off for him.

Costas at work

This is how the scheme works. Costas puts programmes numbered 3, 6, 11, 18, 27, ... in the seats in the front row. On the seats in the second row, he puts programmes numbered with the differences. The first and second rows look like this.

```
3      6      11      18      27
   3      5      7      9
```

He keeps doing this until he finds a row where all the numbers are the same. In this example, it's the third row. Now he has this arrangement.

```
3      6      11      18      27
   3      5      7      9
      2      2      2
```

As soon as the cinema opens, Costas' children and their many friends rush in to grab seats in the third row because – yes, you've guessed it – 2 is today's lucky number.

The unsuspecting customers are surprised and pleased to find that the first two rows are vacant, and fill them up fast. Two minutes into the soundtrack, they realise their mistake, but that is another story …

Working out the formula

If the numbers in the **first** row of differences are equal, then the sequence involves n and Costas will call in DINO to help find the nth term.

If the numbers in the **second** row of differences are equal, then the sequence will involve n^2, and if the numbers in the **third** row of differences are equal then it will involve n^3.

COSTAS stands for Cube Or Square; Times, Add, Subtract.

In the example above, the second differences are equal, so the formula for the nth term involves n^2.

Costas' eldest son – a bright boy – writes down the numbers $n = 1, 2, 3, 4, 5, …$, then underneath he writes the square numbers n^2 (1, 4, 9, 16, 25, …). Then he leaves a line and writes the sequence of numbers in the question under that.

So he writes:

n	1	2	3	4	5
n^2	1	4	9	16	25
	3	6	11	18	27

Now all he has to do is find the link between the n^2 row and the bottom row using TAS (Times, Add, Subtract).

In this case, to find the bottom row he has to add 2 to n^2, so the sequence is $n^2 + 2$.

10

Example 10.14

Find the formula for the nth term of this sequence.

2, 8, 18, 32, 50, ...

Solution

This time Costas' daughter calculates the rows of differences.

```
2       8       18       32       50
   6       10       14       18
      4        4        4
```

The numbers are equal on the second row of differences, so the formula must involve n^2.

Writing out a row for n, a row for n^2, and copying the sequence in the third row gives:

n	1	2	3	4	5
n^2	1	4	9	16	25
	2	8	18	32	50

Using the TAS of her dad's name, she now examines the n^2 row and the bottom row, and finds that if she multiplies the numbers in the n^2 row by 2 she gets the numbers in the sequence.

So the formula for the nth term is $n^2 \times 2$, which is written as $2n^2$.

Example 10.15

Find the nth term of this sequence.

5, 12, 31, 68, 129, ...

Solution

Not to be outdone, baby Costas puts the sequence in the first row and starts writing the differences in the next rows.

```
5      12      31      68      129
   7      19      37      61
      12      18      24
          6       6
```

The numbers in the third row of differences are equal, so the formula involves n^3.

He then writes down the sequence of numbers n, then n^3 on the next row and the original sequence on the third.

n	1	2	3	4	5
n^3	1	8	27	64	125
	5	12	31	68	129

Using TAS of COSTAS, he finds he must add 4 to get from the n^3 row to the bottom row, so the formula for the nth term is $n^3 + 4$.

Exercise 10.6

Find:
a) the next two terms
b) the 25th term (**Hint:** Do part c) first.)
c) the nth term of each of the following sequences.
1 4, 7, 12, 19, 28, ...
2 3, 12, 27, 48, 75, ...
3 2, 9, 28, 65, 126, ...
4 2, 16, 54, 128, 250, ...

Answers

1 a) 39, 52	**b)** 628	**c)** $n^2 + 3$
2 a) 108, 147	**b)** 1875	**c)** $3n^2$
3 a) 217, 344	**b)** 15 626	**c)** $n^3 + 1$
4 a) 432, 686	**b)** 31 250	**c)** $2n^3$

Too easy for you? Ready for something a bit tougher? Try these, then.

Exercise 10.7

Find:
a) the rule for finding the next term
b) the 6th term of these sequences.
1 4, 12, 36, 108, 324, ...
2 5, 10, 20, 40, 80, ...
3 2, 3, 5, 8, 13, ...

TAKE A BREAK

Shape and space
Loci

Example 10.16

The diagram below, drawn to a scale of 1 cm to 1 m, shows a corner of Ma Jinn's lawn. She wants to make a path exactly 1 m wide in this corner. Using the same scale, draw the position of the path.

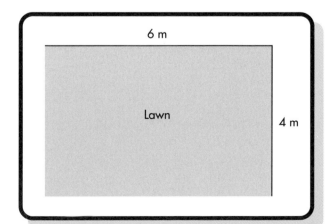

Solution

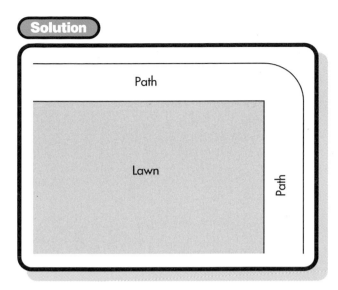

Be careful to round the corners.

Example 10.17

Iona Manshion has invited Millie-Anne Eyre for a visit to admire her new fountains (labelled A, B and C on the diagram). The spray from the fountains reaches distances of 5 m, 9 m and 10 m respectively. Using a scale of 1 cm to 2 m, indicate the region in which Iona should place Millie's chair in order to cause her the maximum discomfort.

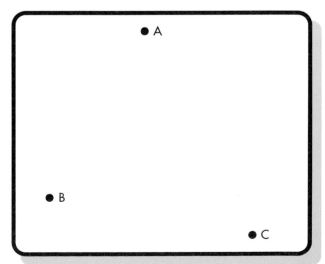

Try it first, before you turn over!

Solution

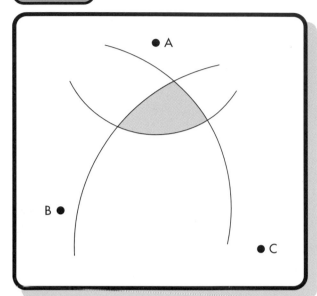

The locus of a point a fixed distance from a point is a circle. The locus of a point a fixed distance from a line is a parallel line on either side, with rounded ends.

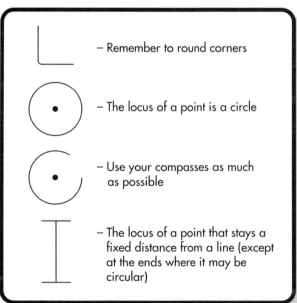

– Remember to round corners

– The locus of a point is a circle

– Use your compasses as much as possible

– The locus of a point that stays a fixed distance from a line (except at the ends where it may be circular)

Pythagoras' theorem

The longest side of any right-angled triangle is called the **hypotenuse**.

The hypotenuse is always opposite the right angle. Don't assume that it is always on the base.

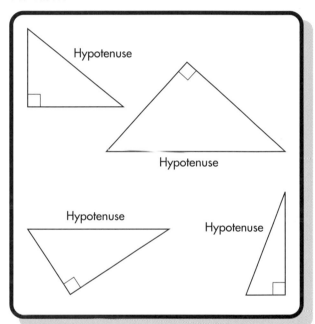

In any right-angled triangle, if c is the longest side, and a and b are the two shorter sides, then:

$$c^2 = a^2 + b^2$$

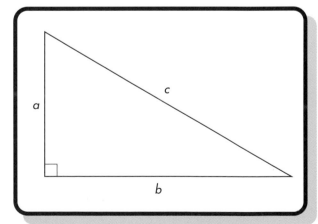

Example 10.18

In the following triangle, which is not drawn to scale, find the length of c, to the nearest cm.

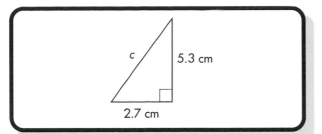

Solution

$c^2 = a^2 + b^2$

$a^2 + b^2 = 5.3^2 + 2.7^2 = 35.38$

$c = \sqrt{35.38} = 5.9$ cm

Exercise 10.8

Find the missing lengths, in cm. Give your answer to 1 d.p. These diagrams are not drawn to scale.

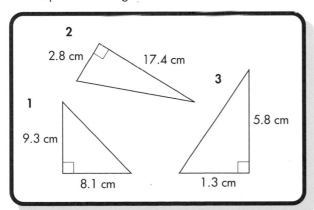

Answers   1 12.3 cm   2 17.6 cm   3 5.9 cm

$a^2 = c^2 - b^2$ and $b^2 = c^2 - a^2$

For shorter sides subtract.

Example 10.19

Triangle DEF is right-angled at E. If DF = 12.5 cm and EF = 4.6 cm, find the length of DE.

Solution

$DE^2 = DF^2 - EF^2$

$DE^2 = 12.5^2 - 4.6^2 = 135.09$

$DE = \sqrt{135.09} = 11.6$ cm to 1 d.p.

Exercise 10.9

Using Pythagoras' theorem, find the lengths of the sides marked x.

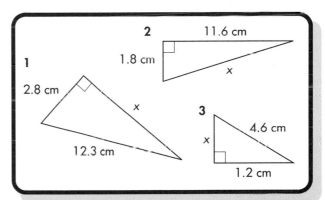

Answers   1 12.0 cm   2 11.7 cm   3 4.4 cm

Volume of a prism

A prism is a 3D shape which you can cut into identical slices. Each slice is called a **cross-section**.

Volume = area of cross-section × length of prism

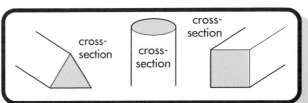

A cylinder is another prism. Its cross-section is a circle, radius r. The length is often called the height (h).

Volume of a cylinder $(V) = \pi r^2 h$

To be absolutely certain of getting this right, it is safer to put r into your calculator, then square it, then multiply by π.

$V = r^2 \times \pi \times h$

Exercise 10.10

1 A cylindrical glass has a radius of 2.5 cm and a height of 7.5 cm. How many millilitres does it hold?

2 A cylindrical tank has a height of 1.2 m and a radius of 45 cm. Find to the nearest half-litre the number of litres it holds when it is half full.

Answers

1 $V = \pi r^2 h$, $V = 2.5^2 \times \pi \times 7.5 = 147.26\,cm^3$
= 147 ml

2 $V = \frac{1}{2}\pi r^2 h$
Change the 1.2 m to 120 cm. The full tank holds 763.4 litres. When half full it holds 381.7 litres
= 381.5 litres to the nearest half-litre.

Castles in the air with Buster Spaid

Buster Spaid regularly wins the weekly sand castle building competition. His favourite design, which he calls a sand castle triplet, looks like this.

You can use Buster's triplets in all sorts of situations.

Distance, speed and time

Example 10.20

Ricky Tea recently took 6 hours to drive Cherie Towtt and the Sand Witches to a gig. He drove at an average speed of 35 km per hour. How far away was the gig?

Solution

Remember Downing Street:
D = distance, S = speed, T = time.

You already know from your work on algebra that

ab is short for $a \times b$ and $\dfrac{a}{b}$ is short for $a \div b$.

Cover or cross out the letter on the sand castle triplet which represents the quantity you are trying to find. This will leave ST.

$D = ST \qquad D = 6 \times 35 = 210\,km$

Example 10.21

Dave Isitt has taken 2 hours to drive 150 km to spend a few hours at New-Mer-a-Sea. Find his average speed in km per hour.

Solution

Cover up the S in the triplet.

You are left with $\dfrac{D}{T}$.

Distance ÷ time = speed

$150 \div 2 = 75\,km$ per hour

Example 10.22

Winnie De Braik drove the same distance at an average speed of 40 km per hour. How long, in hours and minutes, did she take?

Solution

Using Buster's triplet, $\dfrac{D}{S} = T$.

$T = 150 \div 40$

$= 3.75$ hours

You need to calculate 0.75 hours in minutes by working out $0.75 \times 60 = 45$.

She took 3 hours 45 minutes.

Exercise 10.11

1 Rod and Annette went for a cycle ride. They travelled at an average speed of 19 km per hour and stopped after they had travelled 28.5 km. How long had they been travelling?

2 Laurie Lode was driving towards Litter-a-Sea when his vehicle broke down. He had driven for 1 hour 15 minutes and had travelled 30 km. Find his average speed in km per hour.

Answers

1 $T = \dfrac{D}{S} = 28.5 \div 19 = 1.5$ hours or 1 hour 30 minutes

2 You need to change 15 minutes to a fractional or decimal part of an hour. $\frac{15}{60}$ or $\frac{1}{4}$ or 0.25.
$S = D = 30 \div 1.25 = 24$ km per hour

Now that you know Buster's winning formula, you can use the idea in all sorts of situations.

Example 10.23

Remember **ART**:

A = amount, **R** = rate, **T** = time.

Water from the flat above is pouring through the ceiling of Phil Yerbuckitt's home. If he has collected 150 litres in $1\frac{1}{2}$ hours, find the rate in litres per hour.

Solution

$R = \dfrac{A}{T}$

$= 150 \div 1\frac{1}{2}$

$= 100$ litres per hour.

Example 10.24

Remember **D**odgem **C**a**R**s:
D = distance, **C** = circumference,
R = revolutions or turns.
The front wheel on Rhoda Weigh's bicycle has a radius of 18 cm. How many complete revolutions will it make in travelling 55 m?

Solution

The radius is given in cm, and the distance in m. Change one of the units of measurement so that both are the same.

$R = \dfrac{D}{C}$

$C = \pi d = 113$ cm

55 m $= 5500$ cm

$R = 5500 \div 113 = 48.67 = 48$ revolutions

Although you would usually round up this number, Rhoda Weigh has only completed 48 revolutions.

Remember, when working with circles, Buster Spaid's frightened cat (C) likes to sit on the table (π), whilst his furious dog (d) runs round underneath, barking. $C = \pi d$ but $d = \dfrac{C}{\pi}$.

Handling data

Frequency polygons

Frequency polygons are based on bar charts. To draw a frequency polygon, you mark the centre point along the top of each bar, then connect the points up, in order. Sometimes the points at the ends of the first and last bars are joined to the axis on either side. Sometimes they are not.

Check with your teacher whether to join the first and last bars to the axis or not.

Example 10.25

One day in July, Howard Eye-No recorded the ages of people entering the arcade. He showed his results a bar chart like this.

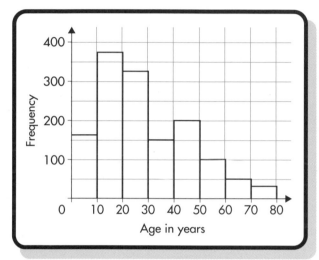

Show this data as a frequency polygon.

Solution

Mark points at the centres of the bars of the bar chart, then connect them up with a ruler. This gives the frequency polygon.

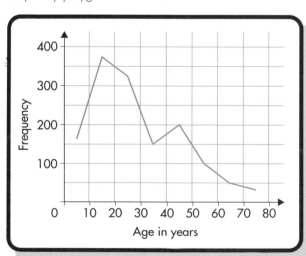

Or, if you need to join the polygon to the axes:

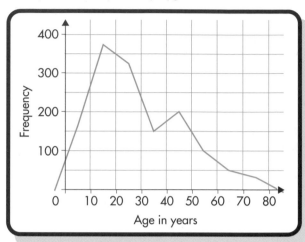

Sampling, surveys and questionnaires

Sampling

Howard Eye-No wanted to find out how the visitors to New-Mer-a-Sea were spending their money. His girlfriend, Candida Pinion, offered to carry out a survey. She said that she couldn't ask everybody who might be affected, so she had to survey a smaller group. This group is called a **sample**.

Samples should be:

- of a suitable **size**, i.e. large enough to give a good estimate
- selected at **random**
- **representative** i.e. chosen from all the different groups affected.

Remember these points, or you will be SoRRy.

Surveys and questionnaires

To carry out a survey, you need to have a list of questions to ask. It is helpful if there are boxes to tick in response to the questions. Remember you must always have an ALIB1 for questionnaires.

ALIB1 will remind you about pitfalls to avoid with questionnaires.

Ambiguous (or having more than one meaning) – sometimes questions have a double meaning, and this can cause confusion. ✗

Leading – questions such as 'Don't you think that the local shopping centre should be open on Sundays?' are designed to influence the person being asked, to respond in a certain way. ✗

Inclusive – response boxes should include the full range of responses. ✓

Biased – as for leading questions, these are worded so that they influence the person being asked to respond in the way the person doing the survey wants them to. ✗

1 and only 1 box can be ticked for each answer. If the respondent to a questionnaire is asked to tick a box, there should be just one box for each possible reply. ✓

Example 10.26

Howard Eye-No conducted a survey on the amount of money people were spending in the arcade. He used the following question.

How much money did you spend in the arcade?

nothing   a little   a fair amount   a lot

a) Why do you think that Candida Pinion said that his question was unsuitable?

b) How do you think that his question could be improved?

Solution

a) Different people have different ideas to what is 'a little' money and 'a lot' of money.

b) By putting amounts of money above the boxes, such as £0.00 to £4.00, £4.01 to £8.00, etc.

Example 10.27

Candida Pinion conducted her own survey on the ages of people coming into the arcade. She asked the following question.

What is your age (in years)?
☐Under 15 ☐15–20 ☐20–25 ☐25–30 ☐30–40

Give two ways in which her questionnaire could be improved.

Solution

Firstly, her boxes are not inclusive (the 'I' in ALIB1). They do not include the full range of responses. What do you tick if you are over 40?

Secondly, there is not just one box (1 in ALIB1) to tick if you are exactly 20, 25 or 30 years old.

Exercise 10.12

1 a) Draw a line of best fit on the scatter graph below.

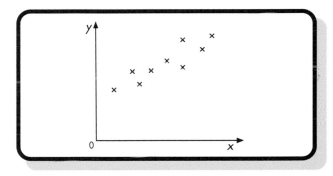

b) How would you describe the correlation?

2 Show the following data in a frequency polygon.

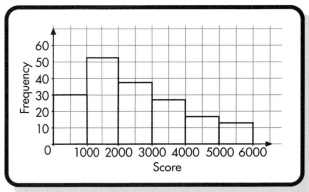

3 Suggest one way of improving the following question. How many times have you visited New-Mer-a-Sea over the last five years?
☐0–5   ☐6–10   ☐11–15   ☐16–20

10

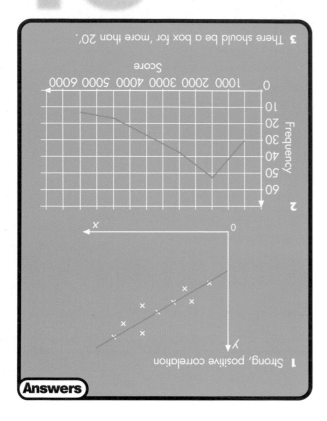

Estimating probabilities

Esther Mait estimates probabilities by repeating an event, and counting the number of times she gets the required outcome.

The estimate of the probability is called the **relative frequency**. It is calculated as:

relative frequency

$$= \frac{\text{number of times the required outcome occurred}}{\text{number of trials (times the event occurred)}}$$

Example 10.28

Rod and Annette went shrimping. Rod caught 60 shrimps, but the holes in his net were so big that 50 fell through the holes.

a) Estimate the probability of a shrimp falling through the net.

b) Estimate the probability of a shrimp not falling through the net.

c) Annette scooped up 24 shrimps. How many of them would you expect to fall through Rod's net?

Solution

a) $\frac{50}{60} = \frac{5}{6}$

b) $1 - \frac{5}{6} = \frac{1}{6}$

c) If $\frac{5}{6}$ of the shrimps fall through the net, then

$\frac{5}{6} \times 24 = 20$ shrimps would fall through.

Exercise 10.13

1 Candy and Floss had a bag of 20 gobstoppers, of which 16 were blue, 3 were green and 1 was red. Candy picked one from the bag without looking at it, tasted it and replaced it in the bag. She did this ten times. Would she have picked out a blue gobstopper every time? Give a reason for your answer.

2 A passenger group complains that trains from Sunchester are late more than 10% of the time.
   a) How would you test this?
   b) Would this be an exact answer or an estimate? Give a reason for your answer.
   c) It was later found that 12% of trains were late. Out of 50 trains, how many would you expect to be on time?

Level 7 review

Number

1 Give the following numbers correct to one significant figure.
   a) 64.7   **b)** 5800   **c)** 28.9   **d)** 0.0098

Algebra

2 Solve these simultaneous equations.
   $3p + q = 14$
   $p + 2q = 13$

3 Use trial and improvement to solve this equation, giving the answer correct to 1 decimal place.
   $x^2 - 9x = 17$
   The first trial is shown below.
   x $x^2 - 9x$
   10   10   Too low

4 Sheila Gree thought of two numbers, x and y. She found that when she added x and y the answer was 30. She also found that y was two more than x.
   a) Write these sentences as two equations.
   b) Solve the equations to find the values of x and y.

5 For the following sequences, find:
   a) the rule for finding the next term
   b) the next two terms of the sequence
   c) the nth term of the sequence
   d) the 12th term.
   i) 7, 11, 15, 19, ...
   ii) 2, 8, 14, 20, ...
   iii) 1, 4, 9, 16, ...

6 Solve the following equations.
   a) $3x - 4 = 17$ **b)** $16 = 5x + 1$
   c) $4 = 20 - 2x$

7 Write down the gradients and y-intercepts of the following equations.
   a) $y = 3x + 2$ **b)** $y = 5 + 2x$
   c) $y = 1 - x$ **d)** $y = {}^-x$
   e) $y = \dfrac{x}{2} - 4$

8 The graph of the line $2x + 3y = 12$ is shown on the grid below.

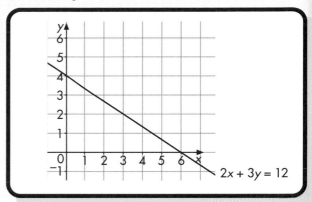

Draw another line on the graph to solve the simultaneous equations:
$2x + 3y = 12$
$y = x - 1$
by a graphical method.

Shape and space

9 A right-angled triangle has a hypotenuse of length 13 cm. If one of the shorter sides is 12 cm long, find the length of the third side.

10 Lil Eepond is still planning to put a water feature in her garden, which needs a circular hole with radius 4 m. What volume of soil will Lil Eepond dig out, if she makes the hole 1.5 m deep?

Handling data

11 A survey was carried out on attitudes to the building of a leisure centre in New-Mer-a-Sea. The questionnaire used is shown below.
   a) Don't you think that the leisure centre will cause crime to fall in New-Mer-a-Sea?
      Yes   No   Don't know
   b) What is your age?
      Under 10 10–15 15–20 20–25 25–30
   Give one way in which each question could be improved.

Answers

1 a) 60 **b)** 6000 **c)** 30 **d)** 0.01

2 $p = 3$, $q = 5$

3 $x = 10.6$

4 a) $x + y = 30$, $y = x + 2$
   b) $x = 14$, $y = 16$

5 i) a) Add 4 to the last term.
   b) 23, 27
   c) $4n + 3$ (using DINO)
   d) $4 \times 12 + 3 = 51$
   ii) a) Add 6.
   b) 26, 32
   c) $6n - 4$
   d) 68
   iii) a) This is the sequence of the square numbers.
   b) 25, 36
   c) The sequence is n^2.
   d) 144

6 a) $x = 7$
   b) $x = 3$
   c) $x = 8$

7 a) gradient = 3, y-intercept = (0, 2)
   b) gradient = 2, y-intercept = (0, 5)
   c) gradient = -1, y-intercept = (0, 1)
   d) gradient = -1, y-intercept = (0, 0)
   e) gradient = $\frac{1}{2}$, y-intercept = (0, -4)

8 $x = 3$, $y = 2$

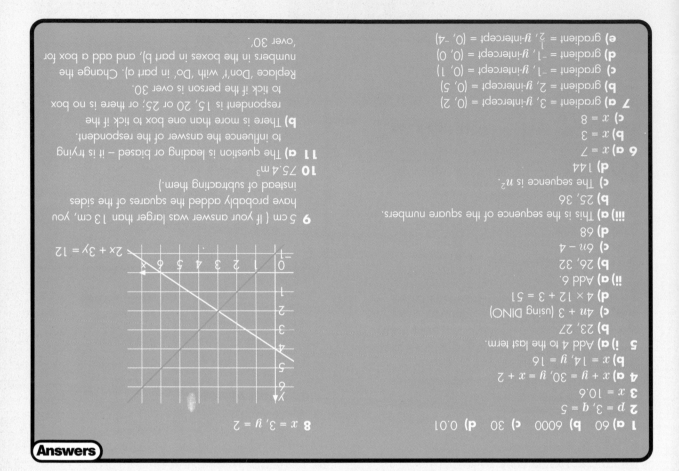

9 5 cm (If your answer was larger than 13 cm, you have probably added the squares of the sides instead of subtracting them.)

10 75.4 m³

11 a) The question is leading or biased – it is trying to influence the answer of the respondent.
   b) There is more than one box to tick if the respondent is 15, 20 or 25; or there is no box to tick if the person is over 30. Replace 'Don't' with 'Do' in part a). Change the numbers in the boxes in part b), and add a box for 'over 30'.

11

Can you meet Howard Eye-No's challenges?

You are nearly at the end of your visit to New-Mer-a-Sea and Howard Eye-No is keen to find out how much you have learned.

Challenge 1

Do not use a calculator for this paper.

1 Put these numbers in order of size, smallest first.
   $^-5$ $^-8$ 7 4 $^-12$ 20

2 Put these numbers in order of size, smallest first.
   5.2 5.06 5.13 5.112 5.009

3 Fill in a number to make the answer 25.
   a) $250 \div \text{☀} = 25$ **b)** $2.5 \times \text{☀} = 25$
   c) $\frac{1}{4}$ of $\text{☀} = 25$ **d)** $90 - \text{☀} = 25$
   e) $8 + \text{☀} = 25$

4 Millie-Anne Eyre bought 16 bunches of roses at £3.50 a bunch to decorate her dining room. She paid for them with three twenty-pound notes. How much did she spend, and how much change did she get?

5 a) Cherie Towtt bought 20 cakes from Victoria Spunj's Olde Worlde Cake Shoppe and gave 15 of them to the Sand Witches. What fraction did she keep for herself? Give your answer in its lowest terms.
   b) What percentage is that?

6 a) A vase contains p flowers. If three flowers are added to the vase, write an expression for the number of flowers it contains now.
   b) Another vase contains q flowers. Another q flowers are added to the vase. Write down and simplify an expression for the number of flowers now in the vase.
   c) A third vase contains $r + 1$ flowers. The number of flowers in the vase is doubled. Write down an expression for the number of flowers now in the third vase. Express your answer as simply as possible.

7 a) A girl holds these four number cards.

   | 4 | 5 | 7 | 12 |

   The mean is 7.
   The girl adds a fifth card to her hand, and the mean stays the same. What is the number on this card?
   b) A boy holds these four number cards.

   | 1 | 11 | 2 | 6 |

   i) What is the median of these four numbers?
   ii) What is the mean of the numbers?
   iii) The boy picks a fifth card, and the mean goes up by 1. What is the value of the fifth card?

8 4, 7, 10, 13, ...
   a) What is the rule for finding the next term in the sequence?
   b) What are the next two numbers in the sequence?
   c) Write down an expression for the nth term of the sequence.

9 Simplify the following expressions.
   a) $6x + y + y + y$ **b)** $5x + 3y + 2x - 5y$
   c) $2(x + 2y)$ **d)** $3x \times 2x$

10 A factory produces equal quantities of five different parts: A, B, C, D, and E.
   A part is picked at random.
   a) Machine 1 uses parts A, B and C. What is the probability that machine 1 uses the part?
   b) What is the probability that it cannot use the part?
   c) Machine 2 uses all the parts. What is the probability that the chosen part can be used by machine 2?
   d) What is the probability that the part cannot be used by machine 2?

11 A tree T is 16 m west of a post, P. Howard Eye-No's dog, Patch, is attached to the post by a lead of length 10 m. Using a scale of 1 cm to 4 m, draw a scale plan to show the tree, the post and the region in which the dog can roam. Label this region R.
A line runs between the post and the tree, equidistant from T and P. Draw this line on your diagram. Shade the area that Patch can reach, where he will be closer to the tree than to the post.

12 Fill in the missing numbers or signs.
a) $7 - \text{\maltese} = ^-2$ **b)** $^-2 + 3 = \text{\maltese}$
c) $^-6 + \text{\maltese} = ^-4$

13 How many equilateral triangles would fit round a point?

14 One angle of a rhombus is 55°. Find the other angles.

15 A diagram of a square with sides 8 cm is to be enlarged by a scale factor of a half.
a) How long will each side be?
b) What will the area of the transformed shape be?
c) What fraction of the area of the original shape is the new area?

16 a) The shortest side of a right-angled triangle is 6 cm, and its longest side is 10 cm in length. Find the length of its other side.
b) What is the area of the triangle?

17 Part of a questionnaire is shown below.
a) How old are you?
☐ under 10 ☐ 15–20 ☐ 21–30
☐ 30–40 ☐ over 40

b) How much do you spend per week at the local supermarket?
nothing   a little   quite a lot   a lot
For each question:
  i) give a reason why it may need changing
  ii) suggest a way of improving it.

18 a) Find the values of x which satisfy the following equations.
  i) $15 = 5x$ **ii)** $12 = 16 - 2x$
  iii) $3x + 1 = 17 - x$

b) The diagram below shows the line $2x + 3y = 12$.

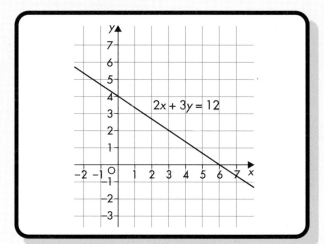

By adding a suitable line to the diagram, solve the simultaneous equations using a graphical method.
$2x + 3y = 12$
$y = x - 1$

Answers

1 -12, -8, -5, 4, 7, 20

2 5.009, 5.06, 5.112, 5.13, 5.2

3 a) 10 b) 10 c) 100 d) 65 e) 17

4 She paid £56.00 and had £4.00 change.

5 a) $\frac{5}{20} = \frac{1}{4}$ b) 25%

6 a) $p + 3$ b) $q + q = 2q$ c) $2(r + 1) = 2r + 2$

7 a) 7

b) i) The median is halfway between 2 and 6, i.e. 4.

ii) 5

iii) The new mean must be 6. The five cards must total $5 \times 6 = 30$. As the four cards total 20, the fifth card must be 10.

8 a) Add 3. b) 16, 19 c) $3n + 1$

9 a) $6x + 3y$ b) $7x - 2y$ c) $2x + 4y$ d) $6x^2$

10 a) $\frac{3}{5}$ b) $\frac{2}{5}$ c) 1 d) 0

11

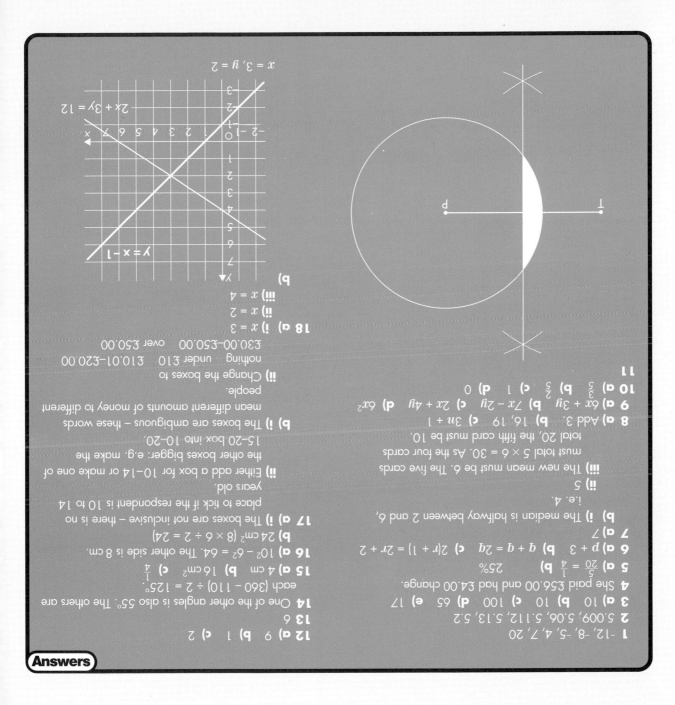

12 a) 9 b) 1 c) 2

13 6

14 One of the other angles is also 55°. The others are each $(360 - 110) \div 2 = 125°$.

15 a) 4 cm b) 16 cm² c) $\frac{1}{4}$

16 a) $10^2 - 6^2 = 64$. The other side is 8 cm.

b) 24 cm² $(8 \times 6 \div 2 = 24)$

17 a) i) The boxes are not inclusive – there is no place to tick if the respondent is 10 to 14 years old.

ii) Either add a box for 10-14 or make one of the other boxes bigger; e.g. make the 15-20 box into 10-20.

b) i) The boxes are ambiguous – these words mean different amounts of money to different people.

ii) Change the boxes to

nothing   under £10   £10.01-£20.00

£30.00-£50.00   over £50.00

18 a) i) $x = 3$

ii) $x = 2$

iii) $x = 4$

b)

$x = 3, y = 2$

11

Challenge 2

On this paper you may use a calculator whenever you need.

1 Ray Lyng's barrier represents 15 m.

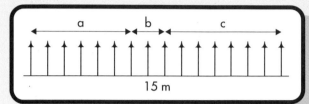

What distances do a, b and c represent?

2 Tanya Leggz and Liza Round have each bought a bottle of suntan lotion. Tanya Leggz paid £9.20 for 750 ml and Liza Round paid £13.50 for 1 litre. They planned to pour the liquid into small bottles each holding 250 ml and give them as presents to the Sand Witches.
   a) How many small containers each holding 250 ml could they fill from the bottles?
   b) How much did each pay for 250 ml?

3 Big Hilda Klime is planning to bake a large cake for Ena Phizinuff's birthday. Her recipe requires 450 g of flour. Big Hilda Klime has 275 g of flour in an opened bag to finish up first.
   a) How much flour will she need to take from a new 1 kg bag?
   b) What fraction of the new bag will she have left?

4 a) Howard Eye-No wants a new carpet for his office. The room is a square with sides 4 m. How many square metres will he need?
   b) The mayor has said that Howard Eye-No can have his old carpet which is a rectangle with the same area. If it is 3.2 m wide, how long is it?
   c) Howard is not very pleased with this idea, and decides instead to buy a square carpet which he sees in a sale. If the area of the carpet is 12.25 m², what is the length of each side?
   d) Ma Jinn suggests that he leaves the same amount of floor round each side of the carpet. How wide should this border be?
   e) Howard Eye-No decides to paint the area of floorboards that will be showing. What area is this?

5 The lighthouse at Decimal Point is due north of the bandstand in the park, and 4 km away.
   a) Ma Jinn's guest house is due east of the bandstand and 7.5 km from it. Make a scale drawing showing this.
   b) From your drawing, work out the distance of Ma Jinn's guest house from the lighthouse.

6 Find the value of x in the following equations.
   a) $x - 4 = 6$
   b) $2x - 3 = 11$
   c) $3(x + 2) = 15$

7 The start of a number sequence is shown below.
   2, 6, ...
   Find three different ways of continuing this number sequence.
   For each chain, write down the rule and the next three terms of the sequence.

8 3, 7, 8, 5, 6, 4, 7, 3, 6, 7, 2, 2
   a) For the set of data above, find:
      i) the mean   **ii)** the median
      iii) the mode   **iv)** the range.
   b) i) A number is chosen at random from the set of data above. What is the probability that the number is a 3?
      ii) What is the probability that it is not a 3?

9 The diagram below shows the graph of the straight line $y = 2x + 1$.

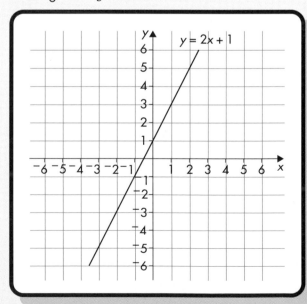

a) Draw the graph of the straight line $y = 2x$. Label your line $y = 2x$.

b) Write down the equation of another straight line which is parallel to $y = 2x + 1$.

c) i) Draw the line $y = x - 4$ on the diagram.

    ii) Write down the gradient and the coordinates of the y-intercept of the line $y = x - 4$.

10 Two remote-controlled cars, A and B, are tested against each other. A distance–time graph of the results is shown below.

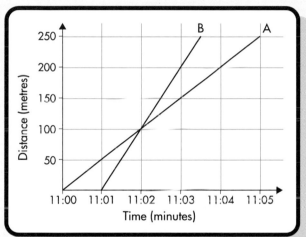

a) One car is given a head start. Which one?

b) What is the gradient of line B?

c) What does this gradient represent?

d) How far have the cars travelled when they are both the same distance away from the starting point?

11 a) Millie-Anne Eyre said that she would make a donation to the Gaudyville Theatre's Retired Artistes' Fund. If she promised £5000 to the nearest £1000, what is the smallest amount she could give?

b) If she promised £5000 to the nearest £100, what is the largest amount she could give?

12 a) Iona Manshion found that if she took the price in pence of a pencil, doubled it and added 7, it was the same as if she took the price from 148. Taking the price of the good in pence as x, she wrote down
$$2x + 7 = 148 - x.$$
Solve this equation for x.

b) Paul E. Payde counted the money in his pocket. He found that if he took this amount in pounds, multiplied it by 3 and then subtracted 21, it was same as if he subtracted 7 from the amount.

    i) If y is the number of pounds Paul has, write this statement as an equation.

    ii) Solve this equation.

c) Solve these simultaneous equations.
$$3p + 5q = 27$$
$$p + 2q = 10$$

13 a) A number of saloon cars were tested. The engine size and fuel economy (in miles per gallon) were plotted on the graph below.

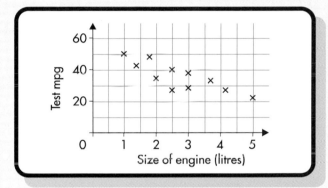

    i) Draw a line of best fit on the graph.

    ii) How would you describe the correlation between the engine size and the fuel economy?

b) Sixty people were asked how many pets they owned. The results are shown in the table below.

Number of pets	0	1	2	3	4	5	6
Frequency	5	18	21	8	5	2	1

    i) Find the mean number of pets.

    ii) Find the modal number of pets.

1 a = 6, b = 2, c = 7

2 a) 750 ÷ 250 = 3, 1000 ÷ 250 = 4, 3 + 4 = 7

b) Tanya paid £3.07 and Liza paid £3.38.

3 a) 175 g **b)** 1000 - 175 = 825g, $\frac{825}{1000} = \frac{33}{40}$

4 a) 16m² **b)** 16 ÷ 3.2 = 5m **c)** $\sqrt{12.25}$ = 3.5 m

d) 4 - 3.5 = 0.5m, 0.5 ÷ 2 = 0.25 (You need half the available amount on each side.)

e) 16 - 12.25 = 3.75 m²

5 a) Lighthouse

		4 km	
Bandstand	7.5 km		Ma Jinn's

b) 8.5 km

6 a) x = 10 **b)** 2x = 14, x = 7

c) 3x + 6 = 15 (expanding brackets),
3x = 9, x = 3

7 Suggested answer:

i) Add 4; next three terms are 10, 14, 18.

ii) Multiply by 3; next three terms are 18, 54, 162.

iii) Add the last two terms together; next three terms are 8, 14, 22 (because 2 + 6 = 8, 6 + 8 = 14, 8 + 14 = 22).

8 a) i) mean = 5

ii) median = $5\frac{1}{2}$ or 5.5 (Remember to arrange the values in order. The median is the 5.5th value i.e. halfway between the 6th value, 5, and the 7th value, 6.)

iii) mode = 7 **iv)** range = 8 - 2 = 6

b) i) $\frac{2}{12} = \frac{1}{6}$ **ii)** $1 - \frac{1}{6} = \frac{5}{6}$

9 a)

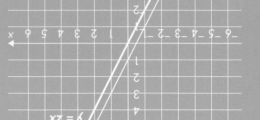

b) y = 2x + 2, or y = 2x + 3, or y = 2x - 1, etc.

c) i)

ii) gradient = 1, y-intercept = (0, -4)

10 a) Car A **b)** 100 **c)** speed in metres per minute

d) 100 metres

11 a) £4500 **b)** £5050

12 a) Hint: First add x to both sides to give:
3x + 7 = 148
This will then give x = 47

b) i) 3y - 21 = y - 7 **ii)** y = 7

c) p = 4, q = 3

13 a) i) The line of best fit should be downward sloping. (A good rule of thumb is to have the same number of points on either side of the line.)

ii) Negative

b) i) Set up a new row.

| f × x | 0 | 18 | 42 | 24 | 20 | 10 | 6 |

Mean = 'fxs over frequencies'
$$= \frac{0 + 18 + 42 + 20 + 10 + 6}{60} = 2$$

ii) The modal number of pets = mode = 2 (the number of pets with the highest frequency)

12 Just when you thought it was safe ...

Don't let these sharks gobble you up.

1 What's the difference between an acute angle and an obtuse angle?
2 How do you turn a fraction into a decimal?
3 What is 75% as a fraction?
4 How do you find an eighth of a number?
5 What's the difference between finding the sum of two numbers and finding their product?
6 What's a digit?
7 What's the correct term for Z angles?
8 How do you find the range of a set of numbers?
9 What's the mathematical name for a diamond shape?
10 What's the easiest way to find 15% without using a calculator?
11 How many sides does an octagon have?
12 What do we call a quadrilateral with one pair of parallel sides?
13 What percentage is the same as $\frac{1}{4}$?
14 How do you find the exterior angle of a regular polygon?
15 When can you **not** use DINO?
16 When you are working out probabilities, what must all the possible outcomes add up to?
17 What fraction is the same as 0.5?
18 πr^2 is the formula for finding what?
19 What is the mathematical term for F angles?
20 What is the smallest prime number?

Answers

1 An acute angle is less than 90°, an obtuse angle is greater than 90° but less than 180°.
2 Divide the numerator (top number) by the denominator (bottom number).
3 $\frac{3}{4}$
4 Divide the number by eight or multiply by $\frac{1}{8}$
5 You **add** the numbers to find their **sum**. You **multiply** the numbers to find their **product**.
6 A digit is a figure or single number.
7 Alternate angles.
8 Highest value minus the lowest value.
9 Rhombus.
10 Divide the quantity by 10 to find 10%. Divide this by 2 and find 5%. Add the two amounts.
11 8
12 Trapezium.
13 25%
14 360° ÷ number of sides of the polygon.
15 When the numbers in the sequence are not equally spaced.
16 1
17 $\frac{1}{2}$
18 The area of a circle.
19 Corresponding angles.
20 2

Feel free to add any personal 'sharks' to this list!

Looking ahead

If you are sitting SATS at levels 3–5, 4–6 or 5–7, your visit to New-Mer-a-Sea should have prepared you for anything which you might meet. However, some of you may be venturing into Levels 6–8, where you will find the following topics.

Level 8

- trigonometry
- standard form
- algebraic formula rearrangement
- cubic graphs
- dimensions
- cumulative frequency
- probability with AND/OR
- quadratic equations solved algebraically

Fortunately there is a guide book to help you. It's called *Revise GCSE Maths – Intermediate Level.*

The Extension Paper

If you are sitting the SATS extension paper, you will also need to know about:

- rational and irrational numbers
- sine and cosine rule for non-right angled triangles
- congruent triangles
- length and area of circular arcs
- volumes of cones and spheres
- histograms with unequal intervals
- sampling
- standard deviation.

You will find all you need to know about these topics in Revise *GCSE Mathematics – Higher Level.*

Index

BUZAN TRAINING COURSES